LOU BENFATTI · CRAIG FAYAK · KI-JANA CARTE
O'HORA · SEVER "TOR" TORETTI · WALLY TRIPLETT · JIM DOOLEY ·
BOB MITINGER · DAVE ROBINSON · GLENN RESSLER · JERRY SAN
EAL SMITH · JACK HAM · LYDELL MITCHELL · DAVE JOYNER · JOH
TTLE · JIMMY CEFALO · MATT BAHR · TOM BRADLEY · KEITH DO
FARRELL · MIKE MUNCHAK · CHET PARLAVECCHIO · CURT WA
LTON · MICHAEL ZORDICH · SHANE CONLAN · BOB WHITE · RA
ERRY SMITH · O. J. MCDUFFIE · LOU BENFATTI · CRAIG FAYAK · K
OWN · LARRY JOHNSON · MICHAEL HAYNES · ADAM TALIAFERRO
A · SEVER "TOR" TORETTI · WALLY TRIPLETT · JIM DOOLEY · ROSEY
MITINGER · DAVE ROBINSON · GLENN RESSLER · JERRY SANDUSK
SMITH · JACK HAM · LYDELL MITCHELL · DAVE JOYNER · JOHN
JIMMY CEFALO · MATT BAHR · TOM BRADLEY · KEITH DORNEY ·
MIKE MUNCHAK · CHET PARLAVECCHIO · CURT WARNER · TODD
AEL ZORDICH · SHANE CONLAN · BOB WHITE · RAY ISOM · JOHN
O. J. MCDUFFIE · LOU BENFATTI · CRAIG FAYAK · KI-JANA CARTE
RY JOHNSON · MICHAEL HAYNES · ADAM TALIAFERRO · ZACK
R "TOR" TORETTI · WALLY TRIPLETT · JIM DOOLEY · ROSEY GRIER
R · DAVE ROBINSON · GLENN RESSLER · JERRY SANDUSKY · TED

WHAT IT MEANS TO BE
A NITTANY LION

JOE PATERNO
AND PENN STATE'S GREATEST PLAYERS

LOU PRATO AND SCOTT BROWN

TRIUMPH
BOOKS

CHICAGO

Library of Congress Cataloging-in-Publication Data
What it means to be a Nittany Lion : Joe Paterno and Penn State's greatest
   players / [edited by] Lou Prato and Scott Brown.
      p. cm.
ISBN-13: 978-1-57243-846-0 (hard cover)
ISBN-10: 1-57243-846-0 (hard cover)
      1. Penn State Nittany Lions (Football team)—Interviews. 2. Football players—United States—Interviews. 3. Pennsylvania State University—Football—History. 4. Paterno, Joe, 1926– I. Prato, Lou. II. Brown, Scott, 1971–

GV958.P46W48 2006
796.332'6309748—dc22

                                                                    2006007310

This book is available in quantity at special discounts for your group or organization. For further information, contact:

Triumph Books
542 South Dearborn Street
Suite 750
Chicago, Illinois 60605
(312) 939-3330
Fax (312) 663-3557

Printed in U.S.A.
ISBN-13: 978-1-57243-846-0
ISBN-10: 1-57243-846-0
Design by Nick Panos
Editorial and page production by Prologue Publishing Services, Oak Park, Illinois.
All photos courtesy of Penn State Sports Media Relations or Penn State University Archives, Special Collections Library, unless otherwise noted.

CONTENTS

FOREWORD

What It Means to Be a Nittany Lion

I'VE BEEN COACHING FOOTBALL AT PENN STATE since 1950 and have been the head coach since 1966. I still love it. What makes it so much fun and so enjoyable are the young men I have been associated with all this time. Many of them are adults now and successful in their own careers—honest, hard-working mature men, raising their families and being leaders in their communities. They're doctors, lawyers, stockbrokers, school teachers, sales executives, presidents of their own companies, newspaper publishers, and more. I'm proud of what they have accomplished after they left Penn State.

They're all part of our football family, not just the players who made the All-America teams or wear those national championship rings. I mean the walk-ons, too, the kids who rarely played or never played at all—the ones who went to practice day after day after day and never complained because they just wanted to be part of the Penn State tradition.

Maybe a lot of people don't really know about Penn State's great football tradition. It started long before I came here.

The 1912 team was undefeated, and many historians now believe it was the best team in the country that year. They only had one touchdown scored against them (while scoring 285 points), and that included a 37–0 victory over Ohio State at Columbus. The captain of that team, Pete Mauthe, is in the College Football Hall of Fame, along with two of his teammates, Shorty Miller and Dex Very.

Hugo Bezdek, who helped develop the screen pass and played under Amos Alonzo Stagg at Chicago, had teams from 1919 to 1921 that only lost one game. The sportswriters of that day called the 1921 team "the Mystery Team"

In this historic photograph, Joe Paterno celebrates Penn State's first national championship with his players after the Nittany Lions defeated Georgia 27–23 at the 1983 Sugar Bowl.

after they had seemingly come out of nowhere in midseason and tied Harvard (21–21), one of the premier teams at that time. The next year, Hugo's team played in the Rose Bowl against USC. He is also in the Hall of Fame, as well as some of his players, like Glenn Killinger and Harry Wilson.

The reason you might not know about this part of our winning tradition is that it was all but forgotten after what happened in the 1930s. Penn State gave up playing big-time football. The administration, in response to a historic Carnegie Foundation report, agreed there was too much emphasis on intercollegiate sports, particularly in football. So they eliminated all financial aid for athletes and downgraded the playing schedules.

It wasn't until the 1940s that the football team recovered, and World War II helped that. A lot of kids wound up at Penn State for their military training, and they came back after the war was over. Bob Higgins, who had been an All-American himself under Hugo Bezdek, was the coach who went through all this, and his undefeated 1947 team played in the Cotton Bowl, tying SMU 13–13, and finished in the top 10 (No. 4).

I didn't know all this when I came here shortly after Bob Higgins retired. I learned about it as I got deeper and deeper into Penn State football. And, now that I look back, I'm very proud to have followed in the tradition of great coaches like Hugo Bezdek, Bob Higgins, and Rip Engle.

I've told the story many times, how Rip was my coach at Brown and how I agreed to come here in his first year to help him and then go back to law school. I remember thinking that this was the boondocks to a kid from Brooklyn.

Football was changing in the 1950s, and the single-wing was going out of fashion. Rip brought the wing-T to Penn State, and the transition wasn't easy. Rip knew we had our work cut out for us to make Penn State competitive with all the good teams on our schedule. But we got a big break when the Penn State administration began giving financial aid again [in 1949].

I still don't think people realized how good those teams were. Army and Navy were still considered the best teams in the East, and we had to play our way up the ladder. I think our game at Illinois in 1954 opened up everyone's eyes. The year before, we had opened the season at Wisconsin, which had won the Big Ten championship in '52. We lost [20–0], but Lenny Moore had a long touchdown run called back on a questionable [motion] penalty.

This statue sits outside of Beaver Stadium to honor Joe Paterno with these words: "Educator...Coach... Humanitarian...They ask me what I'd like written about me when I'm gone. I hope they write I made Penn State a better place, not just that I was a good football coach."

So, when we started the next season at Illinois, I don't think anyone gave us a chance. Illinois had been [co-]champion of the Big Ten in 1953 and had a couple of All-Americans, J. C. Caroline and Abe Woodson. We upset them [14–12] and started to get noticed.

We continued to surprise people, especially when we upset Ohio State at Columbus 7–6 in 1956. The defense was outstanding, particularly our line-backers, [All-American] Sam Valentine and Dan Radakovich. I remember Milt Plum had a great day, not only at quarterback but also his punting, and it was his extra-point kick that won the game. Rip said, "We never had a bigger game," and he was right. I think that's when people started to realize what good football teams we had.

We had a great team in '59 when Richie Lucas was our quarterback. He won the Maxwell Award and almost won the Heisman Trophy. We lost to Syracuse, which won the national championship, but we went to our first bowl game under Rip Engle and beat Alabama. We went to three more bowls after that, and our players were now starting to get some recognition.

I think we had the two best defensive ends in the country in 1961 with Bob Mitinger and Dave Robinson. They both became All-Americans and both played on championship teams in the NFL and AFL. A lot of our kids were now playing in the pros and making a name for themselves. By the time Rip retired and I took over in 1966, I think Penn State was just about there. And I almost blew it.

I started with a 5–5 record and was so stubborn that I didn't listen to the staff. I worked the kids too hard and was impatient, and I confused them. I spent the entire summer trying to design a new defense and came up with the 4-4-3 that nobody had used before. Then, when we were upset by Navy in our first game [23–22], I replaced some of those seniors with sophomores down at the Miami game, and that was the turning point.

I'll always be grateful to those kids in '67, '68, and '69, because they were the ones who took this program to the next level. I don't like to mention one player without mentioning them all, but the leadership on those teams was outstanding from players like co-captains Steve Smear and Mike Reid, and Ted Kwalick, Dennis Onkotz, Neal Smith, Charlie Pittman, and Chuck Burkhart. They were not only smart players but smart in the classroom, too.

We had great players who were also good students, kids who would play and win against the best but would also excel in their academics. They would have a full and normal college life like any other student, going to

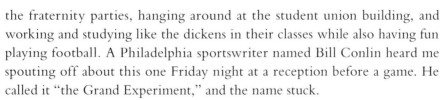

After the 1986 team won Penn State's second national championship, the players and Joe Paterno presented President Ronald Reagan with a No. 1 jersey in a White House ceremony.

the fraternity parties, hanging around at the student union building, and working and studying like the dickens in their classes while also having fun playing football. A Philadelphia sportswriter named Bill Conlin heard me spouting off about this one Friday night at a reception before a game. He called it "the Grand Experiment," and the name stuck.

Hopefully, you'll find out yourself when you read what some of those players and many others tell you in this book. And it still works. Just look at Paul Posluszny, who won the Butkus Award last year as the best linebacker in the country and was also an Academic All-American [with a 3.66 grade-point average in finance]. When I see Paul, I also see Dennis Onkotz, another All-American linebacker [in 1968 and 1969] who was on the dean's list in biophysics and even went to class Saturday mornings before our games. They tie it all together from the beginning of our "Grand Experiment" until this very day.

That's all part of our tradition. Education comes first, football second. It's right there with our plain white uniforms and black shoes.

If there is one question I have been asked over and over in the past 30 or 40 years, it's why we don't have names on our uniforms or why we don't have fancier uniforms. I sometimes ask if they want us to go back to Penn State's first colors, pink and black, back in 1887. Now, wouldn't we look cute in pink?

Those white uniforms are who we are. Hardworking, regular people who play by the rules and do it the right way. And we are a team. We may be individuals, but we play as a team. The team comes first. There is one name on the uniforms. Penn State.

I've also been asked why we don't retire numbers. John Cappelletti wore No. 22, but so did Chuck Burkhart and Milt Plum and Tor Toretti, who was one of my assistant coaches. They didn't win the Heisman Trophy, but in their own ways they were as much a part of Penn State as Cappy.

I have always believed that no one player is above any other. Some of our players are in the College Football Hall of Fame and many have been

Joe Paterno and his wife, Sue, have been a philanthropic couple, leading major university fund-raising projects and giving millions of their own dollars to Penn State. A new library wing dedicated in 2000 is named after them.

Joe Paterno has become such a national icon that in 2004 he was featured on the front of Wheaties cereal boxes, a prestigious honor reserved though the decades only for the super elite of national sports figures.

All-Americans. But they also are members of the team. And it all starts and ends with the team.

Fitting in with the team has been important to the success of Penn State, and it's more than what happens on the field or in the locker room. I think one of the best examples of this is when I came here with Rip. I knew I was out of place, a smart-aleck kid from Brooklyn plunked down in this small town in the middle of nowhere. That's when I met Steve and Ginger Suhey.

Steve had been an All-American guard for Bob Higgins on that '47 team, and then stayed here and married one of Bob's daughters. Steve was helping Rip as a graduate assistant, and he and Ginger invited me to rent one of the bedrooms in the two-bedroom apartment they had moved into. We became good friends, and they introduced me to all of their friends. I could never thank them enough for how they welcomed me and helped me become a part of this community.

Later, as most people know, I coached their sons Larry, Paul, and Matt, and now I'm coaching the third-generation Suhey, Paul's son. We have also coached the sons of many other players, like the Joyners and the Pittmans and others. That's what I mean by being part of a team that goes beyond the game. And it's part of the Penn State tradition, too, because through the Suheys and Bob Higgins I am linked all the way back to Hugo Bezdek and Dick Harlow, who helped Coach Higgins when he played and later became Rip Engle's coach at Western Maryland. Dick's in the Hall of Fame, too.

We've been fortunate since I became the head football coach to have five undefeated teams, and we have come close a few other times. We've won two national championships [in 1982 and 1986] and might have won more if given the opportunity to play for it.

I don't know why, but we always seem to have to prove ourselves. I remember after we had undefeated seasons in '68 and '69 and won the Orange Bowls, and we still didn't get voted No. 1.

When we got into the Big Ten in 1993, there were some people who wondered if we belonged, that the Big Ten played better football than we did with our eastern opponents. But we won the Big Ten championship in '94 and beat a good Oregon team in the Rose Bowl [38–20]. Those kids deserved a national championship, just like those teams back in '68 and '69, and Cappelletti's team in '73. We had one of the great offensive teams in college football in '94. More than 10 years later, guys like Kerry Collins, Kyle Brady, Bobby Engram, Jeff Hartings, and Marco Rivera are still at their prime in the NFL. That should tell everyone how good that team was.

We are proud that when we won those championships back in the '80s we played as tough a schedule as anyone, and I think the Big Ten today is as tough a conference as any of them. We had some rough years recently, but I've always looked to the future and I still do, particularly after what our players did last year. I can't say enough about Michael Robinson, Alan Zemaitis, Tamba Hali, the senior and junior leadership, and the rest of the squad, especially those freshmen. I'm also happy for all my assistant coaches who hung in there and worked their butts off, despite all the criticism and the outside pressures we had.

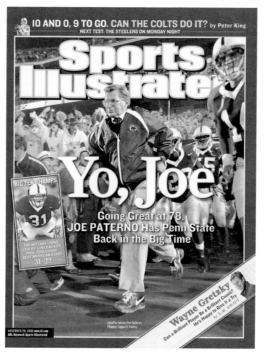

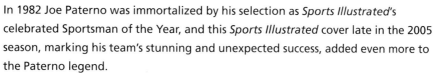

In 1982 Joe Paterno was immortalized by his selection as *Sports Illustrated*'s celebrated Sportsman of the Year, and this *Sports Illustrated* cover late in the 2005 season, marking his team's stunning and unexpected success, added even more to the Paterno legend.

That team may have had to overcome more than any team I've ever coached, and that's saying a lot. They brought our winning tradition back to the top and they deserve the credit. That's what Penn State football has always been about—all those players and all the assistant coaches down through the years who went out there every day to practice and to the classroom, to learn or to teach, and who, on a few Saturdays every fall, would play and coach their hearts out to win a football game.

I've often been asked why I stayed put for so long. I can honestly say that if I had left, I wouldn't have been around the kind of people I've been around here. We have a great University, great alumni, and great fans. I can't think of any school that has more loyal fans. I have a love affair with Penn State. It's a great place.

—Joe Paterno

When Penn State beat Ohio State 29–27 on October 27, 2001, at Beaver Stadium, Joe Paterno surpassed Alabama's Bear Bryant as the winningest coach in Division I-A with his 324th win. The players carried him off the field.

In May 2006 Joe Paterno was elected to the College Football Hall of Fame. Penn State's victory over Florida State in the 2006 Orange Bowl gave Paterno his 354th career victory, the most in history for any coach at one NCAA Division I school and second on the all-time list. He holds the record in bowl appearances with 21 wins, 10 losses, and one tie. In 2005 he was the consensus Coach of the Year and won the American Football Coaches award for an unprecedented fifth time. And early in 2006, the NCAA selected Paterno, a quarterback at Brown University in the late 1940s, as one of the 100 Most Influential Student-Athletes in history.

ACKNOWLEDGMENTS

THE EDITORS WOULD LIKE TO ACKNOWLEDGE all of those people who helped make *What It Means to Be a Nittany Lion* come to fruition. Neither one of us knew what an undertaking this would be. On more than one occasion, we wondered just what we'd got ourselves into as we tried arranging interviews with the players who are scattered all over the country and busy with their own lives. We came close to getting everybody we wanted, and we are confident—given the nearly 70 players who cover eight decades—we have put together what equates to an oral history of Penn State football in the modern era.

First and foremost, we couldn't have done this without the players who were gracious enough to share their time and memories with us, as well as Joe and Sue Paterno, whose support of this project was vital. Bobby Engram, as big a playmaker as anyone who ever suited up for Penn State, epitomized the kind of cooperation we received from the players.

Less than a week before his Seattle Seahawks were scheduled to play in the NFC Championship—easily the biggest game in franchise history and arguably the biggest in Engram's NFL career—Engram did a lengthy interview with one of the editors. The same can be said of John Cappelletti, the only player from Penn State to win the Heisman Trophy. Cappelletti turns down most requests for in-depth interviews because he is inundated with them. But Cappelletti was so enthused about this project that he spoke for nearly an hour about his days at Penn State with one of the editors.

To Cappelletti, Engram, the Paternos, and all of the players as well as others who are in the book, we are truly grateful. Thank you for putting up with all of our phone calls and emails and, ultimately, for agreeing to be a part of this. The families of two players who are deceased were especially cooperative in helping us get their stories into this book. Marilyn Mitinger, the widow of Bob Mitinger, and Peggy Robinson and her three brothers, the children of Jim O'Hora, provided us with newspaper articles and other memorabilia that formed the basis of the Mitinger and O'Hora chapters.

Dr. Paul Suhey, a linebacker in the 1970s whose family legacy goes back to his grandfather, All-American end and Hall of Fame coach Bob Higgins, put us in touch with his brother, Matt; and former soccer coach Walter Bahr and his wife, Davies, brought us together with their famous sons, Chris and Matt.

We also want to acknowledge the efforts of many, many others who helped us in contacting players. Fran Ganter, who played at Penn State and was later the offensive coordinator before moving into athletics administration following the 2003 season, was particularly helpful, as was Penn State athletics director Tim Curley. Others on Penn State's coaching staff who helped include Dick Anderson, Tom Bradley, Larry Johnson, and Jay Paterno. Thanks also to Joe Paterno's staff assistant, Sandy Segursky, for her efforts in coordinating Coach Paterno's foreword.

Some of the players in this book, such as Trey Bauer, Dr. Dave Joyner, Mark Markovich, O. J. McDuffie, Lenny Moore, Chet Parlavecchio, and Leo Wisniewski, aided our efforts to contact fellow players, as did former Nittany Lions wideout Tony Johnson.

Reaching Penn Staters currently in the NFL was not easy by any means, and the efforts of folks like Mai Davis of the Detroit Lions, Dan Edwards and Ryan Robinson of the Jacksonville Jaguars, Paul Kirk of the Denver Broncos, and Burt Lauten of the Pittsburgh Steelers are greatly appreciated. Allyson Turner, who works with O. J. McDuffie, also merits mention for her assistance (and patience with us).

We also had help from Penn State's sports information department, especially director Jeff Nelson and his assistant directors Barry Jones and Brian Siegrist, and staff assistant Valerie Cingle, as well as Jackie Esposito and Paul Dryzak at the Penn State Paterno-Pattee Library Sports Archives.

A special thanks also goes to Triumph Books, particularly managing editor Tom Bast and this book's editor, Amy Reagan. Tom had enough faith in this project that he twice extended our deadline after we encountered difficulty reaching some of the players in the book. Amy was also patient with us and was always quick to answer any questions we had.

In lieu of a dedication, Lou would like to thank his wife, Carole, for her moral support and her copy-reading efforts, while Scott would like to thank his father, Scott, mother, Gretchen, and sisters, Melissa and Ali, for the love and support they have always shown him.

INTRODUCTION

WHEN WE WERE ASKED BY TRIUMPH to be involved in this book, we agreed wholeheartedly. We are both Penn Staters of different generations.

One of us, a one-time Pitt fan from Indiana, Pennsylvania, remembers seeing his first football game in 1955 when future NFL legends Lenny Moore and Jim Brown went head-to-head at Beaver Field. Penn State won 21–20 in what is now considered one of the greatest individual performances by two opposing players in Nittany Lions history, and Lou was hooked. When Lou started dating his wife, Carole, that year, he learned she had been a devout Penn State fan almost from infancy because of her grandfather, Bob Harpster, who used to drive over the mountains from his home outside of Lewistown with friends and family to see games in the 1930s and 1940s.

The other one of us wasn't even born until decades later, but he had blue and white in his genes long before that. His father, also named Scott, didn't graduate from Penn State, but just about everyone else did in the Brown family of Greensburg, Pennsylvania. Younger Scott vividly remembers one of his first games at Beaver Stadium in 1982. He burst into tears as he watched the hated Pitt Panthers take a 7–3 lead into the locker room at halftime with the opportunity of ruining the Lions' chance to play for the national championship. A Todd Blackledge–to–Kenny Jackson touchdown pass helped make for a happy ride back down the mountain.

Both editors wrote about the football team for the college newspaper, *The Daily Collegian.* Lou was there when Joe Paterno was Rip Engle's assistant and Penn State was trying to break into the national limelight as it became one of the elite teams in the East. After college, Lou covered many Nittany

Lions games as a reporter, including several bowl games, and then wrote a book about the history of the program, *The Penn State Football Encyclopedia.*

Scott covered the shock-and-awe offense of the Big Ten champions in 1994 and later had the privilege of telling how that incredible offense came together in a book titled *Lion Kings.* Both editors still consider it a shame that the '94 team didn't get a share of the national championship with Nebraska. Lou also believes the great undefeated teams of 1968, 1969, and 1973 were also treated shabbily by the pollsters. The perceived bias against Penn State over the years comes through in some of what the players say.

Even though the editors did not meet until a few years ago, they are tied directly together through Scott's uncle, Tom Brown, who has been Lou's good friend since their days as Theta Delta Chi fraternity brothers. Penn State football was a lot different when Lou and Tom first met in the mid-1950s, and it has changed even since Scott started going to games in the 1980s.

When Lou was in school, the home games were played before crowds of about 30,000 or less, and Beaver Field was in the middle of campus, literally across the street from Lou's dormitory window when he was a freshman. By the time Scott was raking leaves as a fraternity pledge outside of Phi Kappa Psi during the 1991 Notre Dame–Penn State game, the roars from the stadium could be heard miles away. The games were drawing capacity crowds of more than 96,000 in the renamed Beaver Stadium, which had been reconstructed on the eastern fringe of the campus. Today, with further expansion, crowds frequently exceed the seating capacity of 107,282.

Tailgating was unknown in the 1950s. In that era, you could park your car downtown, have a late breakfast or early lunch, and then walk a couple of blocks to the Beaver Field ticket booth and buy a couple of seats for that day's game. Nowadays, you can't park near Beaver Stadium unless you have a reserved parking pass because the dozens of parking lots surrounding the stadium are filled every game day with dedicated Nittany Lions fans tailgating from early morning until late night.

Back in 1960, when they moved the home field from the middle of campus to the edge of the cow fields, one of Penn State's assistant coaches was very vocal in opposing the switch. Joe Paterno still talks about his belief back then that the move "will destroy the great game-day atmosphere we have here." Okay, so he missed that one, but he hasn't missed on much else since becoming the Nittany Lions' head coach in 1966.

It has been during the Paterno era that so many of the Nittany Lions football traditions began. Take the cheer of "We Are…Penn State!" that reverberates throughout Beaver Stadium—and elsewhere—on game day. Or the "flip" by the Blue Band's drum major that precedes the march of the band into the electrified stadium before each game.

But though it may be difficult for younger fans to believe, some of the traditions started long before Paterno came on the scene. For instance, the white helmets and plain white or blue uniforms without names on the jerseys. That goes all the way back to 1888. Well, not the helmets. They didn't wear helmets until years later.

Of course, back in that era no one wore colorful uniforms with names on the jerseys. Most of the teams didn't have numbers on the uniforms either. Numbers began appearing on Penn State uniforms in the early 1900s, but names on jerseys, never. Nowadays, whenever anyone sees those uniforms on television, they know automatically who is playing without having to be told. And the Nittany Lions who have worn those blasé uniforms over the last 50 years love that tradition more than anyone. Many of them write about it in this book.

Some of the players also remember the rides from their practice locker room to Beaver Stadium on game day in those sterile, uncomfortable blue school buses or the trips in the same swaying buses to the hotel on the eve of the game. In his own inimitable, free-spirit style, All-American Greg Buttle, one of the premier graduates of Linebacker U, describes one such bus ride as a freshman in 1973.

The players also tell how they were recruited and why they decided to play football at Penn State:

- Lydell Mitchell, who played his way into the College Football Hall of Fame, decided to go to Ohio State because he felt more comfortable there than at an "out-of-the-way place" in the middle of Pennsylvania's mountains, until one particular football coach challenged his manhood.

- Fun-loving defensive end Greg Murphy had committed to Michigan because he felt "it was meant to be" after he accidentally walked through a plate glass hotel lobby window during a snowstorm while on his recruiting visit to Ann Arbor. But then an assistant coach at another Big Ten school named George Paterno intervened and asked Murph to talk to his older brother Joe at Penn State before making his final decision.

- All-American running back Ki-Jana Carter grew up an avid Ohio State fan in the shadow of the famed "Horseshoe" stadium in Columbus, and he was not a fan of Penn State's plain uniforms. He accompanied his coaches to Penn State one summer day before his senior year of high school, met star wide receiver O. J. McDuffie, and started a friendship that continues to this day between the next-door neighbors in South Florida.

Naturally, the players remember some of the great games they played in:

- Milt Plum and Dan Radakovich recall the major upset of Ohio State, 7–6, in 1956 that moved the Penn State program to a higher level virtually overnight.

- Ted Kwalick, Dennis Onkotz, and Jack Ham, all enshrined in the College Football Hall of Fame, reminisce about the Orange Bowl victories in 1969 and 1970, when Paterno's unbeaten teams became the talk of the nation.

- Kenny Jackson, Gregg Garrity, John Shaffer, Shane Conlan, and others remember the national championship teams of 1982 and 1986, and Todd Blackledge has a special memory of the fans greeting the players on the way back to State College the day after the 1983 Sugar Bowl.

- Michael Robinson, Tamba Hali, and Paul Posluszny take readers right up to the shocking turnaround season of 2005, when the Nittany Lions came out of nowhere to win the Big Ten championship, the Orange Bowl, and the No. 3 ranking in the country.

Today, Joe Paterno is synonymous with Penn State football. The Nittany Lions have become one of the nation's elite teams under him and, as the 2006 season gets underway, he is the second-winningest coach in NCAA Division I-A history. No man has ever won more games as the head coach of one Division I-A school.

Almost all of the stories in this book are told by men who played for Paterno. That includes nine players who were there when Paterno was an assistant coach for his mentor, Rip Engle. Two of those nine, Dan Radakovich and Jerry Sandusky, later coached for Paterno, as did two players from the

1930s who are now deceased, Jim O'Hora and Tor Toretti. The memories of O'Hora and Toretti are in their own words as they reminisced years ago in interviews with sportswriters. So Paterno's presence is integrated through the stories that all the players tell.

They remember Paterno's shrill voice with a high-pitched Brooklyn accent, his sporadic temper outbursts on the practice fields, and how they occasionally argued about what he told them or challenged his authority behind the scenes. They also remember his kind words after losing disappointing games and the frequent inquires about their mothers and fathers that still continue and now include their wives and children.

They recall how they listened to his talks about life and heard his repeated sayings, but behind his back sometimes mocked him and thought he was full of beans. Today, they tell their sons and daughters what he told them, even repeating some of Paterno's favorite sayings.

"Joe would always say, 'Keep your poise and understand with hard work and in time, things will work out,'" All-American defensive back Michael Zordich remembers. "These lessons are the same ones I try to drum into my own kids' heads."

As Penn State's only Heisman Trophy winner, John Cappelletti writes, "Joe was a good person to have in your life for those four years, whether it was on or off the field."

The players also remember the Penn State assistant coaches in their lives. They were recruited by them and usually were almost always closer to them than they were to Paterno. Many of them had been Nittany Lions themselves, but all of them had the players' interests at heart—from the seriousness of Frank Patrick or Bob Phillips to the fun-loving nature of J. T. White or Jerry Sandusky.

It was this diverse group of assistant coaches as much as Paterno who made sure the players went to class and studied. If there is one major theme that intertwines throughout the players' thoughts of what it means to be a Nittany Lion, it is the education they received at Penn State.

This was expressed best by Dave Joyner, an All-American in football and wrestling as well as an Academic All-American and now a member of Penn State's Board of Trustees: "We were always taught by Joe and the other coaches that athletics were part of academics, not a separate piece. A lot of people say it but not all of them believe it. We live it. That attitude prevails from the top down, and I mean from the [university] president and not just the athletics director and head coaches."

But this book is more than what the players remember about Joe Paterno and the other assistant coaches. It's about what Penn State University stands for beyond its football program. Standards. Integrity. Class. And it's also about being a leader in one of the major social issues in this country's history: race relations.

Wally Triplett describes what it was like to be Penn State's first black football letterman in the mid-1940s and how his all-white teammates stood behind him and voted not to play a game at Miami in 1946 because of segregation.

Lenny Moore and Rosey Grier recall their experiences almost a decade later on the still mostly white Penn State campus, and how they truly felt like Nittany Lions because of the kindness of the coaching staff as they continued to encounter racism on and off the football field. Moore, a member of the Pro Football Hall of Fame, describes the letter he received from a Texas woman after he, Grier, and Jesse Arnelle were the first black players to play in Fort Worth in 1953.

Dave Robinson remembers not being allowed to play in the 1959 Liberty Bowl because all-white Alabama dictated that only one black player be on the field. Robinson also writes about the class of Georgia Tech coach Bobby Dodd when Robinson became the first African American to play in the Gator Bowl at Jacksonville two years later.

Playing football for the Nittany Lions is something special, and many of those in this book did not realize how special until years after they left. They discovered strangers giving them a little more respect when they learned they had played football at Penn State. They found their teammates and coaches in pro football constantly asking them about Penn State and Joe Paterno and whether they really had to study and go to class, and whether they really had to wear coats and ties on road trips and really weren't allowed to wear hats inside buildings.

All-American guard Steve Wisniewski found out that Joe's rule about hats is still enforced, even after a player has left the program. He was wearing a hat indoors while visiting some of the coaches one day when the eight-time NFL Pro Bowler heard that familiar strident voice barking at him about the transgression.

Like Wisniewski, the players find themselves returning more and more to campus, perhaps to see a game but more importantly to get back with their old teammates and remember together the joys and heartaches of putting on that plain blue and white uniform, riding those noisy blue school buses, and running out onto the stadium grass and hearing the multitude of fans.

"I gained more understanding on a recent visit back to Happy Valley," writes Keith Dorney upon his return to Penn State in the fall of 2005 after his election to the College Football Hall of Fame. "It was then that my epiphany hit me like a 300-hundred-pound defensive lineman." Dorney is one of two players who actually wrote about himself without the help of this book's two editors. The other player is Greg Buttle, and his chapter is a beaut.

We also have included the memories of three men who never played football, but they, too, are true Nittany Lions. Retired broadcaster Fran Fisher is as well-known by Penn State fans as any player, and he saw his first game long before almost all of the players in this book were born. Equipment manager Brad "Spider" Caldwell represents the staff behind the scene, the "grunts" who keep the football team going from decade to decade, befriending the players and neutralizing internal strife. Gene Wettstone, better known to the Penn State fan as a legendary gymnastics coach, comes the closest to being a "real" Nittany Lion because he was the third official Lion Mascot in 1939 and he tells how it happened.

If the editors have one regret, it is that we could not include more players in this book. Penn State has had a lot of great players, and these stories represent just a small segment of that revered galaxy. Their memories will now be yours, too.

The
THIRTIES
AND FORTIES

YEARS OF CHANGE

1930s–1940s

THEY'RE ALMOST ALL GONE NOW. They were the hardened men who played football for Penn State in the decade of the 1930s.

The country was emerging from a depression, and life was tough where they came from. Their fathers and uncles worked deep underground in the dirty, dimly lit coal mines or sweated profusely in the heat and grime of the steel mills.

Without their skills on the high school football fields of Pennsylvania, they would have been there, too, just like some of their brothers and cousins. Most of them were the first in their families to attend college. And it wasn't easy.

If they wanted to play football and get a degree, they had to wash dishes in the fraternities that they could not join. Or clean up at the downtown stores where they couldn't afford to buy anything or at the rooming houses where they lived. Or do one of the other menial jobs set up for them. That paid for most of their room, board, and tuition because there were no scholarships.

Athletic scholarships for incoming freshmen had been eliminated in 1928, and so they had all ended by 1930. A football team comprised of everyday students was fine, the administration declared, but education is the priority. Many alumni were not happy, particularly some former teammates of Coach Bob Higgins, who had been a two-time All-American end before and after World War I. The Hig's friends were the ones who conceived of the work program and an innovating fund-raising scheme to circumvent the administration's idealistic policy.

The effects of the policy were almost immediate. Penn State had one of the nation's best teams in the previous two decades, even playing in the 1923 Rose Bowl game against USC, but after the last scholarship players graduated, the football program plunged into near disarray. A 2–8 season in Higgins's second year, 1931, and a 2–5 record the next year was too much for the coach's one-time classmates and friends. They developed a resourceful plan for subsidizing players and they went to work.

They scoured the coal regions of northeastern and western Pennsylvania and the mill towns across the state. They found kids with names that were sometimes hard to pronounce: Cherundolo, Mikelonis, Stravinski, Gajecki. By 1940 Penn State was back in the limelight, with a 6–1–1 record that almost got them into a postseason bowl game.

Of all those dozens of determined young men who wore the blue and white in that decade, two epitomize what it means to be a Nittany Lion— Jim O'Hora and Sever "Tor" Toretti. That's because they not only played at Penn State but they returned years later to help coach the players who turned the Nittany Lions into a national powerhouse. No one was more loyal to Penn State or as dedicated to the team. Their names are mentioned frequently by many of the players in this book, and their influence has been immeasurable.

Both were sons of coal miners. O'Hora was from Dunsmore and played center from 1933 to 1935. Toretti, from Monongahela, followed O'Hora, starting at guard or tackle from 1936 to 1938. They also were coaching colleagues, with O'Hora's tenure as defensive line coach or defensive coordinator from 1946 to 1976, while Toretti was there as offensive line coach, chief recruiter, or assistant athletics director from 1949 to 1979. Toretti died in 2000, and O'Hora passed away in 2005. If still alive, both would have told their own stories of what being a Nittany Lion meant to them.

We do have the words of both men, taken from newspaper articles their families had saved over the years and the special Sports Archives collection at Penn State's Paterno-Pattee Library. We think these chapters not only speak for O'Hora and Toretti but for all the other assistant coaches who spent most of their life's work molding callow, unsophisticated young men into proud, industrious, and worldly Nittany Lions.

JIM O'HORA

CENTER   COACH
1933–1935   1946–1976

WHEN I FIRST CAME TO PENN STATE [TO PLAY FOOTBALL], it was a down time for us. Scholarships had been abolished [in 1928], and there was a feeling that the bottom had fallen out of the football program. The coaches were discouraged because there weren't any blue-chip athletes around.

Bill Griffiths, Casey Jones, [Jim Gilligan], and some other alumni got interested in bringing football back to where it had been. That was the start, and each year it got better.

I never played or coached on a losing team at Penn State. We had a losing record when I came here as a freshman, but we didn't have any losing seasons the three years I played under Bob Higgins and we haven't had one since I've been here coaching.

[As a player, O'Hora had the misfortune of playing center at the same time as one of Penn State's greatest players of the era, Chuck Cherundolo, who later spent 11 years in the NFL. Following graduation, O'Hora coached high school football and returned there after his service in World War II, before Higgins hired him in 1949.]

I remember when I came back as an assistant coach [in 1946], we needed to find somewhere for many of the players to eat. Earle Edwards, Al Michaels [two other assistant coaches], and I went around to the fraternities. We'd sell

Penn State's coaches in 1936 were all former Nittany Lions players, and they lined up for the photographer in the positions they played. Jim O'Hora is the center. The others are (from left): Earle Edwards, Marty McAndrews, Joe Bedenk, Bill Miller, Al Michaels, and head coach Bob Higgins.

the idea that they'd be helping football players of renown like [Sam] Tamburo and [Elwood] Petchel. Most houses turned us down right away. A few agreed to feed a player or two. The players would have to go around at 6:30 and eat anything left over. When Rip Engle came, we had scholarships. He set up a training table during the season in the dormitories, and the players would eat with the females.

When I first came here [in 1946] I thought I'd stay a few years to get some experience and then coach at some small college. Gradually, I began to see great growth possibility here. I said to myself, "How high is up?" I looked at what I saw ahead for Penn State and decided that's how high I wanted to go.

I've kind of raised Joe. When he first came to Penn State [in 1950], he lived with my family. He was one of us. [Paterno was a bachelor and still living with the O'Horas 12 years later.] It was in 1962, I think, when I talked to him.

My parents had come to this country from Ireland and later were joined by cousins. They would take them in. After the relative became settled down, financially able to take care of themselves, my father would say, "Now it's time for you to go out and find a place of your own."

I knew it was a time at which Joe was getting to the age where maybe he had to have a change. So I told him the story of my father and his relatives. Joe said, "I got the message." He moved out and, less than a year later, was married.

I always saw Joe as one of the outstanding coaches in the game. He was ahead of his time and all he needed was the chance to prove himself. I think Joe and I get along so well because we respect each other's ability as well as respect each other as persons.

I wanted to be a head man back earlier in my career. Later, I began to feel there was no better situation, so I stopped thinking about it. I've enjoyed my association with the coaches and the others in the athletic program, but for me, the real joy was working with the kids, seeing their courage, their enthusiasm. Most of the time, I couldn't wait to get to work.

In looking back at our great players, at defensive end it's almost impossible to eliminate Dave Robinson. Jack Ham has to be the top outside linebacker. The down people that are the most memorable are Mike Reid, Glenn Ressler, and Mike Hartenstine. The best inside linebacker would have to be Dennis Onkotz. And the best secondary man is Neal Smith.

Lenny Moore was an outstanding defensive back. And I'd have to put Richie Lucas up there, too. We've had so many great inside linebackers, people like John Skorupan and Eddie O'Neil, but the one I would have to put next to Onkotz is Danny Radakovich. And I would rate Sam Tamburo just a bit higher than Bob Mitinger at the other defensive end.

A defensive lineman must have the willingness, the desire to hit. He can't be satisfied to just tackle his opponent. He must want to destroy the opponent's usefulness. Rosey Grier loved to have a play come his way. He would smile and say, "lovely, lovely," after the tackle.

He was good on offense, too. I'll never forget that 20–20 tie we had against Purdue at Beaver Field in 1952. We were down on their 6-yard line late in the game when a play was called to Rosey's side. He destroyed his side of the Purdue line.

One of the games I remember was beating Ohio State 7–6 in 1956. We noticed in scouting that their No. 64 [on offense] positioned his hand and feet wherever the play was going. [Assistant coach Tor Toretti was the scout who helped Penn State upset the heavily favored No. 5 Buckeyes at Columbus.]

The 1969 team was one of our best, but the one I remember the most was our 1964 team. That season really stands out. We had hard luck early in the season, but we went from 1–4 to 6–4. The Ohio State game that year stands out in my mind. [The Nittany Lions upset the No. 2 Buckeyes at Columbus, this time 27–0.] We had some people who knew adversity but came back to be as good a team as there was in the country. That was as good a team as I've been around and it was thrilling and satisfying to be a part of it.

I know I'll miss coaching—that's natural—but the physical demands of the game today [in 1977] are great. It's a different game today. It's a young man's game. Football has become so much more complex. The teaching today is specialized in each area so that the player with potential can come closer to reaching it. Every aspect of his game is brought forward. [But] it takes more out of an individual to coach. The demands on your time on and off the field have increased tremendously.

I've enjoyed my years here. When I see the kind of kids we have here now, I'm glad I never left.

Credits: Jim O'Hora's words were taken primarily from articles written by Ronnie Christ of the Harrisburg Patriot-News, *Frank Bilovsky of the now defunct* Philadelphia Bulletin *and the* Centre Daily Times, *with additional material from* Beaver Field Pictorial *and a personal interview with the editor.*

7

Jim O'Hora never had a winning or losing season as a player because when he played center from 1933 to 1935 Penn State finished with three straight records at .500. Before joining the Bob Higgins coaching staff in 1946, he had been a high school coach and naval officer. O'Hora began to make his name as the defensive line coach for Rip Engle and later as the man in charge of the Nittany Lions' outstanding defensive teams of the early Paterno era. When he retired in 1977, an award was created in his honor that now is presented annually after spring practice to a defensive player for exemplary conduct, loyalty, interest, attitude, and improvement.

IN MEMORIAM

SEVER "TOR" TORETTI

GUARD/TACKLE

1936–1938

COACH/STAFF

1949–1979

WHEN I CAME TO PENN STATE I had to work for my room and board. I worked at the Rathskeller for my meals and made beds in the dormitories. A lot of the fellows worked as waiters and dishwashers at fraternities. We didn't have the dining hall set-up we have now [in 1979]. You have to give credit to the fraternity system for the help they gave us.

[As a senior, Toretti played on the 1938 team that set four NCAA defensive records—including one that was still unbroken in 2005—but wound up with a losing record of 3–4–1. After one year as a graduate assistant, he went into high school coaching and returned there after his air force service in World War II. In 1949 Joe Bedenk took over as head coach from the retiring Bob Higgins, and Bedenk, who had been Toretti's line coach as a player, hired Toretti for the staff vacancy.]

We didn't even have grants-in-aid. I asked Joe Bedenk what kind of grants he had, and he told me none. Oh, we had a fund for athletes; we raffled off a car, and we'd take care of a kid's tuition or something like that. But no full rides. I used to hate that, having to sell [raffle] tickets for that car [every year at the Pitt game].

We went to Sam Hostetler, who was the controller, and proposed a program [similar to Notre Dame's] where they got the football players jobs as dormitory monitors. Sam was a businessman and he knew what we needed. I call him the father of Penn State football.

They were rebuilding Beaver Field. Steel for 35,000 seats was a big chunk of cash, and we needed a winning team to keep those seats filled. Sam took our proposal to the Board of Trustees meeting in Harrisburg in January. When he got back, he called us and said our proposal had been turned down flat.

Hostetler said, "However, they are aware that aid is important because they do feel that a young man cannot participate in high-pressure athletics, do well academically, and hold down a job, too." He said the Board authorized 30 full grants-in-aid per year, authorized 15 more the following year, and 15 more the year after that, so we eventually had 60.

This program began to move when Rip [Engle] came here in the spring [of 1959]. It had become evident to him and those of us on his staff that if we were really going to get the program going, we had to have men who would stay here for four years. Prior to that we had been on a treadmill of sorts. We had a certain academic mortality rate.

But we felt that unless we got a boy who was going to stay here for four years, someone who had been around, who knew the problems and would provide the leadership for the younger kids, we weren't going to get anywhere. It was tough at first because we weren't recognized as an outstanding football school and we were not getting the outstanding student-athlete.

We'd go recruiting and ask a coach about a certain boy. He would say he was saving him for Notre Dame or someone like that. I'll tell you, there were many a night when we'd come back up these hills in the middle of winter with our hearts broken. Our program wasn't built overnight. A lot of hard work by people like Frank Patrick, Jim O'Hora, and others went into it.

I figured we had arrived when it got to the point where we would go see the same coach and he'd say, "Hey, we have a good boy for you." Heck, there was a time when a lot of kids didn't even know where Penn State was. I think

9

things really started to turn around in 1956, after we beat Ohio State 7–6 out there. Before that, people would say, "Penn State? Where the hell's that?"

We began to win on a national scale. We began playing people who were recognized as top powers and were able to do more than hold our own against them. We beat Alabama [7–0] in the first Liberty Bowl in 1959 and then went down to the Gator Bowl and beat Georgia Tech [30–15] in 1961. We ran into some polite snobbery in Jacksonville. People wanted to know what right we had coming down there to play an SEC power like Georgia Tech.

Of course, we've been winning key games, doing it with outstanding men who are better-than-average students. We're to a point now [in 1977] where if there is a good kid, his coach will tell him he should take a look at what Penn State has to offer before making up his mind. Now our program is recognized everywhere and we get kids from all over the country wanting to come here.

[Toretti was such an outstanding recruiter that in 1963 he was named assistant athletics director with full responsibilities for football recruiting.]

The letter of intent [introduced in 1964] was one of the best things that ever happened. There was a time when even after a prospect had made up his mind, he was not above changing at the last moment. Before the letter, you never knew who you were getting until they actually enrolled, and sometimes they'd leave after they had enrolled. You had to keep an eye on these kids all summer. We lost Mike Ditka [to Pitt in 1956] like that. We thought he was coming here and he changed his mind in August.

I remember when we were recruiting Mike Reid [in 1964]. I went down to Altoona on the first day of preseason practice in his senior year, took him aside between the morning and afternoon sessions, and told him how much we wanted him to come to Penn State. He said he already knew what he wanted to do and I sort of sucked my breath and waited for him to tell me. He said he already had decided he was going to Penn State.

Then, just as I was getting ready to go, he said he had something he wanted me to do. I thought, "Uh-oh, here it comes." Then he said, "Go out and get some good players. I don't want to play on a loser."

To illustrate the human error involved [in recruiting], there's no better case than Neal Smith. He came to us without a scholarship [in 1966]. We overlooked him in scouting for players. Neal came out for football on his own and wound up an All-American defensive back his last year in [1969].

Tor Toretti was what is now termed "a player's coach" because he could communicate with the players on their level with sensitivity, compassion, and with their basic interests at heart.

Steve Smear came into my office one day in April of 1966 and asked what we were going do about Jack Ham, if we knew anything about him. I said, "Yeah, sure we know about him." But we didn't. [Toretti had recruited Smear from Johnstown's Bishop McCort High School the previous year. Ham was on the same team but had diverted to a military prep school with the intention of enrolling at Virginia Military Institute.] Steve told me how tough Ham was and how fast he was.

After he left, I called Jack's coach. He said if we had any rides left we should give it to Ham. So I called Jack down at Massanutten Prep and asked if he'd come up for a visit. We made up our minds that if he was 6'2", we'd take him. When he came in, we stood him against the wall and he measured 6'2¼", so we gave him a grant. It was the last one we had that year.

[Reid, Smith, Smear, and Ham formed part of the nucleus of one of the greatest college defenses of all time, in 1968 and 1969, leading the Nittany Lions to back-to-back unbeaten seasons, two Orange Bowl victories, and consecutive No. 2 national rankings.]

Our idea here at Penn State is to make an honest attempt to provide the boy [being recruited] with all the information we can give him with regard to the academic, social, and athletic life. We use a very low-key approach, no hard sell. We want to make sure a boy has a chance to evaluate the university without pressure. Not every boy wants to come to State. Some want the big city life. You can't satisfy everyone. Our reputation is such that I've had recruiters at other schools tell me that if Penn State is after the same kid they're after, they can't beat us on a fair deal.

There's nothing wrong in trying to get the best student-athletes to come to your school. Where the problem comes in is some people want to do it contrary to the rules. Everyone has their own standards, but if they say they are adhering to the rules and then break them, that's where they are wrong. As I see it, winning at any costs could be the end of college football.

Years ago, [Penn State President] Dr. [Eric] Walker said nothing unites the alumni, the faculty, the student body, the townspeople, and friends like a fine athletic program, primarily a fine football team.

The average fan has taken to Penn State as the team to follow. You don't realize this until you go out there and walk into some of these homes and see nothing but Penn State things. And these are not alumni. They are eager for any scrap of information you can give them on this team, that player, how Joe is doing. It's a way of life for them.

It's been a great tenure. I made lots of friends, established some great relationships. Penn State has been my life. The school has given me a fine education, I met my wife here, and my children have graduated from here. I love Penn State.

Credits: Tor Toretti's words were taken primarily from articles written by Ron Bracken of the Centre Daily Times, *with additional articles written by John Travers and Ronnie Christ of the* Harrisburg-Patriot News *and Donna Clemson for* Town & Gown *magazine.*

Tor Toretti called the defensive signals for the 1938 team that set three NCAA pass-defense records, including one for fewest yards passing allowed per game (13.1 average) that was still the record as of this writing in 2006. He was a successful high school coach in Steelton and Williamsport before returning to Penn State in 1949. Toretti became known for his development of offensive linemen and his scouting reports on opposing teams. When he became the Nittany Lions' first full-time recruiting coordinator in 1963, his reputation as a first-class recruiter surpassed everything else and helped propel Penn State into the elite of college football.

WALLY TRIPLETT

HALFBACK/WINGBACK

1945–1948

I WAS THE FIRST BLACK PLAYER TO EARN a varsity football letter at Penn State and I feel proud of what I did as a student and athlete there. I'm also proud of some of my teammates who stood with me in fighting the prejudice that was socially acceptable at the time.

I had met the great Paul Robeson in 1942 when he appeared at my Elkins Park Junior High School, and so when I went to Penn State in 1945, I was very conscious of being one of few blacks in State College, and I was "cautious," as State College was prejudiced, to put it bluntly. It was not "Happy Valley" at that point in time.

My entrance was not pleasantly accepted by the coaching staff of Bob Higgins and assistant coach Joe Bedenk. They were hoping I was going to try to be the replacement for probably one of the greatest athletes to enter Penn State, Dave Alston. [Dave Alston was Penn State's first black player and played on the 1941 freshman team. He was a multiple-threat player who could run, pass, kick, and play defense with great skill. Before his scheduled debut with the varsity as a sophomore, the press touted him as a sure-fire All-American, but he died unexpectedly before the 1942 season of complications from tonsillectomy surgery.] The Hig always wanted to compare me to Dave Alston, and I didn't like that because I wasn't the player Dave Alston was. Hig didn't like my attitude about this, and we got into it a lot.

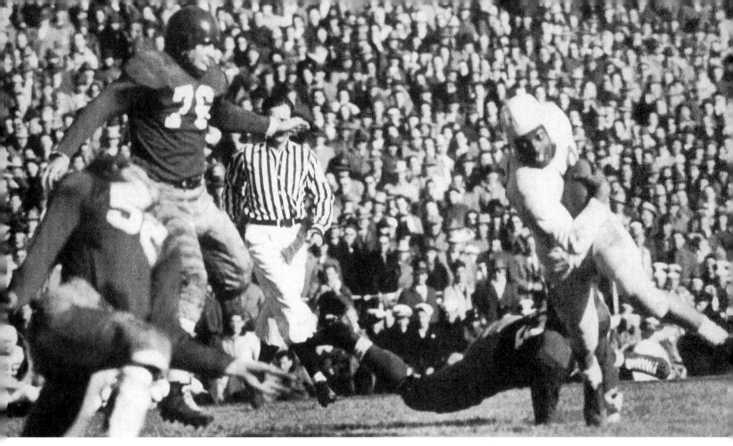

Wally Triplett was first and foremost a trailblazer in the pursuit of civil rights, but on the playing field he was an outstanding runner and defensive back in an era when college football was played by hardened, mature men who had served in World War II.

I went to Cheltenham High School. It was a racially mixed school in suburban Philadelphia that was very high on academics. I had made the All-State, All-City, and All-Suburban teams, but we weren't recruited much in eastern Pennsylvania. There wasn't that big of a deal in recruitment. Everybody just sent letters. I had a letter in January from Miami [Florida] telling me they had a beautiful program, played a nice schedule, and were interested in getting eastern kids. I knew they didn't have any blacks on their team because of segregation. I wrote a very stinging reply, and they wrote me back, apologizing, but I was angry. Then I had a letter from Higgins, saying, "Would you like to come up to Penn State?" When the letter from Hig came, I just replied that I would be up.

I didn't even know where Penn State was. I convinced my dad that I should go up there and see what this is all about. At the railroad station, I almost bought a ticket for Lewisburg and the wrong train, instead of for Lewistown, which served State College and Penn State. Classes had already started, and I had to take an examination to get in, but it was really just 10th-grade stuff from my school. The football scholarships at Penn State at the time were mostly for players from western Pennsylvania [and the hard coal region], and they had work programs with fraternity houses to help the players. I had won a Senatorial scholarship and had the promise of financial help from my church and family.

When I arrived in State College, I checked into the Corner Room Hotel, which was the class hotel at the time. When I met Higgins the next day, he was surprised I was at the Corner Room, and he sent me to see if they had a room at a house they called Lincoln Hall. This was the house that all the black guys lived in, if you could get in. The lady had a room for me with Barney Ewell. [Barney Ewell was one of America's star sprinters in the early 1940s and had returned to the campus to get his degree after service in World War II.] I then went up to talk to Hig. On my way I was able to get a dishwashing job at the bus terminal near to where I was going to live. So when I met Coach Higgins, he was impressed that I was settled in on my own.

The Hig and I got into it right from the start. He told me he wanted me to fill the shoes of Dave Alston. I said I knew all about him. In fact, knowing about Dave kind of made me want to come here. But I told Hig I was just going to try and do what I could do because I couldn't be that style of ballplayer Alston was because he could do everything.

We were single-wing, and Dave was the tailback, and everything centered around the tailback. I was always coming off the wing and I was good at blocking. I didn't mind hitting those big tackles. I said that's what I felt my position should be. The Hig didn't like that and he said, "Aww, I heard about you, Wally. You're going to have to get along." So, right there it all started. Hig and I never did see eye-to-eye. I was ready to fight at the drop of a hat and I got into a couple of fights, especially at the beginning.

I didn't play much in my freshman year but I did start against Michigan State late in the season, and they beat me up pretty good. I earned my first letter in '46, when I played both wingback and halfback. Dennie Hoggard [another black player] had come back after being in the service. He was the son of a wealthy minister and was from a Philadelphia high school, but he was older. He had played with Dave Alston but had not lettered, and we became very close friends.

Even before the '46 season started, we both knew there were going to be problems because we were scheduled to play at Miami [Florida] in our last game in early December. Dennie and I knew Miami wouldn't allow us to play. The other guys started talking about it, too, and the practices got a little rougher for me and Dennie. About midseason, *The Daily Collegian* made it all public and said we should take a stand and not play the game. So the Hig called a meeting presumably to "let the team decide."

Hig said we had this problem about Miami having these segregation rules and he would leave it up to the players to vote on whether we play the game or not. Dennie and I had some friends on the team, particularly the older guys who had been in the army, and the guys from western Pennsylvania like Sam Tamburo, Rip Scherer, and Chuck Drazenovich who had played with and against blacks in high school. But we didn't know how the vote would go, with the sunshine of Miami against the heavy winter snow of State College also being an issue.

Surprisingly, the guys spoke up, like John Nolan and Johnny Potsklan, guys I had been wary about. Someone said, "We don't need Miami." I was shocked. They were going to ask Dennie and me to leave the room, but somebody said, "No, they're part of the team and their vote counts." So the hands went up slow and we had a majority. That's when someone said, I think it was Sam Tamburo, "Let's make it unanimous," and the guys said, "Yeah, let's get it over with and get on out of here."

They didn't understand at that point the significance of what they did. I didn't either. For years, none of them thought they had done anything. That started to give me a whole new perspective on Penn State. It united us and made us a better team. We only lost two games that season, and the next year we went undefeated and the question came up again.

There were only four bowl games at that time. The Rose Bowl was the only bowl blacks could play in, and Michigan was playing there. The Sugar and the Orange Bowls wouldn't allow us. Higgins wanted a meeting again, and the guys like Sam and Nolan said, "Our position is already known. We don't have to have a meeting because we're on record."

The big question was the Cotton Bowl because there was no city ordinance preventing blacks and whites from playing in the stadium at the same time. It was Southern Methodist that broke the color line by agreeing to play us in the Cotton Bowl, and they should be applauded. But we couldn't stay in the hotels in Dallas. That again was a city ordinance. They said there was

17

a naval air base nearby that had a field and all the equipment and locker rooms to support us, and we would be able to stay there, it being a government facility. That's what we did. Again, some of the guys didn't realize what they had done. Of course, they didn't understand what prejudice was. I had to tell them many years later that that was a big thing.

Down through the years the civil rights movement went on, but there's never a mention in sports of this thing Penn State did that really helped turn it around. We changed the course for a lot of other schools. They followed our lead and said they weren't going to submit to the prejudice anymore.

We tied SMU 13–13 in the Cotton Bowl, and I had a pretty good game. I scored a touchdown on a pass and just missed catching a pass deflection at the end that would have won the game. I also remember making a tackle that saved a touchdown.

We had another good year the next season, finishing 7–1–1, but we lost to Pitt at the end, 7–0, and that cost us another bowl game. I had my best year and led the team in all-purpose yards. [Triplett had 440 yards rushing, 90 yards receiving, and 220 on punt returns while scoring 36 points.]

While I was going to Penn State, I had a lot of regrets. But when I got to the pros, I had another whole new perspective, and I have learned a lot over time. I think that we had opened up some doors at Penn State and caused some players to go there. They had good teams after that. It became a really notable place, particularly after Joe Paterno came in and really got it on the map. With the history of that, it is very encouraging when you say you are from Penn State. They always give you a little more respect. I am glad Penn State turned out to be the school that it is, and I'm very proud I'm from Penn State.

In 1949 Wally Triplett became the first black NFL draft choice to play in the NFL, first with the Detroit Lions and then with the Chicago Cardinals. Blacks played in the NFL prior to Triplett, but they were personal selections of teams. His professional career was disrupted when he became the first NFL player to be drafted into the army for the Korean War. Later, he became a businessman, a teacher, and the first black mutual clerk in Michigan racing history. Triplett married Leonore Bivins of Philadelphia, and they raised four children. He is now retired and lives primarily in Detroit.

The
FIFTIES

JIM DOOLEY
CENTER/LINEBACKER
1949–1952

PENN STATE FOOTBALL SHAPED MY LIFE in many ways. It not only provided me with an education, but I also met my wife, Nancy Higgins, whose father was Bob Higgins, a two-time All-American and head football coach at Penn State. Coach Higgins's two other daughters also married Penn Staters—Mary Ann, a Blue Bander, and Ginger, a football player, Steve Suhey. The Higgins sisters have children and grandchildren who are Penn Staters. In fact, Paul Suhey, Ginger and Steve's son—and Matt's brother—has a son, Kevin, who is a fourth-generation Penn State football player.

I was also part of a unique recruiting class. When we were recruited, we were the first scholarship players at Penn State since about 1930. I understand football was de-emphasized, but Bob Higgins brought the program back in the 1940s, using guys who worked for their tuition, room, and board. Bob retired after the '48 season, and Joe Bedenk was the coach for 1949.

Joe Bedenk had already announced his resignation while I was at California State [in Pennsylvania], but fortunately for me, he had hired Sever Toretti. Earle Edwards and Bedenk had been vying for the head-coaching job at Penn State. When Bedenk got the job, Edwards left for Michigan State and Bedenk hired Toretti. He had been the high school coach at Williamsport, and I knew him indirectly because my high school, South Williamsport, used to scrimmage against Williamsport.

Jim Dooley (No. 52) was part of Penn State's long tradition in developing good linebackers. He was good on both sides of the ball, earning second-team All-America honors his senior season, and then playing in the Senior Bowl.

Photo courtesy of Jim Dooley

Sever became my mentor at Penn State, but I was recruited by Al Michaels, who was an assistant coach. It was in the spring of my senior year when Al Michaels visited for the first time. That had something to do with the introduction of football scholarships late in the recruiting season in 1949. I already had other opportunities to go to schools far away from Williamsport, like Indiana and Pitt. I also wanted to visit Miami because we had a couple players from Williamsport who were at Miami and another from South Williamsport. My mother told me, "You can't go visit those schools." I asked why not, and she said, "Well, you aren't going to go there."

"Where am I going to go?" I asked. And she said, "You can either go to Bucknell or Penn State." Both of them are close to Williamsport, and I elected to go to Penn State because it was farther away.

It was clearly spelled out that we would not go to the main campus our freshmen year but would be sent to California [State Teachers College], which was near Pittsburgh. From 1945 through 1949, freshmen were not accepted at the Penn State main campus because there wasn't enough room. [Because of the influx of World War II veterans, Penn State worked out an arrangement whereby all Penn State football freshmen would spend their initial year attending California.] My wife, Nancy, was actually in the first class of 500 women accepted on the Penn State campus in 1949. I think they needed women up there because the ratio of men to women was about 8- or 10-to-1.

Going to California for the first time was quite an experience. My father had an old automobile and didn't think it could make the trip. So I got on a bus in Williamsport, and the bus made seven stops before it left town. I was 17 years old, and when I got off the bus in Pittsburgh, I was shocked by what a horrible looking city it was. I ended up going in the wrong direction before I found the trolley that took me down the Monongahela River to Monessen. Then an old rickety school bus took you from Monessen to California. At that particular time, there was a coal strike going on, and they were shooting at trucks. I had not been exposed to the ethnic variety of people that you see in southwestern Pennsylvania, so it was quite a cultural shock for me.

We had some extremely good football players. It was a mix between California upperclassmen and Penn State freshmen, and I'd say 80 to 90 percent of the starters were freshmen. My roommate was Ted Shattuck from Warren, Pennsylvania. Ted was an outstanding athlete and later became a fighter pilot. Unfortunately, he was killed in Vietnam. Ted was one of our top players. Paul Anders, Joe Yuccia, Don Barney, and Davy Simon were some of the others. I think we had about 25 scholarship players from Penn State.

Earl Bruce was our coach. Earl was originally from Brownsville, which is right over the hill from California. He had been recruited by Bob Higgins to run the show there. Earl had been there for four years, and I don't think he lost more than two games.

We were playing in a fast league [the Pennsylvania State Teachers College Conference] that was still composed of World War II veterans. We were really kids playing against men who were in their mid-twenties and some even older than that. We won all our games except one. I was the starting center and a linebacker. We had used the single-wing in high school until my last year when we switched to the T formation. Penn State was still running the single-wing at California and at Penn State. That didn't change until Rip Engle arrived in 1950.

We had some very good athletes, but because of the lateness of the university getting back into the scholarship business, I don't think the group was chosen well for academics. The academics were rigorous at that time—the schools were overflowing and the teachers were demanding. I think only eight or nine of us finished school. Many of the players left after their freshman year.

When Bedenk quit, there was a group pushing Earl Bruce for the head job, and some of the players were trying to get a petition around, but it didn't go anywhere. In the 1950 spring semester the group that was still around went up to Penn State for spring practice even though we were students at California. It was the week during spring vacation. There was some accommodation so that we could get to meet the new coach, Rip Engle, and convert from the single-wing to the T formation. That's why Joe Paterno got involved. He was brought in to help us adjust from a single-wing to the T.

Preseason practice was quite different back then. Before the 1950 season, we had five regular scrimmages, almost games. I remember we scrimmaged at Cornell and Colgate. Bucknell and Duquesne came here.

We had fair seasons in my sophomore and junior years [Penn State was 5–3–1 in 1950 and 5–4 in 1951]. In our last year, we had a 7–2–1 record, but, unfortunately, Ted Shattuck and Paul Anders dropped out of school and went into the air force and marine corps. They were big, strong runners. Paul was a fullback at 220, and Ted had been a tailback at 210. If they had stayed, I think we could have made a run at a high national ranking.

In our second game, we tied Purdue 20–20. I played a lot at linebacker, and Purdue threw the ball a lot. That was probably my most enjoyable game at Penn State. We played at Michigan State [four games later]. Michigan State had been undefeated in '51, and that year they would win the national championship. We had a good game with them, although we lost 34–7. But we had a pony backfield. Neither Matt Yanosich nor Dickie Jones weighed over 175 pounds soaking wet. Then we lost at Syracuse 25–7. It was a poorly played and poorly managed game. At least one of those two losses probably would not have happened with Ted and Paul.

I sure felt I got a good, sound education at Penn State, and it prepared me well for life after. Penn State always had its feet on the ground as far as the academics, being in charge from an administration point as opposed to the athletics. In the end, that may be the best part about being a Nittany Lion.

23

Jim Dooley was a second-team All-American and All-East in his senior year when his line coach, Sever Toretti, called him "the best offensive center in the country." After two years in the army, he went into the insurance business, which he continues to operate today. He lives in Allentown with his wife, Nancy, and with several of his children and grandchildren nearby.

ROSEY GRIER

TACKLE

1951–1954

IF IT WEREN'T FOR THE NITTANY LIONS, I wouldn't have graduated from college. It means that much. It made a difference in my life. I was a young man coming out of high school, not really knowing what I was going to do until I was given an opportunity to go to Penn State University. While there, I learned a lot of good things. I learned that it takes hard work to pursue anything, whether in the classroom, on the football field, or just in the overall involvement in the college campuses. It taught me how to get along with people. It taught me how to search for things that I was seeking in my life, and it also gave me a good education.

More than anything else, it taught me about leadership. I became a track captain at Penn State because I really wanted to inspire the other players and other participants of the track team. It helped me to start growing up. Penn State put me on a course. It made me proud because I was the first member of my family ever to go to college and the first one to get out of college with a degree. That meant a lot to me. Penn State taught me how to get along with coaches and it taught me how to get along with players. It taught me the essence of being on a team, and that's something that I use today.

People might be surprised to learn that I went to Penn State on a track scholarship. Norm Gordon was a track coach, along with Chic Werner, and Norm was the guy who recruited me for Penn State. Norm had a way of

Although Rosey Grier became better known as a football player, he went to Penn State primarily for track and field and was an All-American in the shot put in 1954 and 1955, winning a Penn Relays championship in 1955 and IC4-A titles in the shot put in '54 and '55 and the discus in '55.

saying things that put you at ease and made you want to listen to him. I was an All-American in high school in track in Roselle, New Jersey. I was a shot putter, javelin thrower, discus thrower, and a runner. I also played football and basketball. I had about 28 schools after me. I don't remember most of them, but one was Virginia State. I didn't meet the Penn State football coaches until I went there in the fall, but I went to Penn State on a track scholarship, knowing I was going to play football.

Rip Engle was our coach. Rip didn't yell and scream. He spoke gently. Anyone yelling at me is not going to get anywhere with me. Rip spoke gently and he could probably get me to do anything because of the way he told me how to do it. I don't mean that he was always on your side. Sometimes you messed up. But he wouldn't scream and yell at you and make you feel like nothing.

We had a pretty good freshmen group, like Jesse Arnelle, Charlie Blockson, and Danny DeFalco. Penn State did not have the tradition it has today, but they were building it. I knew it was the beginning of a change. I knew that there were a lot more players coming up here, black ballplayers particularly.

When I went to Penn State, they didn't talk about football. They talked about the college in terms of education, and I really liked that. They didn't talk about what kind of team they had—they wouldn't sell me on the team. They were selling me on the fact that if I came to Penn State, I'd get a good education, and that education would be recognized. That's what I liked.

I played my freshman year, but what I remember most is being ineligible after my first semester. Yeah, it was my grades. I went into the wrong curriculum. I went into music, although I had never studied music one day. They gave me a cello, and I thought I was going to go crazy. I didn't know anything about A, B, C, D, E, F, or G, and I was out there trying to compete with kids who had six and seven years in music before they even went to school. Some people may find that funny now because, after I left Penn State and went to play pro ball, I got involved in a singing part and even went on tour and sang in nightclubs. But then all I had to do was learn how to follow music and I had bands, so it worked out really fine for me. I really enjoyed that, too. Anyway, in the second semester I switched to physical education and psychology.

I also remember one day as a freshman we were at football practice where I guess they decided to test me out. I was ruining every play that came my way, so one of the linemen, Earl Shumaker, decided to try my chin and see if I would stand up. I was on the right side because I was really fast off the ball and I was a good defensive player, as well.

Every time they came my way, I'd mess up the play. One play, he just hiked the ball and leaped for my chin and knocked me over. I thought I was seeing all kinds of stars. It really, really hurt. When he hit me, I was determined that they were not going to run any play to my side again. Any time they came my way, I was going to ruin it. I got really angry and fought back, but not by doing what he did. I also learned that when I went to the pros. A guy did that to me in the NFL, and I went after the guy later, not at that moment but in that same game. I went after him, and the referees separated us—the guy realized that he couldn't do that to me and get away with it. So they taught me a good lesson up at Penn State.

My good friend Lenny Moore wrote a book recently about the problems the black players had there because it was a rural town. I didn't have any problems because I was born in Georgia. Things that other people might notice, I don't pay attention to because I've been through that. But I remember I got to be friends with one of the daughters of one of the white professors there, and I used to go to their home all the time. One Sunday morning one of the coaches called me in my dorm and said he wanted to talk to me. Someone made a remark that wasn't even close to being true, and I let it go but I didn't stop seeing my friend. No one tells me who my friends can or cannot be and I don't care who they are. That's one thing I still use today.

I'll tell you something else I learned at Penn State. We had a kid named Roy Brudridge who was a hurdler. I'd just see him practicing, practicing, and practicing. He wasn't the best hurdler, but, boy, he got really, really good because he practiced all the time. He was always stretching, always working to make himself a better hurdler. It all comes from hard work. If you don't like the way things are going in your life, you must work hard to correct that weakness and make it your strength. And I guess I learned in high school that a big guy can be as fast and as agile as small guys but he has to work at it. So I would always compare myself with little guys and work at it. In fact, the little guys were usually my friends.

The game I remember most at Penn State was the one at Illinois [in '54] where they had all these great runners, J. C. Caroline, Mickey Bates, and Abe Woodson. We upset them 14–12 and gained a lot of notice, but I got hurt.

That was the first time that I got hurt on the field. I hurt my knee, and I had that bad knee the rest of my career in the pros. I had to begin watching my knees. From that point on, I was always cognizant of the fact you were very vulnerable in your knee area.

I can also say my playing at Penn State made me better prepared for the pros in the sense of knowing the game. I learned a lot of stuff playing both defense and offense, and when I went to the Giants, I didn't feel like there was anyone I ever played against who was better than me.

I don't get back to Penn State very often because it's a little far for me. I was back for an Alumni Fellows award several years ago, and before that I was back for a campaign with Bobby Kennedy [in 1968]. I'm sure there was a time after that, but I'm not sure when. But I always think about Penn State. I call on the phone, I call the athletics office, and sometimes Joe Paterno's office. I remember Joe being a good assistant coach. He had great knowledge and he wasn't always jumping in the way or anything like that. He did his job and he was supportive of Rip and the team and the concepts, and I really admired him. I always watch Penn State when they're on television, and I saw them play in the Rose Bowl that one year. Once you're a Penn Stater, you always will be a Penn Stater.

Rosey Grier was known as the "Gentle Giant" when he played on the under-rated Penn State football teams of the early 1950s and set several school records in the discus and shot put. He gained greater fame in his 12-year NFL career with the New York Giants and the "Fearsome Foursome" defensive line of the Los Angeles Rams. In 2006 the NCAA selected Grier as one of the 100 Most Influential Student-Athletes in history. A humanitarian, entertainer, and social services advocate, Grier is now community services director for the Milken Foundation in Los Angeles. He lives there with his wife, Margie, and he has a son, Rosey Jr., a daughter, Sheryl, four grandchildren, and three great-grandchildren.

LENNY MOORE
HALFBACK/KICK RETURNER
1952–1955

I'VE BEEN TOLD BY A COUPLE OF PEOPLE that Joe Paterno has called me the greatest football player ever to play for Penn State. That's an overwhelming statement, and I am truly humbled. When I'm told things like that, I wonder how can that be because there have been great ballplayers there for more than 100 years. I feel very honored just to be included in that group.

I'm very happy every time the opportunity comes to go back to Penn State. I get real excited about it and I look forward to driving up there, going over those mountains, getting on College Avenue, and just walking around. It's a far different place than it was when I was going to school, but in some ways it hasn't changed at all. What has changed is for the better. At that particular time, there were limited opportunities for the black players.

I understood at the time what the deal was. You didn't even have a place to get your hair cut, except for one guy on Beaver Avenue. You couldn't go into a lot of the spots. But you knew where you could go and you knew where you couldn't go.

Sometimes we'd go to the HUB [the student union building] or some other place where students would hang out. I found out that when I was around a group of white youngsters, the other students would say things that made me uncomfortable. That made me withdraw from them because I couldn't trust them.

Charlie Blockson, who came from Norristown, was probably my closest buddy. We played against each other in high school and we ended up being roommates. That was probably the biggest influence for me because we could talk and work through the problems. So we made the best of it and got as much out of the college life as we possibly could.

I wanted a full college life, which just couldn't happen and didn't happen. So I was very, very disappointed, and I was bitter at the time. It was just a microcosm of society in those days, and I don't hold that against Penn State because it was the same at other colleges. You didn't have the whole civil rights movement or the public accommodation open until the mid-'60s. It was a sign of the times.

When I was in high school [in Reading] I wasn't even sure I wanted to go to college. My coach, Andy Stopper, wanted me to go to school and he talked to my parents. Bob Perugini, who was coaching the line at Reading, was the coach who influenced me to go to Penn State. He had played for Penn State in '41 and '42. It was his insistence that if we could deal with it that I go to Penn State.

I didn't have any basic interest in where I was going except I particularly didn't want to go to an all-black school because of the lack of exposure. I was a home boy. I wanted to be as close to home as possible, and Penn State hit it better than anyone else. That's when I started checking on Wally Triplett and that group. [Wally Triplett was Penn State's first black letterman in 1945. He tells his own story in an earlier chapter of this book.]

I heard about Wally Triplett when I was in high school. I wanted to find out who the black players were who were out there and what colleges they were with because I wanted to watch these guys. I was very, very happy when I knew Wally Triplett was at Penn State.

Tor Toretti was involved in recruiting me. I loved him. I really did. All the coaches always made me feel like a big part of the Penn State family in spite of some of the little negatives that were going on there. I loved Rip Engle because he was not only my coach but also he was a great human being. I admired him and how he carried himself, and I never heard him curse. Never. You can't say that about a lot of coaches. My backfield coach, Frank Patrick, was excellent. And, of course, Joe Paterno was still the same Joe Paterno that he is now. That's the beautiful thing that I remember about him.

I remember my first game, in my sophomore year. We opened the season at Wisconsin, and they had played in the Rose Bowl the year before. Alan

Lenny Moore's high-stepping running style made him a favorite of fans and sportswriters, but he also was an exceptional defensive halfback and an outstanding punt and kickoff return man. He is still among the team career leaders in both categories. Most Penn State historians believe Moore is the best all-around player in Nittany Lions' history.

Ameche, whom I later played with in Baltimore, was their big back, and I started at halfback. On my first run [in the second quarter] I ran [64 yards] for a touchdown, but it was called back on a motion penalty. I think we could have won if that touchdown had not been called back.

I also remember the last game that year [against Fordham], but not because of the game. The coaches took us to a hunting camp, called Camp Hate-to-Leave-It, the night before the game. There was a big surprise snowstorm overnight, and we had to walk all the way back to the road—almost a mile—to get back to our bus. Rip and the coaches made a path for the ballplayers with the guys who were starting, like me, bringing up the rear. The snow was waist high, and we had a long walk, man. [Moore scored two touchdowns, including one on a 54-yard run, as the Lions beat Fordham 28–21.]

The next year we started the season at Illinois, and they had been the Big Ten co-champions. They had J. C. Caroline, who had led the nation in rushing. I made a game-saving tackle on J.C. in the first half and then scored a touchdown just before the half ended. I also made an interception late in the game. [Penn State won 14–12, as Moore rushed for 138 yards on 18 carries.] I think that was my most satisfying game because it let us know that we were a quality team and that we could play with anybody in the country. Because Penn State was an independent, we never got much press, but that game helped us a lot.

The other game I remember in '54 was down at Fort Worth when we played TCU. Rosey Grier, Jesse Arnelle, and I were the first black players to play a game in Fort Worth. My buddy Charlie Blockson was hurt, or he would have played, too. Unfortunately, we lost [20–7]. But I got the sweetest letter from a lady who was in the stadium. She said, "We were so proud of the way you all handled yourselves," meaning the black players on the team. She said, "You were perfect gentlemen, and I was very discouraged at the remarks that were ringing around the stadium and the things that I overheard, and I had to write you and let you know that. I apologize." Those are the things that bring the reality to where it needs to be.

Now, the game everyone still talks about is our Syracuse game when I was a senior. People still come up to me and tell me it was one of my best games, but I never really thought about it in those terms. I think they remember it because Jimmy Brown played for Syracuse.

We always had a big rivalry with Syracuse. We beat them at Beaver Field in my sophomore year. I remember making an interception [at the 11-yard line] late in the game and then being pushed out of bounds into the Syracuse bench. They started a fight, and the next thing I knew everybody was jumping around and kicking and all that kind of stuff. We won 20–14, but Jimmy Brown didn't play against us until the next season when we beat them again [13–0] at Syracuse.

Jim Brown was turning the corner as a player in his junior year when we played Syracuse back in Beaver Field in '55. We both played defense and offense, so we were at each other all day. They were ahead 13–0 near the end of the half. Jimmy scored both their touchdowns and kicked an extra point, but we blocked the kick after the second one. Then we scored after intercepting a pass.

Jimmy got the kickoff in the second half, and he might have scored if I hadn't made an ankle tackle at midfield. But he got another touchdown a few minutes later and made the extra point. We came right back, and I scored a touchdown on a short run. Jimmy almost scored again in the fourth quarter on an interception, but he was tackled by Milt Plum, who was our quarterback. Then Milt intercepted in our end zone and we went downfield for a touchdown, and I carried the ball a lot. Milt kicked the extra point that won the game 21–20. [Moore rushed for 145 yards and a touchdown on 22 carries, while Brown gained 159 yards on 20 carries, caught two passes, returned three kickoffs 95 yards, and scored all of Syracuse's points.] Jimmy and I talked about the game later in the pros. He said, "You had a very good game, man." And I said, "So did you."

Once I left Penn State, I didn't go back very often. There was no reason. I was just involved in other jobs, in other things. Many years later, I was misquoted in a newspaper article talking about the black situation at Penn State. I said it would be nice if they would recruit more blacks for the university because, if you look at the overall campus, there's maybe 2 percent black. I was talking about the entire campus and not the football players. We didn't even talk about the football players. But he twisted it around to say that I was attacking the football team.

I called him up and, man, I laid him out, but the damage had been done. *The Daily Collegian* picked up the story, and I wrote them a letter to state exactly what I told the sportswriter. I also said this is not an apology because

33

I don't have anything to apologize for. I went up there shortly after when Rip died and, man, I got some hard looks.

Too many people believed that article, and I think it hurt my relationship for a while. But it's all forgotten now, and I'm happy about that. I've been told I helped change the racial atmosphere at Penn State, but I'm not sure that's true. I know it's a lot different at Penn State than it was when I was there. There are many more black people in town and not just football players. So, if I had anything to do with helping to make that happen, I can look back and thank the Penn State coaches.

That was the beginning of the real growth of Lenny Moore because of the people I was around, namely Rip Engle, "Poppa" Tor, Joe, and the rest of the coaches. I'm definitely proud of my time at Penn State.

When he left Penn State, Lenny Moore was the all-time rusher, with 2,380 yards, and was still 11th all-time in 2006. His 1,082 yards in 1954 was the season record until it was broken by Lydell Mitchell in 1971, and it also still ranks 11th in team records. Moore went on to greater fame in the NFL with the Baltimore Colts, where he was the Rookie of the Year in 1956, the Most Valuable Player and Comeback Player of the Year in 1964, and a member of two NFL championship teams. He was inducted into the Pro Football Hall of Fame in 1975. For years he worked in community relations for the Colts. He is now a prevention intervention specialist for the Maryland Department of Juvenile Justice. Moore has eight children and lives with his wife, Edie, in Randallstown, Maryland.

MILT PLUM
QUARTERBACK/SAFETY/KICKER
1953–1956

MY LIFE AS A KID WAS BASEBALL. As a catcher, I threw harder than most pitchers.

When I went to Penn State, the head football coach, Rip Engle, said I could play baseball after my first spring practice. So I said, "Fine, that gives me three years of baseball."

But my sophomore year, there were three of us going after the starting quarterback job, and they say the coaches pretty much make up their minds on who starts during spring practice. So I thought I better concentrate on football. My junior year, the coaches changed offensive systems, so I didn't play baseball that spring, either.

I was a physical education major, and my senior year I had baseball coach Joe Bedenk for one of my courses. One day I happened to be in the old Rec Hall and a St. Louis Browns scout came by and said, "Milt, how are you doing?"

He was walking with Bedenk and apparently he said, "How come Plum isn't out for baseball?" I'm glad the class was over because after that, Bedenk wouldn't talk to me. He didn't know about my baseball exploits before that. I think the way I handled myself in class—covering the bag, pivoting, stuff like that—he might have known that I knew more than the Average Joe. But nothing ever came of it like him asking, "Have you ever tried baseball?"

Milt Plum was a triple threat quarterback who could run, pass, and kick as well as play excellent defense, but he received little notice nationally until he became a first-team quarterback for the Cleveland Browns.

In fact, I came close to not going to college and pursuing a career in base-ball coming out of Woodbury High School in southern New Jersey. We didn't have letters of intent that you had to sign, and I didn't make up my mind about going to Penn State until, I think, June. I didn't want to go too close to home because I knew I'd be coming home all the time, but I didn't want to go too far away, either.

Auburn was hot after me, as was Maryland. Notre Dame and the University of Pennsylvania, which was right in my backyard, also recruited me. I never heard from Rutgers.

Joe Paterno was the quarterbacks coach when I got to Penn State. Rip had coached him in college, and Joe was a basics guy. I became the starting quarterback my junior year in 1955. I was the only one left, I guess, although I had some pretty good people behind me, including Richie Lucas. I rarely came off the field, as I also played safety, punted, and kicked off.

I used to kid my son. He was a defensive lineman at East Carolina University, and after games he'd say, "Man, I'm tired." I'd say, "David, you only played half the game." I had seven interceptions in 1956, and not to blow smoke, I knocked two down on purpose because they were on fourth down.

The big highlight for me that season came when we went to Ohio State and upset them. Eastern teams didn't beat Big Ten teams back then. We got there on a Friday, and Woody Hayes had his TV show and he mentioned Penn State, but then it was "and then next week we've got Texas Christian."

We went down to breakfast the next morning, and the hostess said, "Well, boys, give it your best." We beat them 7–6, and I felt like going back and asking her if that was good enough. The stadium held about 80,000, and the game was televised and aired across the street in the gym. After we scored and made the extra point, Ohio State came marching down the field.

Ohio State scored a touchdown, but it had 12 men on the field when it attempted the extra point. It missed the kick after the penalty.

We lost at Syracuse later that season in bizarre fashion. No one I tell this to believes it, but they had a rule in 1956 that if you came out of a game, you could only come back in if you had started the quarter.

We were losing 13–9 in the fourth quarter. I had Les Walters run a deep in, and it went off his fingertips. I asked him if he had any more gas left, and he said, "Yeah." I had him go to the other side and run a down and out, and it was again off his fingertips.

With a couple of minutes to go, we punted the ball to Syracuse. Rip Engle took me out to give me instructions in case we got the ball back. We got it back, and I ran on the field and Syracuse coach Ben Schwartzwalder yelled, "Twenty-two is illegally substituted."

Suddenly I was out of the game, and I was like, "Whoa, whoa, whoa, wait a minute." I had started the fourth quarter! They ran film back on Monday and, being a safety, I didn't show up on the film.

We played Pittsburgh the last game of the year. We had a fullback named Babe Caprara and we were in a 7–7 tie near the end of the game. Pitt's coach said, "No. 34 is illegally substituted." And he had been playing fullback and linebacker.

The official came into the huddle and said, "Sir, as a gentleman and a scholar, are you illegally substituted?" And Babe said, "Sir, I am not." The official said, "Play ball." That was the last year that rule was in.

I got out of college in June, and my thinking was to try pro football. If the Cleveland Browns had cut me, I would have talked to some people about trying to play baseball. That was my long-range thinking.

Football is so different nowadays that it's almost like talking about a different sport. There's so many reads, not only for the quarterback, but linemen and receivers, as well. The players are also bigger and faster.

I've been lucky in my life and have no regrets about going to Penn State.

Plum's seven interceptions in 1956 tie him for sixth on Penn State's single-season list. He led the Nittany Lions in passing, punting, and interceptions that season. Plum played 13 seasons in the NFL for the Cleveland Browns, Detroit Lions, Los Angeles Rams, and New York Giants, and appeared in two Pro Bowls. The 110.4 passing rating he had for the Browns in 1960 was an NFL single-season record until Joe Montana broke it in 1989. Plum is retired and living in Raleigh, North Carolina. He has three children and five grandchildren.

DAN RADAKOVICH
LINEBACKER
1953–1956

I PLAYED FOR RIP ENGLE, COACHED FOR ENGLE with Joe Paterno, and then coached for Joe. I'm the only player who did that, so I have a unique perspective about being a Nittany Lion. I guess you also might call me the father of Linebacker U…or maybe the grandfather. I was the linebackers coach for some of the first players who gave us the reputation as Linebacker U, like Ralph Baker, Bill Saul, Jim Kates, Dennis Onkotz, and Jack Ham. I also assisted Joe in developing the four-linebacker scheme that helped his early teams win all those games in the late 1960s. People don't realize what a great defensive coach Joe is.

Joe was a young coach when I played here and wasn't a legend when I coached with him. We argued and yelled a lot, but I considered him a good friend then and now.

Penn State had a good tradition before I went there, but no one seems to remember that. The '47 team went to the Cotton Bowl, but it was probably a growing tradition. When we beat Ohio State 7–6 in my senior year in '56, the coaches said that it changed a lot of things. Winning that game helped change the perception of Penn State in the eyes of the rest of the country, and especially the high school coaches. When our coaches went to see a player, instead of getting their second-best player, the high school coach would show them their best player. In previous years, we'd say, "Well, how about this kid?" and they'd say, "Oh, no, he's going to Michigan State," or

"He's going to Ohio State," or "He's going to Purdue," or something. So the Ohio State game was a turning point. [The undefeated, fifth-ranked Buckeyes had been national champions in 1954 and were a 21-point favorite in Columbus.]

I had a pretty good game that day, although I got knocked out in the last quarter. They had a player named Don Clark. I made a tackle in which he went over the top of me and his knee kept hitting my chin, like a machine gun—*ratatattattattattat*. He must have hit me six or seven times. Rip told me later he had a guy write to him or call him, saying he'd never seen a human being get hit as hard as I got hit with that "*ratatattattattattat*." Rip said, "I told him, did you see who made the next tackle?" On the next play, I made the tackle, but when we went out, I never went back in because I didn't know where I was. I had a concussion. The other thing I remember about the game is sending a postcard before the game to my wife, who was my girlfriend at the time, and saying "There will be 87,000 people. What an audience to make faces at," or something like that.

We also won another big game that year against North Carolina State at Beaver Field. Earle Edwards was NC State's coach. He had played at Penn State and had been a longtime assistant to Bob Higgins. Two of his assistants [Al Michaels and Bill Smaltz] also were Penn Staters. Three minutes were left in the game, and we were still scoreless. We both scored touchdowns, and then [Nittany Lions end] Les Walters scored with a couple seconds left, and we won 14–7. Some of our coaches said it saved their jobs because we beat the previous Penn State coaches. I played pretty well and I was on a high. After the game, I hitchhiked in the rain to Easton and back and asked my wife to marry me—we had dated but had never gone steady. I guess you would say I was a little bit off the wall. Maybe that's why they called me "Bad Rad."

The other game I remember was against Syracuse [at home] when I was a junior. I didn't start it but I went in and helped stop Jimmy Brown. He had, like, 160 yards and scored three touchdowns and a couple of extra points. I played almost the entire second half, and we came from behind. We were down 20–7 in the third quarter but managed to win it by one point, 21–20, and we were on their 3-yard line when the game ended. Lenny Moore had a big game for us. [Moore rushed for 146 yards and a touchdown and saved a touchdown when Brown broke away on the opening kickoff of the second half.]

As a player, Dan Radakovich earned the nickname of "Bad Rad" for his style as a linebacker on Penn State's defense. Although his All-American linebacker teammate Sam Valentine received more press coverage, Radakovich was a vicious tackler who was all over the field.

I lived in Kennywood and I was captain of the football and basketball teams at Duquesne High School. I was recruited by about 20 schools. I remember I visited Navy, Boston University, Pitt, and Penn State. Notre Dame and Indiana University came to see me play, but when they found out how skinny I was, they fell off. I had to mail plane tickets back to Indiana. Pitt called me 12 times in one week, but I really didn't want to go to Pitt. I told them, "There's nothing there. It's just a big, tall skyscraper."

I decided to visit after all because they told me about the Serbian nationality room. They told me to report to the field house at 8:30 in the morning. They had us 40 recruits lined up outside of the training room, stripped down to our jocks and socks. They were weighing and measuring us in front of seven Pitt football coaches who were sitting there. The guy in front of me stepped on the scales and he was 6′6″, 285 pounds with about an 18-inch neck. Then I stepped on the scale and I was 6′1″, 169 pounds. Red Dawson, the head coach, yelled out, "Radakovich, do you play basketball at Duquesne?" I said "yes," and he said, "You guys must have one hell of a fast break." Everyone laughed, including me.

After I got dressed, I was talking with two players from McKeesport when Captain Tom Hamilton [Pitt's athletics director] came over and asked me if the streetcar went anywhere near where I lived. I said "yes," and he said, "Well, here's a dollar for transportation home." He then put his arms around the other two players and said, "Let's go to lunch," leaving me with my dollar. I never did see any nationality room.

Frank Patrick recruited me for Penn State. There were a couple of players from my high school who were up there, Pete Schoderbek and Ed Kleist. So, when I came up, I liked it. When Rip saw me, he did the opposite of what Pitt did. He said, "Oh, you're going to be a big guy." I eventually played at 180.

In those days, we practiced and played our games at Beaver Field, which was very convenient because it was right next to Rec Hall and the West [Halls] where I lived. Beaver Field only seated a little over 30,000 fans but was a beautiful place, with trees overhanging the stands and two full-grass practice football fields just outside the stadium. The old water tower that was converted into a locker room was almost right up against the stands and was used by the freshmen. Varsity locker rooms were under the stands, and we used the same locker room for practice as we did for games.

I majored in business and I wasn't a very good student. After my senior football season, I dropped out of school, withdrew, played in the Blue-Gray game, and got married in January. I went out for the Eagles and made the final cut but was released when two guys came out of retirement and I was the skinniest guy on the team. So I went back to Penn State, became a good student (I was married now), and finished my degree the next year while helping coach the freshmen. During the winter, I was in the coaches' office, and they were having an argument about how the linebackers play. They called me in to see what I thought, and I got into an argument with them on how to play linebacker. I remember Joe saying, "Well, if you're so smart, why don't you come out and coach in the spring." So I started out coaching the varsity linebackers in 1958. I became a graduate assistant coach that fall and a full-time staff member in 1960. I got an MBA in 1964. I left after our two straight undefeated seasons, 1968 and 1969, to go to law school. That is when Jerry Sandusky took over.

Being a Nittany Lion is like belonging to a private club. Everybody seems proud of their school and they're always happy to see each other. I coached a lot of different Penn Staters in the [National Football] League as offensive line coach or linebackers coach, and I think they were better coached and smarter than the normal group of players. I enjoy going back to the campus and I enjoy seeing people whom I knew well at one time. Penn State's provided a pleasant experience in my life, and I'm proud to be part of the football tradition.

After leaving Penn State, Dan Radakovich became one of the most sought-after assistant coaches in college and professional football. He is credited with helping to develop the Pittsburgh Steelers' Steel Curtain defensive and offensive line techniques that have changed the way the game is played. He has coached in three Super Bowls. For the last several years, he has been the assistant head coach at Robert Morris University and lives with his wife, Nancy, in suburban Pittsburgh.

RICHIE LUCAS

QUARTERBACK

1956–1959

I GREW UP IN GLASSPORT AND WENT TO Glassport High School. Back in those days, it was unusual for somebody in Glassport to get a grant-in-aid to play football. I was a Pitt fan. Pitt was in my backyard, about 18 miles away. I was recruited by Pitt. No other big name schools recruited me.

I was a running quarterback in high school but I also played halfback. Back in those days we played both ways, offense and defense. When they were looking at people, they were looking for people who could play both ways. I was a good defensive halfback, there's no doubt about that. Overall, that was my strength.

When a college coach was in town to look at somebody, the whole team would show up to meet the coach. Then afterwards, they would have a couple guys stick around. I was introduced to Penn State through Earl Bruce. Earl called a couple of times, and I think Joe Paterno and probably Rip Engle came by my house and met my parents. Rip was just a super nice guy. The situation at Penn State was pretty nice. It was 130 miles from Glassport, so if my parents wanted to come up, they could. If I wanted to go home, I could. Judge Sammy Weis, who was also an NFL official, suggested that Penn State would be a good place to go. We had a few people from Glassport who went to Penn State, and they seemed to have a great time up there. And, once you saw the school—back in 1956 there were 15,000 people on campus—it was

Sportswriters nicknamed Richie Lucas "Riverboat Richie" for his gambling play-calling and running style that made Penn State a contender for the national championship in 1959, when the Nittany Lions went to their first postseason bowl game in 12 years.

really a nice, nice place. I decided somewhere along the line that I would go to Penn State.

Freshmen weren't eligible to play varsity ball. That was okay with me because once a week we would scrimmage or have some sort of competition with the varsity. Those guys were just bigger and faster and much more mature than we were. And we knew that. I was pleased not to be able to play and I really didn't want to.

I was on the second unit as a sophomore until the fifth game against Syracuse. Al Jacks, the quarterback in front of me, got hurt [in the first half], and I had some success against Syracuse. It was up there and it was a big, big game for us. And we beat Syracuse [20–12]. From that point on I think I was maybe the starting quarterback, primarily because Al had a separated collarbone, so it wasn't something that healed overnight.

But back in those days, Rip had a thing; he didn't want to call it first team or second team. He called it "A" team and "B" team. He was nice that way. The "A" team would generally play about two to two-and-a-half quarters and the "B" team about a quarter and a half. And if it was a good ballgame and we were involved in the game-scoring situation, we would play two-and-a-half quarters, perhaps. But we didn't play more than that because it wasn't a matter of being tired, Rip was just trying to keep us fresh.

Playing both ways was nice because you got to know more of the coaches than you did as a one-way player. Frank Patrick was our defensive coach, Joe was our backfield coach, and Rip was our head coach. But I knew Sever Toretti, who was the line coach, J. T. White, the receivers coach, and Jim O'Hora, who coached the offensive line. There was something special about those coaches.

I called my own plays. To fake a punt was always part of the game plan. We didn't call many audibles. We had some but we went on the quick signal so we couldn't call them. When I went to the pros, I had trouble adjusting to a different style of calling signals because we would go on a quick play at Penn State. Here again, Rip's idea was based on what Oklahoma did because they would run off, like, 100 offensive plays a game. And we were trying to get to 100 plays. By doing that you don't waste time on the line of scrimmage by making any calls. We had a quick signal. I don't know if we ever got 100, but we came pretty close

Someone told me Joe said I was the best running quarterback Penn State ever had. I didn't know that. We had a roll-out offense. Everything was built around attacking the outside. I always had an extra blocker because when I handed the ball off to one of our running backs on an outside run, I would go in the other direction. If I rolled out on a pass play, if one or two of the defensive guys did something, I would run and pick up four or five yards because the guy wasn't there. If he attacked me, I would throw to the short receiver, only about a seven- or eight-yard pass. But I always realized that if I needed four yards, I could probably get four yards because I had three or four guys in front of me.

There are two games that stand out in my senior season. The first game, we were playing Missouri out there. What I remember most was the airplane we took to Missouri. We had to bus from campus to the airport in Phillips-burg. So the plane landed and the pilot got out. He had this post in his hand and he put it under the nose of the airplane, so that the plane would not tip forward when everyone got on it. Rip asked the pilot, "What did you fly with before you flew us?" He said they flew cattle. You put a seat belt on but the seat wasn't attached to the floor. So when we got to Missouri they terminated the contract of that airline right there. They got a TWA plane to pick us up after the game.

I was lucky in that game. We played an offense that not many people were familiar with, and playing Missouri was outside our region. It was a week before the football season actually started, so there were a lot of newspaper guys there. I think I missed one pass, going 10-for-11. We won the game [19–8], which was the big thing. We had extra time in the airport because we were waiting for a plane. And Jim Tarman, the sports information director, got this great idea of getting these postcards with a riverboat on them. He sent a card to all the newspaper people who covered us and he signed it "Riverboat Richie." And that's what everyone started calling me.

When we played Syracuse in November, we were both undefeated. It was a sellout crowd, and you couldn't get a ticket. At some point, Roger Kochman returned a kickoff 100 yards. Andy Stynchula blocked a punt. We recovered the ball and went in for a touchdown. But we didn't make an extra point in that game and we lost [20–18]. We had them on the run with five or six minutes to go, and they just ran the ball right down our throats. They became national champions. We didn't recover from losing that game because we lost to Pitt and I don't recall the Pitt game at all. I can recall there was some disgruntlement on the team about playing in the Liberty Bowl, and sometimes we didn't play as well as we could have because some of the people were not happy with the situation.

We played in the first Liberty Bowl, and back in those days the Liberty Bowl was the sixth bowl. Now there are 25 or 30 bowls. We beat Bear Bryant's Alabama team [7–0]. Sam Stellatella, who organizes our reunions, keeps referring to us as the only Penn State team to beat Bear Bryant, which is okay with me.

I found out I came in second in the Heisman when I was at an airport going someplace. It was in the paper. I actually had no idea what the Heisman was. They didn't have any big celebration beforehand or a banquet. Billy Cannon of LSU won the Heisman that year.

Getting inducted into the [College Football] Hall of Fame [in 1986] was nice because, back in those days, it was pretty unusual for Penn State. I remember this was the first time my dad flew on an airplane and the first time he rode in a cab when he wasn't driving. My dad was a steel mill employee, and I think some of his experience in the steel mill rubbed off on me. We were all close to our parents way back then, so this was something special.

When I left pro football, I came back to Penn State to work and I was in the athletics department [for 35 years] until I retired in 1998. I really, really enjoyed the work with the coaches and the trainers. I'm happy to be here.

Richie Lucas won the Maxwell Award in 1959 as the nation's outstanding college player and played two years for the Buffalo Bills before an injury ended his career. He was Penn State's first player of the 1925–1960 era to be inducted into the College Football Hall of Fame. When Lucas retired from Penn State, he was the associate athletics director in charge of men's sports teams. Lucas lives in State College.

The
SIXTIES

BOB MITINGER
END
1959–1962

EDITORS' NOTE: Bob Mitinger was born to play football. Bob's father, Robert Mitinger Sr., was a tough All-East guard for Lafayette in its football heyday of the 1920s, and his older brother Joe was captain of the 1952 Yale team, winning the national Swede Nelson Award for sportsmanship as a senior.

Bob's uncle, Charlie Berry, was a Walter Camp All-American end at Lafayette and a teammate of the senior Mitinger. Berry went on to catch 709 games in major league baseball before becoming a renowned American League umpire and National Football League official. In fact, that's how Bob's father met his future wife, Lucy. She was Charlie's sister, and at one time held the scoring record for women's basketball in New Jersey.

The Mitingers were from Greensburg, not far from Pittsburgh. It was in these western Pennsylvania coal mining and mill towns that professional football was born, and Bob's paternal grandfather, Joseph, was in the thick of it. The first professional football game on record was on November 12, 1882, when the Allegheny Athletic Association paid Yale's Pudge Heffelfinger $500 for its game against the Pittsburgh Athletic Club. Heffelfinger later played for

Bob Mitinger was an outstanding end on offense and defense. In 1967 Chet Smith of the *Pittsburgh Press*, who covered Penn State football for more than 50 years, selected Mitinger to his All-Time Penn State team.

the Latrobe team against the Greensburg Athletic Association, managed by grandfather Mitinger.

Bob's father coached some of the great high school teams in the Greensburg area in the late 1920s, and when Bob played at Greensburg High School three decades later, his head coach was Bobby Williams, one of the star running backs of Penn State's World War II teams and the unbeaten 1947 team that played in the Cotton Bowl. Bob might have followed his dad to Lafayette, but he wanted to play big-time college football and Lafayette had stopped that long ago.

Bob Mitinger made an immediate impact at Penn State. Players had to play both offense and defense, and Bob was more like a tight end on offense, but his forte was defense. In the middle of his sophomore year he started for the first time, as a defensive end in one of the most significant games in Penn State history—the so-called "Battle of the Unbeatens" against Syracuse, which won the game, 20–18, and went on to win the 1959 national championship.

In his senior year, a Miami sportswriter called Mitinger "a killer" because of how he manhandled the Hurricanes' star quarterback, George Mira, incensing the hometown Miami crowd to near hysteria. A month later, before a homecoming crowd, Mitinger's play was so devastating in a 33–16 win over California that Cal's coach Marv Levy called Mitinger "the best college football player in the United States."

At the end of the 1961 season Mitinger was named to several first-team All-America teams, a rarity for Penn State players at that time because he was just the 13th Nittany Lion selected since they started playing football in 1887. He was the third-round choice of the Washington Redskins but chose to play with the San Diego Chargers of the upstart American Football League as their fifth pick.

Mitinger was a starting linebacker on the 1963 Chargers team that won the AFL championship and included future Hall of Famer Lance Alworth and such All-Pros as quarterback John Hadl, running back Keith Lincoln, and defensive linemen Ernie Ladd and Earl Faison. His pro career was disrupted when called into the army, but even that turned out to be fortuitous because he was assigned as a military policeman at West Point. He helped coach the Plebe team as a volunteer and became friends with a little-known assistant coach named Bill Parcells and the Army basketball coach, Bobby Knight.

After playing with the Chargers for six years, he retired at the end of 1968 and followed his father by becoming an attorney in Greensburg. He later moved to State College to be closer to his Nittany Lions, opening his own practice and becoming a community leader, an adjunct professor at the university, and a major booster of the football team. That's where he lived with his wife, Marilyn, a San Diego native, as they raised their two daughters, Michelle and Christine, and his law firm thrived.

Marilyn remembers that one of the things Bob treasured the most was his meeting with Bear Bryant after the Liberty Bowl game in 1959. She told us, "He liked to tell people how Bear Bryant came up to him on the field, shook his hand, and said, 'Young man, I believe you could play for Alabama.' Bob considered that one of the greatest compliments he ever received. He was very, very proud of Penn State." Unfortunately, Bob passed away from cancer on September 24, 2004, after battling a mysterious illness for two years. If not for his death, Bob would have told his own story for this book. But, with the help of his family, we have his words from newspaper stories written about him in the past.

★   ★   ★

I lived beside the football field back home and I spent a lot of time running around there when I was small. I used to clean the field after the games on Friday night. They gave me a quarter for spearing pieces of paper on a long stick.

My brother Joe played for the high school team, so naturally I began to hang around. I started playing organized football in the midget leagues. I was a halfback then. When I played freshman ball in high school, I was a guard, but they switched me to end in my sophomore year.

Once I made All-WPIAL, I got letters from all over the country. I never seriously considered Lafayette. There was talk of going to Yale in my family. Even my mother took sides with Joe and wanted me to go to New Haven. Maybe Yale was real football when Joe was there—it must have been to hear him tell about it. I didn't want to go to Yale as "Joe Mitinger's kid brother." I wanted to do it on my own, not my brother's name. I [also] didn't know whether I could do the scholastic work in the Ivy League, but now I know that I could.

When it was time to choose a college, it was between Pitt, Vanderbilt, and Penn State. I was really impressed by the campus here and I felt the coaches were the type I wanted to play for. I decided on Penn State because I was on such friendly terms with Earl Bruce [the freshman coach]. My dad was real disappointed in me that first year [of 1958]. He said I would never make the grade in college football.

Football's a tough game. I just like to play football for all it's worth. If I didn't try to do the job all the way, I'd quit. This is a game of kill or be killed, and if a player isn't on his toes, he's going to be hurt—hurt physically and hurt by the other team which will take advantage of a mistake.

[When I went after George Mira in '61], I didn't rough him up. I just tackled him like I'd tackle anybody else. Just before halftime, I brushed against him and he slipped right under me. I wasn't even near him and he was flopping all over the ground yelling, "Oh, get off me. I'm hurt. I'm hurt." He stirred up the crowd against us. I'd call him a ham or an actor. I think he was putting on a show for his hometown crowd.

Every time after that, Jim Smith and I really rushed him. One time when I hit him I knew that he was hurt. Even if he hadn't had bruised ribs he would have felt that one. Mira's got to expect a little punishment. Just like everyone else, we're out to get the first-team quarterback, legally, that is.

Their cheerleaders and one whole section of their stands kept shouting, "Savage! Savage!" in the second half. Then this writer comes out and calls me "killer" in one paper. Don't misunderstand me. I don't particularly like being called "killer." I just laughed at it all. [Tommy Devine of the *Miami News* vigorously defended Mitinger, criticizing the "wholly partisan and idiotic reaction by the crowd" and adding that "it is ridiculous to label Penn State's tactics as dirty." But the Lions lost 25–8.]

Our loss to Pittsburgh [in '59] was the bitterest dose I ever had to take. Beating Pitt twice [in 1960, 14–3, and 1961, 47–26] was my biggest thrill in football. [Pitt upset Penn State 22–7 in 1959. Mitinger was singled out for his play by sportswriters in the other two games, scoring a rare touchdown in 1960. Both victories sent the Lions to postseason bowl games, where they beat Oregon 41–12 in the Liberty Bowl and Georgia Tech 30–15 in the Gator Bowl.]

I never dreamed of being an All-American. I'm very happy. When I was a kid, my big ambition was to play in the East-West game. [The 1961 East-West game was played the same day as the Gator Bowl, but Mitinger later did get to play in the Hula Bowl.] You read about this [becoming an All-American] in magazines, but you have to make your own name as you go along. I'm sure Rip Engle is quite pleased. He had to be instrumental in getting anything at all for me.

I tell young fellows when they graduate from high school and go to college, "Leave your press clippings at home. At college, there will be 30 to 35 players who can run as fast as you can, will be as big as you and as smart as you. The main thing is to get your education and don't go overboard on sports. When you leave school, you can't eat football or serve basketballs to your family, and you can't buy food with your looks."

Credits: Bob Mitinger's words were taken primarily from newspaper articles written by Sandy Padwe and Jim Karl of The Daily Collegian, *Herb Werner of the* Altoona Mirror, *Doug McDonald of the* Centre Daily Times, *Ray Crawford of the* Miami Herald, *Rusty Cowan of the* Harrisburg Patriot-News, *Frank Yeutter of the* Philadelphia Bulletin, *and Huddie Kaufman of the* Greensburg Tribune-Review.

In 2004 the Penn State Quarterback Club established an award for Penn State football players in honor of Bob Mitinger, a former club president who spearheaded the effort to bring women into the organization in the late 1980s. The award goes to the player who exhibits outstanding courage, character, and social responsibility.

DAVE ROBINSON
DEFENSIVE END/TIGHT END
1959–1962

I ALMOST DIDN'T ATTEND PENN STATE because of a mix-up.

Getting recruited out of Moorestown High School in southern New Jersey, I had it down to Penn State and West Virginia, or I was going to play Ivy League ball at Pennsylvania, which was 35 miles from my home, or Columbia. I went down to visit West Virginia, and one of the assistant coaches said, "You can be a big frog in a little pond or a little frog in a big pond." He told me, "If you go to West Virginia, you'll be the first black player in West Virginia. If you go to Penn State you'll be a little frog in a big pond." I looked at him and said to myself, "If I go to Penn State, I can be a big frog in a big pond."

It got down to Penn State and the University of Pennsylvania. I was really set on going to Penn State, but Penn State had stopped recruiting me. I later found out there was a small white guy named Dave Robinson from Philadelphia and he had been accepted to Penn State.

The football office thought it was me and marked me off the list as coming to Penn State. He went up for an interview with his counselor, and he got a call from the football office saying the coaches wanted to take him to dinner. He had played a little football in high school, we both were taking engineering courses, and so they saw "Dave Robinson, engineering" and figured it was me.

The other Dave Robinson later told me he could still see the faces on the coaching staff when he walked in. He said their mouths dropped open and they took him to dinner anyway. Then they got on the phone with me and I said, "I haven't heard from you guys in so long I'm already committed to the University of Pennsylvania." I ultimately decided to go to Penn State because it was big-time football, not too close to home yet not too far away, and its engineering department was ranked number three in the nation.

Penn State played in the very first Liberty Bowl game my first year, and since freshman season was over [NCAA rules prohibited freshmen from playing for the varsity], I could dress for the bowl game. So the game was played in Philadelphia right near my home, but we were playing Alabama.

A week before the game Alabama sent a letter saying they would not be allowed to play against Penn State because the SEC would not allow the team to play against black ballplayers. The game was going to be canceled, so they went back into negotiations. We had one tackle who was instrumental to our offense, Charlie Janerrette, and they said, "Okay, Charles Janerrette is the only person who can play in the game." So I was unable to dress for the game. It was a very interesting game, too. We won, 7–0, and Rip Engle was proud to say he never lost a game to Bear Bryant.

57

During the spring of my freshman year, we had four ends coming back, both juniors and seniors, so they wanted me to play offensive and defensive tackle. I weighed 209 pounds. It was the only time in my whole career that every time I went to practice I knew someone was going to kick my butt. The next lightest tackle was Stew Barber, and he was 235 pounds. When they saw me in line for drills, everyone fought to be one-on-one with me. I think they toughened me up as a tackle because I had a great time at guard. In the seventh game, we started losing guys left and right with knees and shoulders and everything else, so they moved me to end again.

I came back my junior year and was an end. We were invited to the Liberty Bowl again, but Rip didn't want to go because people were starting to call it "the Penn State Bowl." So we accepted an offer to the Gator Bowl to play Georgia Tech, which I think was undefeated at the time. I was the first black guy to play in the Gator Bowl, which I didn't know until right before the game, and it shook me up.

The team voted to go to the game and I voted against it. Rip and Joe Paterno pulled me aside and had a discussion with me. They said, "We know

58

Although he played end at Penn State, becoming the Nittany Lions' first black All-American in 1962, Dave Robinson's career as a linebacker with the Green Bay Packers made him an early graduate of "Linebacker U." Rip Engle called him "the greatest lineman and greatest athlete I ever coached."

you have concerns and if we go to Jacksonville we'll make sure everybody stays together." I said "Okay," and they said, "We're going to announce the vote as 100 percent." The reason I voted no is I had a job over Christmas break working at the post office and I wanted to make some money. I didn't even think about going South; I was simply a poor kid.

So we get down there and there's a law against integrated living in Jacksonville, so we had to stay in St. Augustine. We beat Georgia Tech 30–15, and I had a good game. After the game they told me they wanted to interview me upstairs at a hotel. They took me up in the freight elevator and one guy came and talked to me. A couple of guys told me I had a great game and they voted for me for MVP, which I didn't get, of course.

The play that everyone remembers came when one of their guards tried to take my legs out. He was coming so low I just went over him. I was still airborne when I struck the quarterback and he fumbled the ball. I would have scored, but in those days you couldn't advance a fumble. It was one of the turning plays in the game.

All in all, it wasn't a real pleasant experience. We stayed in St. Augustine, where much later the mayor went down and poured acid in the city pool and said, "If blacks want to swim, go ahead and get in the pool." So it wasn't a piece of cake either. The only time I really felt at ease, where no one said anything, no one inferred anything, was the 60 minutes we were on the field.

Later, Bill Curry told me that before the game Georgia Tech coach Bobby Dodd told his team, "I know a lot of you guys have never played against a black guy before. You remember you're the gentlemen from Georgia Tech and I want you to act like gentlemen on the field." There were no incidents on the field whatsoever. There was a lot of hard hitting but nothing out of the way. I've been a big fan of Bobby Dodd from that day on. He and Rip Engle were just great human beings.

I didn't start that game and I found out why afterwards. In one of the first letters that had been written to me, this guy said he was an army sharpshooter and that if they introduced me, he was going to shoot me on the 50-yard line on national TV. I had been hurt that year and missed about four games. Rip came to me before the game and said the senior that had replaced me had done real well in my absence. They were going to let him start and play the first series and I'd come in for the second series. He said, "We'll go to another bowl game next year and you can start and be on national TV."

There were some very interesting letters and, after the game, Joe gave them to me. I just read about half of them; they were so repetitious I stopped reading them. Then in my senior year we went back to the Gator Bowl, this time we lost to Florida 17–7. I guess they felt a little kinder about that so they gave me the outstanding defensive player award.

Everything you imagine a great football program to be was up at Penn State. I get goose bumps when I think about it. For me, it was ideal because it was close enough that I could get home in case of an emergency but it was far enough away that I had to grow up. I went to Penn State as a kid. When I left Penn State, I'd like to think I was a man.

After catching 17 passes for 178 yards in 1962, Dave Robinson earned first-team All-America honors. He blossomed into a star at linebacker after Green Bay took him with the 14th overall pick of the 1963 NFL draft, helping the Packers win Super Bowls I and II and making the All-Pro team three times. Robinson, who has been named to numerous all-time Packers teams, got inducted into the College Football Hall of Fame in 1997. He and his wife, Elaine, live in Akron, Ohio, where Robinson is part owner of a beer distributorship.

GLENN RESSLER
MIDDLE GUARD
1961–1964

WHEN I PLAYED AT PENN STATE, it was a different time. Rip Engle was the coach. Joe was an assistant coach. Sever Toretti, Jim O'Hora, J. T. White, Frank Patrick, and Earl Bruce also were there as assistant coaches. They were the heart of the program, and I have to tell you they were the coaches who made the current program what it is today. Joe may be the head coach now, but most of them came along with Joe and they were an integral part in getting him started in his coaching career. It was a carryover from Rip. Of course, Joe has his own coaches now, but they're carrying on what those coaches did when I played.

I'm not the type of guy who looks into the past very much. I was raised on a small farm in Leck Kill, which is not far from Sunbury. There's a post office there and that's about it. We didn't have much, but we raised some vegetables and had some chickens and eggs. So when I went to school I majored in agriculture education. I got my teaching degree and I had planned to be an ag teacher.

When some Penn State fans tell me they remember me as "Paul Bunyan and his Ox," I'm not really into it. [In 1964 sportswriters referred to Ressler and running back Tom Urbanik by the nickname of "Paul Bunyan and his Ox" as Urbanik's running behind the blocking of Ressler led the Lions to a dramatic comeback after they started the season with three straight losses.

The nickname was the creation of Penn State administrator Ridge Riley after watching Ressler and Urbanik the previous year.] I think that came up when Tom and I were juniors.

What happened was, in my senior year I played both ways, but the transition was already going in the other direction where we were primarily becoming one-way players. I was basically a defensive player, playing over the center at middle guard, but on offense I was a center and always played on short yardage. So that's where the name came from. Actually, Rip always called me "Zeke." I figured he could never remember my name. There was no reason for it. So when the writers started calling me Paul Bunyan, I just figured that was another name that writers felt happy writing about. It didn't particularly mean anything to me because I played primarily on defense, except on short yardage. I felt pretty good about that because in the pros I played on offense.

People also tell me about the photograph they see of me being double-teamed in some game. I really don't remember the game, but I have seen the photograph. I think it's in the All-Sports Museum. As you get more notoriety you tend to draw more attention. That's just natural, so I don't think it's anything special. I don't think I got double-teamed any more than anyone else did. But being in the middle, sometimes you would get blocked by the guard and center in some sort of a post-type block. That's just the way it is.

I didn't start out here as a middle guard. I was a linebacker. Then in my junior year they moved me to middle guard, and I played the rest of the time there. When I was in high school I played everywhere—guard, center, tackle, linebacker, nose guard, defensive tackle. You played wherever they needed you, but I was primarily a center. I went to Mahonoy Joint. It's now Line Mountain. I wasn't really that heavily recruited because we were a small school—I think there were 88 in my class. The only player who came out of our conference at the time with any notoriety was Gary Collins, who played for Maryland and then went with the Cleveland Browns.

I had some letters, but other than Jim O'Hora I don't think anyone ever came to recruit me. I remember I had a letter inviting me to visit Wichita, and we went there. I was just happy to receive a letter that someone might have some interest in me because, back then, you actually went to school with the idea of getting an education and determining what career you wanted to pursue after graduating. I never really gave a whole lot of thought about playing

Penn State never had a two-way lineman better than Glenn Ressler, who could dominate a game on both offense and defense. He usually was double-teamed on defense, and he often took on two blockers on offense, which is where he played in the NFL.

pro football. When I started in '61, it was only three years after the Giants and Colts pro game that really got pro football going and put it on the map. It's not like today where kids pretty much determine where they want to go to college by the type of program the school has, what type of offense they're running, and where they fit in, ultimately, as a pro. I didn't think about pro football until my senior year. After my junior year I was nominated as an All-American and I got to thinking that maybe I do have the ability to play at another level.

Coming from where I did, Penn State was just right for me. They put education first and football second. I think we played three games as freshmen—Pitt, Army, and Navy. I think that was it. Other than that, we practiced with the varsity squad. It was a learning experience, it really was. Dan Radakovich was our line coach as freshmen. He had been a player at Penn State and taught me how to play football.

Spring practice is not like it is now, but I started with a yellow jersey, which was the fifth or sixth team. You had to work your way up, and when we opened the [1962] season, I worked my way up to the green team, which was basically a traveling team. We traveled and we got to play. I remember how frustrating it was because I had my knee injuries that year. I would get fluid in my knees and I would have to get them drained every day. I kept wondering if it was really worth all the pain, but I just kept at it. After a while it paid off, and I got to play. In my junior year I became a starter.

I had a lot of great experiences. Obviously, the Ohio State games were the highlights. We upset them in Columbus in my junior and senior years. They were the No. 2 team in the country in '64, and we lost four of our first five games. We finally started playing well as a team and we went out there and won 27–0, and I played both ways. Our center was Bob Andronici, and I was his backup on offense and the middle guard on defense.

After that we had a whole lot of confidence. We finished 6–4, and that was the difference. We had a chance to play in the Gator Bowl but the players voted not to. We had been there two years before and we had some tough workouts. The training facilities weren't the best and it really wasn't that great of an experience. We lost that game [in 1962 to Florida 17–7], and everyone had a bad taste in their mouth, so we didn't go.

I won the Maxwell Award [as the outstanding player in college football], but honestly I didn't know how big that award was. It was a big deal, a nice honor, but I really didn't know what it represented. It was just another award ceremony. Today everything is on TV and they make a big event out of it. Back then they didn't do that a whole lot and so you just didn't think about things like that.

Getting inducted into the [College] Football Hall of Fame is different. That's pretty special because now you realize you are among an elite of less than a thousand folks who have been inducted and that makes an impact on you. It means a whole lot to me, particularly later in life when you have an opportunity to appreciate it more. You really don't think about football anymore other than strictly being a fan, and then to have this happen. It turned out to be one of the greatest experiences I've ever had in my life. And in the touch football game they have [at the enshrinement ceremonies] in South Bend, I scored a touchdown. That was great because it's the first time I ever scored any points going back to high school.

Being a Nittany Lion means being part of a great tradition. You go all the way back to the very beginning, the players that started the program and the coaches that got the program going. It's a tradition that's been handed down through the years. What it's really all about is school spirit, being proud of Penn State and being proud of the program. I was just proud to be part of that and, hopefully, that I made a contribution to that tradition in a positive way.

Glenn Ressler was a consensus All-American in 1964 and one of only seven linemen to win the Maxwell Award. He was inducted into the College Football Hall of Fame in 2002. During his 10-year career with the Baltimore Colts, he played in two Super Bowls. After nearly 30 years of owning and operating several restaurants in the Harrisburg area, he went into semi-retirement and is now a real estate broker in central Pennsylvania, where he lives with his wife, Sandy.

JERRY SANDUSKY

END

1962–1965

Penn State fans think of me more as a coach, but I played end for Rip Engle in the early 1960s. I knew I always wanted to coach, but I never dreamed that I would get such a reputation for coaching linebackers. Some sportswriters have called me "the father of Linebacker U." I never looked at myself that way, but I did coach some of our greatest athletes.

I actually played linebacker for a bit in my junior year when we had some injuries and I was switched from defensive end. The defensive end position at Penn State was somewhat like a linebacker because it had some of the same characteristics. We played both ways back then, so I also played on offense, but it was confusing because the substitution rules changed a lot when I was here.

Freshmen were ineligible, and we played two freshman games. In my sophomore year I played tight end and defensive end. You basically had two teams—a first unit and a second unit—and both played. You weren't out on the field for 60 minutes. But I was better on defense than offense.

I remember the first pass that was ever thrown to me hit me in the back of my head. And the real highlight came against the University of Pittsburgh, my favorite team to beat because that was my home area. I was supposed to run a down-and-out pattern. I went down and I broke deep. I'm tearing up the sideline and I run right into the yard marker and fall flat on my face, bending the yard marker out of shape. But I also scored a touchdown there in that game, so I guess I made up for my earlier embarrassment.

Then, in my junior year, the rules changed and you would play either offense or defense. That was the beginning of two-platoon football. But there were still some crazy scenarios where you actually could get caught and had to play offense, and we really didn't practice it.

One time I was playing linebacker, and the corresponding offensive position was guard. I never played guard in my life, and we got caught out on the field and we had to be in there on offense. Glenn Ressler was the center and he was a great football player. I remember asking him, "What'll I do?" He points to this big lineman and says, "Block him." So he's telling this big lineman what I'm gong to do. And I say, "Oh no. I think I'm going to pull." It wasn't pretty. In my senior year we went totally to two platoons, so there was no way you could get caught where you had to play any offense.

I certainly wasn't a great athlete, but I was a good player. I played on a great high school football team at Washington [Pennsylvania]. We actually had six Division I players on that team and two professional players. We ran the single-wing and double-wing. I was the blocking back in the single-wing and left wingback in the double-wing. Then I played linebacker and defensive end. They recruited me as possibly a defensive end, linebacker, or tight end.

I was very naïve about colleges. I thought colleges were resorts. Earl Bruce recruited me for Penn State. My first visit was to Penn State, and it was in the winter. I was looking for the palm trees and everything, and this wasn't the resort that I thought it was. In those years, recruiting went on forever. I wasn't sure whether Penn State was very interested in me and I don't think they were real sure either.

As recruiting went on, I visited Tennessee, which was the first time I ever flew, and it was Friday the 13th. I thought, "Oh, oh." Three of us [from high school] visited Kentucky during spring practice, and they had just changed coaches. Charlie Bradshaw, who had played for Bear Bryant, had come in and he wanted to turn that thing around quickly, and actually 40 players quit that spring. I also visited West Virginia—I would have probably gone to West Virginia if I had not gone to Penn State.

I remember playing in the first game of my sophomore year at Oregon. Dick Anderson, who was a redshirt senior, would have been the starter, but he got hurt, and so I started [at end]. What I remember most was the first play of the game when [running back] Gary Klingensmith, who was almost totally deaf, went in motion and was five yards into the Oregon secondary before the ball was snapped. He thought he saw the ball snapped and just took off. We upset Oregon [17–7] and the next week we played at home against UCLA.

We kicked off, and I was all excited and fired up. I did not pay close enough attention to the kick return that UCLA ran, and they kind of crossed their linemen for blocking. I ran full steam downfield and was oblivious to what was about to happen. A guy hit me and knocked me clean out of bounds, and then he jumped on top of me. I was lying at the feet of Dick Anderson and he stood there looking at me, shaking his head and laughing. Rip Engle was screaming, and I was furious because this guy killed me and I was trying to get him off me. On the next play I was really upset, and the tight end hooked me and they went around my end for about a 20-yard gain. I had a feeling it wasn't my day. And the player I was playing against, Mel Profit, was named the *Sports Illustrated* Lineman of the Week [but Penn State beat UCLA, anyway, 17–14].

The game that stands out the most was our upset at Ohio State in my junior year in 1964. We played them in my sophomore year and had upset them [10–7]. They were very talented and executed so well and were so disciplined, but they were quite predictable. They weren't ranked that high, so this wasn't as big of an upset.

The next season we got off to a terrible start. We lost four of our first five games. We hadn't come together, and the quarterback situation wasn't good. Then we went down and played West Virginia, and all of a sudden everything just started clicking.

We beat West Virginia [37–8] and then [Maryland 17–9], and now we had a lot of confidence. Ohio State had been ranked No. 1 and then they had a very close game and went down to No. 2. We were big underdogs. But we just totally dominated that game. Our offense controlled the football. They just methodically went down the football field. So we were in three plays and we were out for five, six minutes. The first-team defense was only on the field for nine series of three plays and a total of 27 plays. In the fourth quarter we substituted when it was 27–0, and that was when Ohio State got its first first down. They never did score, and I remember Woody Hayes throwing the phones down. That game was special to me because I was playing against my high school teammate and great friend, Bob Stock, and we were lining up opposite each other.

After I graduated, I stayed on for a year as a graduate assistant and then left to be an assistant coach at Juniata. I was an assistant at Boston University in

Jerry Sandusky's self-effacing, whimsical personality made him a lifelong friend for most of the players he coached and played with, and many of them return to Penn State annually to participate in Sandusky's golf tournament that raises money to help fund his charity, Second Mile.

1969 when Joe had an opening and brought me back to help coach the offensive line. Dan Radakovich was the linebackers coach and had actually coached me when I played linebacker as a sophomore. Rad wanted to become a defensive coordinator, and before he left the next year, he and Joe asked me if I wanted to coach linebackers. Joe told me I'd be stupid if I didn't do it.

It was just perfect timing. When I was a graduate assistant I had worked with Denny Onkotz, Jim Kates, and that group. The first linebacker I coached I inherited from Radakovich. That was Jack Ham, who was bound to be an All-American because he had had a great year the year before. We also had Gary Gray, who was exceptionally bright, and a young sophomore named John Skorupan. They also taught me.

I had the good fortune that Rad was here for a while before he left. Rad and I put together a book that had all the defenses and the schemes. Then he went over techniques with me. That was the beginning. Then it started rolling. We established such a reputation that we were able to get some really good players to come here.

I'm often asked who is the greatest linebacker I've coached, but I really don't want to answer that. They all think they're the greatest linebacker—heh, heh, heh—and they should because they were all good. Some of them were great collegiate players who didn't even get recognized in professional football. Some of them had great athleticism, some had great toughness. All of them had a great deal of confidence and belief in themselves. They are like quarterbacks. They all were bright people capable of leading others and guiding and directing an entire football team. Even today, when I see a lot of them at our Second Mile Golf Tournaments, they're still fun to be around.

But I have to tell you about one who was a special challenge from the first day I saw him, Greg Buttle. Greg came here thinking he was the greatest linebacker. That first day he swaggered in here with his sunglasses on, I said, "Wow, this is going to be fun. If it's the last thing I do, I'm going to humble this guy." Well, four years later he walked away with the same swagger and probably the same sunglasses. But he also left with the team record for tackles [in a career and season].

I'm just thankful I had the opportunity to work with so many great coaches here. I especially had the good fortune of being around good defensive coaches. Jim O'Hora, J. T. White, Frank Patrick, and Dan Radakovich were special and I learned so much from them. J.T. was my personal coach as a player. He called us all "knuckleheads" and he had tremendous influence on me. He was a real character and we had a lot of fun fooling around with him.

Being a Nittany Lion can be summed up in two words: "plain" and "proud." The plain aspect comes from basically a fairly conservative approach to football. Nothing flashy. Very plain uniforms. The foundation for a lot of blue-collar football players. And from my experience, first-generation college students. Plain people, yet very proud. They are proud of a tradition that demanded academic excellence but also allowed them to excel and succeed on the football field. I am very proud to call myself a Nittany Lion.

Jerry Sandusky earned a national reputation as a linebackers coach and defensive coordinator. His name became synonymous with Penn State's nickname as Linebacker U. He retired after the 1999 season, after spending 31 years on the coaching staff, including the last 22 years as defensive coordinator. He now spends his time running the Second Mile Foundation, a charity for disadvantaged children that he founded. Jerry and his wife, Dottie, raised six children and they continue to live in State College.

TED KWALICK
TIGHT END
1965–1968

I WAS RECRUITED BY RIP ENGLE, and Joe was an assistant in 1965. I really didn't know much about Penn State. Pretty much all the schools around the country recruited me. My dad and I talked, and I decided with him to take only six trips. I can't remember all six.

Penn State was one of them and Michigan State, Notre Dame, Florida State, and I think Minnesota.

Bob Phillips was my high school coach at Montour High School in McKees Rocks, outside of Pittsburgh. Bob was like a second father to me and the ideal high school football coach. He didn't drink. He didn't smoke. He didn't cuss. Penn State, Pitt, and Notre Dame started recruiting me in my junior year, and my grades were not real good. Coach Phillips came to me and said, "If you get your grades up your senior year, you might have a chance to go to Penn State." I worked hard my senior year and got my grades up. We had good football teams back then.

Joe came to my house, met my parents, and my mother made him a nice home-cooked meal. Essentially, when I went to college, I wanted to get an education and be a high school football coach. I wanted to study physical education. It's one of the reasons I didn't go to Notre Dame. Michigan State was a little far away and I wanted my parents to be able to come and see the games. I visited Penn State and liked what they had to offer. They were sincere. They

Ted Kwalick, an outstanding receiver and blocker, turned himself into a prototype of the modern tight end position in the 1960s when he became Penn State's first two-time All-American in nearly 50 years.

72

were honest. Joe and Rip and all the Penn State family were just up-front. They said you're not going to get any cars here and you're not going to get any freebies. You're going to get $15 a month and a great education.

I came from a large family, and my parents worked really hard. My mother had 13 brothers and sisters and my dad had two brothers, so I had a bunch of cousins. I was the first one to go to college out of that whole group. I was excited just to be able to go to college, get an education, and play football. When I was playing high school football, Dad took a second job so they could go to the games. He had a bar and restaurant that he owned with his brother and he worked the night shift, from 5:00 PM to 2:00 in the morning. Then he took another job putting up aluminum awnings and siding. He got up at 5:00 in the morning, went out until about noon, came home, took a little nap, and then went and did the restaurant and bar thing. That work ethic carried over when I went to college because Mom and Dad didn't have the wherewithal to send me to college.

Dad and Mom never missed a high school or college football game I ever played in, and that was kind of extraordinary because my father didn't like to fly. He was a bombardier on B-17s in World War II, and they had a couple of crash landings. If you're familiar with the B-17, the bombardier sits right up front, so you know why he hated flying. When he had to fly out to UCLA in my junior year, he had to get a lot of beer in him before he got on the airplane. They almost threw him off the plane. They made it and, you know, the older I get, the more I appreciate all that.

Freshmen were not eligible to play varsity football in '65. We had two freshmen games. I think we played Pitt and Maryland. The emphasis was more on education than football. You had mandatory study hall as a freshman. In Joe's first meeting with us, when he sat down with the freshmen recruits and the guys coming in, one of the first things he told us was that there's more to life than football. He said, "When you come to Penn State, we want you to be people who are good human beings when you leave here. You're going to get an education and you're going to be a very integral part of the community wherever you go." That was something that's been with me all my life. If you ask me what it means to be a Nittany Lion, I think that's the biggest thing that I remember, the emphasis on being a better person overall than just being a better football player.

73

I didn't know Joe was taking over for Rip. We found that out at the end of my freshman year. When Joe got the job, Bob Phillips came to Penn State as the receivers coach. So in my sophomore year, Bob Phillips was my receivers coach. It was a whole new era. It was exciting. Things were changing, and Joe's philosophy was getting into place, not that Rip's wasn't a good one. Rip set the foundation for things that Joe carried on, and then Joe developed some of his own and kind of refined all that. So I was very fortunate. We had great football teams at Penn State. Joe was my head coach, Bob Phillips was my receivers coach, so I couldn't ask for anything more. It was just an ideal situation for me.

We had a close group of guys. I attribute a lot of our success not only to the great coaching we had but also to the camaraderie that we had. We had a lot of fun and we would not let each other down. My teammates were not only great athletes but also great people. Chuck Burkhart was our quarterback my senior year, and we had both played for Bob Phillips at Montour. And with the recruiting back then, Joe was able to get great players. I mean, when I was a senior, we had the Jack Ham and Franco Harris group in. They were either freshmen or sophomores at that time. So there was the longevity, and I really think the year after I left [1969], Penn State had the best defense in college football I had ever seen.

I've been told I was in the starting lineup for Joe's first game as a head coach at Maryland but I don't remember that game at all. I thought my first game was against Michigan State at Lansing the next week. They were national champs and I played against [All-Americans] Bubba Smith and George Webster and I thought I was going to have a short college career. But I do remember after the game I had a tough time and Joe supported me, saying, "Hang in there and keep working." Luckily I did and didn't do too badly.

I remember some games like they were yesterday. I remember the Miami game in '67. We went down there and everyone said Penn State didn't have a chance. We thought we could show them because we knew we had a good group of guys. I remember catching a bunch of passes and that touchdown that helped win the game. [Penn State won 17–8 as Kwalick caught nine passes for 89 yards in the game that turned around Paterno's coaching career.] I remember catching a touchdown against North Carolina State when they were ranked No. 3 to help win the game 13–8 in '67. I remember the UCLA game out there in my senior year when we beat them [21–6] with the help of a blocked punt.

People still remember that onside kick I recovered in the Army game my senior year. I went back to Penn State in 1989 for my induction into the College Football Hall of Fame. Penn State had a weekend of events to honor me, and everybody who came up to me said, "Oh, I remember you, you're the guy that ran back that onside kick against Army." [Kwalick's touchdown with less that three minutes left gave the Lions a 28–24 victory that preserved their undefeated streak.] A photo of that was in *Sports Illustrated*.

And, of course, I remember the ['69] Orange Bowl win over Kansas when they had 12 men on the field and we had a second chance to go for two [points] after our touchdown in the last minute. I remember blocking their All-American John Zook to help Bobby Campbell get in the end zone for a [15–14] victory.

I haven't been back to Penn State since my Hall of Fame induction. But I look back at my career at Penn State as one of the best experiences of my whole life, not just from a football standpoint but in terms of maturing and working with people. People back there are like family. Joe has been very gracious to me, and I have mutual respect for him. Maybe I didn't show it as a young kid, but as you get older you realize how much this man was trying to mold your life and help you. You don't understand when you're a 17- or 18-year-old kid when Joe stresses the education and the study halls. But, you know, the older I get, the smarter Joe Paterno gets.

Ted Kwalick was Joe Paterno's first All-American (1967) and first two-time All-American (1968), and finished fourth in the 1968 Heisman Trophy race. He was named to *Sports Illustrated*'s All-Century Team in 1999. Kwalick still holds the team career receptions record (86) for tight ends. After a 10-year All-Pro NFL career with the 49ers and Raiders, he retired in 1979 and now is president of his own voltage protection company in Santa Clara, California.

DENNIS ONKOTZ
LINEBACKER/PUNT RETURNER
1966–1969

PENN STATE DID NOT HAVE THE REPUTATION it does now when I came here in 1966. We were 11–0 two years in a row [in '68 and '69] and not No. 1. I don't think that would happen today. Even the year prior to that, a pretty good Florida State team tied us in the Gator Bowl [17–17]. The reputation is much better nowadays, and with the sportswriters and TV you get so much more coverage. We weren't on national TV very often back then. Today we are.

We really didn't think about traditions. There was no tunnel. We came out from one end, came through the stands, and just ran out on the field. There was no locker room at the stadium. We had to dress in the locker room at the practice field, ride over, and go back. I remember the bus ride to the stadium. That's when you focus. It's awfully quiet. You get off that bus and you're really ready to play football, particularly when you know you're going to beat the other team because you are so much better. The plain white uniforms didn't mean anything either. I guess we liked them because they made us different, but I don't think we even thought about it. It's what they gave us to wear. They were different than the practice uniforms. The ones we had for practice almost looked the same. Our game uniforms had stripes on our pants. We had stripes on our helmets, too. That's as fancy as we got.

When I think of being a Nittany Lion at this point in my life, it's just a good feeling. You come here, you see the stadium, you drive by and you

Dennis Onkotz epitomized the scholar-athlete facet of Joe Paterno's "Grand Experiment" concept. He graduated with a 3.5 GPA in biophysics and was Paterno's first two-time first-team All-American linebacker. On game day he also ran back punts.

know you and the teams you played on had a part of creating this thing, making the stadium grow from 43,000 to 107,000 or whatever it holds now. Penn State's name is thought of in a positive way today, and I think we had a big impact on that. We went to class, we graduated, we did all those things you're supposed to do. We were the symbols of what Joe was pushing, the scholar-athlete. You were expected to go to class. It was the norm. I started out in physics, which was quite over my head. Even when I switched to biophysics, I'm not sure why. I really didn't know what I planned to be. I just assumed I'd go on to graduate school and do a lot of things like that in the area of science. My parents pushed the academics, and that's one of the reasons I came to Penn State.

I played three sports at Northampton [near Allentown, Pennsylvania]. I was the quarterback and safety. We played the short-punt formation, which meant I was the quarterback but I played clear behind the guard and the ball was hiked a distance. I had to have good hands. We weren't much of a passing team, but I ran the ball and usually did all kinds of faking. I hurt my knee my junior year and didn't play very much. Maybe that was why I wasn't heavily recruited. I wasn't recruited by Notre Dame or schools like that. I don't know what would have happened if I would have been because part of my family loved Notre Dame.

I was part of Joe Paterno's first recruiting class as a head coach. George Welsh was the coach who recruited me. Our high school football coach was like Joe. He was there a long time and he was also the gymnastics coach. He would come up here for gymnastics occasionally, and I came up with him once. I remember we went [on] Route 45, this was before Route 80, and it took forever to get here. I also remember coming up here with my parents. They went with Joe, and I went with John Kulka. We did nothing. We went to a movie. I remember going to other schools, especially North Carolina and Maryland. Sometimes I was put up in a hotel and I didn't feel comfortable doing that. Here I stayed in the dorms and it was comfortable. It wasn't a big school back then. I fit right in. I lived sort of at the edge of town [in the Lehigh Valley], so this was kind of living on the edge of town. I don't know if I could have handled the city. I visited Pitt when I was a senior in high school and I just didn't care for that. Joe was easy. They didn't promise me anything. My parents liked him. Back then, we were about three-and-a-half hours from home. There was no thought that this was the biggest football

school around and I'm not sure that's what I wanted. They never told me
where they would play me, but safety is almost like a linebacker here, and I
played linebacker from freshman year on. Freshmen weren't eligible back
then, but we knew we were better than a lot of the starters on the varsity.
The first team couldn't run on us.

I had a pretty good spring prior to my sophomore year and did a lot of
good things. I didn't know what to expect when we started the season at
Navy. I probably got in for four or five plays and I wasn't happy, especially
since we lost a close game [23–22]. I thought, "What kind of a coach is this
guy?" The next game at Miami started the same way, where the upper class-
men were playing. I don't remember everyone else, but all of a sudden I was
in the game. I know I was playing out of position at times because there were
four linebackers and I was the fourth one. I actually went down and probably messed them all up because they didn't know and I didn't know what to
do. But we won [17–8], and I didn't come out and I assumed everyone else
didn't come out. At the next practice we had blue shirts on. I had mixed feelings because if I have a blue shirt, there's someone who doesn't. There was a
disciplinary problem after the game, and Joe had to take some drastic action.
That made it easier for me to play. But it set some kind of standard.

I also ran back punts. Joe's first concern with the person running back
punts is that he catches the ball. That's a big turnover after a punt. So there
was a little bit of a problem that year in getting someone to catch the ball. I
think there were a couple of turnovers. So after I intercepted a pass or two
and had some good returns, they put me back there. I was fortunate in that I
had a couple of good returns. That was fun. I remember one against Pitt in
my senior year. I ran for 60 or 70 [71] yards and I almost scored. I thought I
did. They said I stepped out of bounds on, like, the 3-yard line.

I remember being player of the week against NC State as a sophomore.
That was a big game for us. They were undefeated, and we upset them
[13–8]. I remember the interception that I ran back [33 yards] for a touchdown. No one got close to touching me. I just made one cutback and I
remembered the blocking and went in pretty easily. I also remember helping
to make the tackle on the goal-line stand late in the game.

Of course, I remember our two wins in the Orange Bowl in '69 and '70.
Do I regret we didn't get to play for the national championship, particularly
in '70? In retrospect, it doesn't really mean a whole lot. We're still who we

are. We may have lost. There's no guarantee we would have won if we had played Texas [in '70]. We were a good team and, defensively, a lot of us were together for three years. We had a good time and we had fun playing in the bowl games. It's hard to have regrets.

It's a great honor to be elected to the College Football Hall of Fame and it is a big deal for me to be one of the first in a line of good linebackers from Penn State. It sure does help when the offense had to block the defensive line that I had in front of me, Mike Reid, Steve Smear, and John Ebersole. I was able to roam a little bit, which truly helps a lot. I think the best linebackers or the ones that appear to be the best are the ones that had some pretty good defensive linemen in front of them.

Joe really expected us to go to class and get an education. He believes that, and we believed it. I think Joe's legacy, and perhaps Penn State's, is that you can have a football program that obeys the rules and most of the players will graduate and lot of them will do well after football. I'm glad to have been part of that.

Dennis Onkotz was a two-time All-American (1968 and 1969) and an Academic All-American (1969) who was inducted into the College Football Hall of Fame in 1995. A severe leg injury cut short his pro career with the Jets and Steelers. He married his high school sweetheart, Diane, in 1968, and since 1973 they have lived in the State College area with their five children. Dennis now operates a financial consulting company.

CHARLIE PITTMAN
RUNNING BACK
1966–1969

I'VE BEEN A PART OF WHAT JOE PATERNO calls "the Grand Experiment" and I'm here to say the experiment is successful. I'm a product of it and so is my son, Tony. [Tony Pittman was a starting defensive back on the undefeated 1994 Nittany Lions team that won the Big Ten championship and finished No. 2 in the nation.] What little success I've gained in the business world I can attribute to the fact that I participated in that program.

I haven't scored a touchdown in 35 years, and people still remember Charlie Pittman. It still opens doors. We played for a coach who's very well respected across the nation. He's been highly successful and he actually believes that winning is not the only thing, but how you win and how you prepare and how you compete is important, and that doing it as a top-notch student is equally important.

There's a remarkable amount of consistency between when Paterno coached me and when he coached Tony. I think that model of consistency is just what separates most programs. Even though Joe became a little more flexible when Tony played, he has certain rules that he doesn't yield on, like going to class, like the celebrating and showboating on the field, like the way you carry yourself and dress on campus. That's what separates him from most coaches.

Both Tony and I were good students in high school and we both were Academic All-Americans at Penn State. I graduated 35th in my class out of

Charlie Pittman was the first superstar running back of the Paterno era and is the most underrated of the Paterno running backs since most of his records have been eclipsed by such players as Curt Warner, Lydell Mitchell, and Ki-Jana Carter.

1,000. Now, when kids go to college to play football, most of them go with the expectations that they're going to play in the National Football League. When I went to Penn State, I went with the expectations that I was going to be a successful student and be one of the first in my family to get a college degree. And throughout the time I was there, Joe talked about understanding and enjoying the entire college experience. He said don't let everything be relegated to playing football because there's more to life than that. I bought into that and I believed that.

George Welsh recruited me. I was All-State and All-American, and I was recruited by Notre Dame, Ohio State, Maryland, Penn State, and some Ivy League schools. I really didn't want to go too far from my home in Baltimore. I wasn't a well-traveled young man and I had never been too far from my neighborhood. I really narrowed it down to Maryland and Penn State. I liked Penn State because Lenny Moore, who played for the Colts and was an idol of mine, was a Penn Stater. Then Rip Engle announced his retirement, and I didn't want to go to a program that was going to be unsettled. I didn't know anything about Joe Paterno.

So I called Maryland and told them I was coming to Maryland. Then Joe and Rip called me and convinced me that it was going to be a stable program. They said Joe's been in the program a long time and he wasn't going to change too much, that I didn't have to worry about confusion and changing the philosophy. So I called [head coach] Lou Saban back in Maryland and he said, "Well, if you come to Maryland you can start as a sophomore. Do you honestly think you can start as a sophomore at Penn State?" He doubted my ability and he issued me a challenge. I said, "I'm going to go to Penn State and show everyone," and I went to Penn State with the express purpose of showing that I could start as a sophomore.

83

When I met Joe for the first time, I remember telling my mother, "This guy's too nice a guy to be a football coach." I was used to guys yelling, screaming, ranting, and raving. Boy, was I wrong. Once you're on campus, you see the real coach come out. He laid down the law that this is the way it's going to be. I couldn't believe it the first time I heard him.

Naturally, when Tony was being recruited he thought Joe was a nice guy, too, but he had me to counsel him. I don't think you fear the hard work and the discipline. There are other things that override it, which I think helped Tony. He had seen me be successful there. We were winning and we had two undefeated seasons. They'd already won two national championships by the time he was being recruited. He had seen me launch my career outside of football, so he had more things going for him. He really had Penn State in his blood, so he almost had to go there.

Jim Kates and I were the first two black players Joe recruited, and we bonded. He was my roommate, and we united in an effort to be successful and to help pave the way for other black athletes to come there. We were very close and we helped each other survive the four years, except on Tuesdays when the running backs had to block the linebackers. I thought he would take it easy on me but he never did. He punished me.

I remember in my freshman year I almost quit several times. I would call my mother up and she would say, "Well, if that's how you feel, come on home." Then, my father would get on the phone and say, "You can't come here. What do you want to do, work in the steel mill like I did for 30 years?"

I went there as a high school All-American, an All-State performer, and I couldn't even make the third team on the freshman team. Yet, when we practiced against the varsity, I played the best back for the opponent. I was an All-American every week. We would scrimmage and I'd run 60-yard touchdowns and [freshman coach] Earl Bruce would tell me, "Your stance was lousy." My stance? I felt there was unfairness there, but now, as I look back on it, they were tying to make me a better football player. They were preparing me for greater things ahead.

I started at wingback as a sophomore against Miami and then became the starting tailback when Bobby Campbell got hurt. After we beat Miami, we lost to UCLA, but we never lost again for the next three years. We won two Orange Bowls and were No. 2 in the country both times. As to not playing Texas [for the national championship] in the Cotton Bowl in '69, I have no regrets.

Back in those days, you made the decision of what bowl you were going to go to after the eighth game. Ohio State was like the team of the century and was just killing everybody. We didn't think we'd have anything to gain by going down there playing Texas on their home field. So we made the decision, and then Ohio State lost to Michigan, but by that time we had already made the decision to go to the Orange Bowl. Yes, there was some racial discussion in turning down the Cotton Bowl. We lived in an era when these issues were on the forefront of news and there was a lot of unrest. The Orange Bowl was more amenable to having blacks play in their bowl games, rather than play in the Southwest Conference region. In hindsight, the better decision would have been to play Texas in the Cotton Bowl. But I learned a great lesson from Joe from this—once you make a decision, you live with it, and you don't do a lot of second-guessing.

I learned another lesson in my senior year when I thought I had a real shot at winning the Heisman, and that all I needed was a good year. Then I got hurt in the opening kickoff against Colorado in the second game. When I came back I was still sore, hurting, and I got booed at home. I just couldn't believe anybody would boo me, and my dad got into an argument in the stands. I was giving it my best but it wasn't good enough, but as Joe always said sometimes you can't control what happens but you have to keep working. I finally got healthy and ended up leading the team in rushing for all three years that I played there.

I learned a lot from Joe. I learned how you motivate and lead people. I really believe in setting examples, living the model-type life and then inspiring people to do the very best that they can. I don't focus on the negative side of things. I focus on what people do well and learn to play to their strengths.

I think Joe Paterno was very good at finding out what people did well and then using it to their advantage. I promised Joe I would get an MBA after I graduated and I did. Joe also helped me find my first job when I left pro football. I think that's a real testament also to where Joe's putting his belief out front and not necessarily trying to build his reputation as a football coach but doing the best for his players in general. I am who I am today because of Joe Paterno's Grand Experiment and Penn State.

Charlie Pittman was an All-American running back as well as an Academic All-American in 1969. He played two years in the NFL before injuries curtailed his career. He has spent most of his adult life in the newspaper publishing business and is now senior vice president of Schurz Communications Newspaper Division. He lives with his wife, Maurese, in South Bend, Indiana.

STEVE SMEAR

DEFENSIVE TACKLE

1966–1969

W**HEN** I **PLAYED UP AT** P**ENN** S**TATE** I was a student and an athlete. The guys around me belonged in college as students and they also were athletes. I was proud of that fact when I was there, but it really, really hit home when I went on to the Canadian Football League. Most of the guys didn't have degrees back then. Now, I look back as an older guy at having been in school with a bunch of guys who graduated in four years and I am even more appreciative.

Now, you have to understand, I was one of those guys who almost didn't make it. We were on the quarter system, and in my first quarter I did very poorly. I didn't go to class. Joe called me up to the office and just lit into me. He told me what a great disappointment I was to him. My father was deceased, and Joe said he had promised my mother I would get an education and graduate from Penn State. He said he was upset with me and that I was letting him and my mother down. He told me I wasn't there just to play football and I'd better go to class. He really straightened me out. I always felt he wanted you to do well academically and he wanted you to graduate.

Sever Toretti recruited me. Back then he was Penn State's main recruiting guy. Tor was tremendous. He was so dapper. I was from Johnstown and played for Bishop McCort. Back in 1966, anybody could get a job in the steel mill. You didn't need any "pull" to get into the mill because everybody got hired. Tor knew the vice president of Bethlehem Steel, so he took me down

Steve Smear was a determined and aggressive defensive tackle on the field but a friendly and amiable man off it. Joe Paterno said Smear was "one of those unspectacular type of players who does a great job, play in and play out."

87

there for an interview. We're sitting there in this big palatial office, and Mr. Walton says, "Well, Tor, we can do this one of a couple of ways. We can give him a fairly easy job or we can give him a hard job." Tor looks at him and goes, "I want you to put him in the worst place in the mill." And they stuck me in the coke plant and the open hearth. I had buddies who just walked down to Bethlehem Steel and got into the car shop and places where you didn't even get dirty. I had dirt in my pores all the time and it would take me two days to get cleaned.

I played tight end in high school, so they started me out as a tight end. We played two freshmen games, against Pitt and West Virginia, and we were on the foreign team. All we did was get beat up by the varsity all the time. Right after the season, before we went into winter workouts, Joe called me in and said they were going to make me a defensive tackle. And I thought, "Oh my God, there's no way. I'm going to get my brains beat in." In the spring, I just got killed. I was really discouraged. One of my best friends is the Hammer [Jack Ham]. We played together at McCort, but he didn't have many [scholarship] offers, so he went to a military prep school after we graduated. Hammer came up for the spring game and I was lucky I wasn't taken away in a hearse. They were just beating the crap out of me. After the game I said to Hammer, "Geez, I'm never going to play here. You want to go to IUP [Indiana University of Pennsylvania] because they have a good football team there?" Then Joe called me up to the office and I knew it wasn't about my grades because I had done real well in the second and third quarters. He said, "I know you're discouraged, but we have confidence that you can play defensive tackle. Hang in there and trust me." Then he asked me about Hammer. One of their scholarship players had backed out and so they gave their last scholarship to Hammer.

Joe always used to say, "If you keep hustling, something good will happen." That's what I still tell my kids today and it's the way I still conduct myself. In the spring of my sophomore year, everything started clicking. I worked hard and I was well-coached by Jim O'Hora, who taught me how to read things in front of me. And I won the [Red] Worrell Award [as the team's most improved player]. When we opened the season at Navy I was on the second team. We get beat and Joe goes ballistic. He said, "There's going to be some drastic changes. A lot of people are going to be promoted and a lot of people are going to be demoted, and that's the way it's going to be." So myself and seven or eight other guys, mostly from my class, were promoted. It was a tough locker room, as you can imagine, when you bench seven guys that were seniors. Of course, we go down to Miami, and we play really, really well, and the rest is history. [Paterno's insertion of several sophomores provided the spark to a 17–8 upset over Miami that turned around his faltering coaching career.] That really calmed the locker room down because the older guys couldn't say anything. We had done the job and they just had to live with it.

In the next game, we played UCLA at Beaver Stadium. They were undefeated and their quarterback was Gary Beban, who won the Heisman Trophy [that year]. If the punt we blocked hadn't gone through the end zone and we had fallen on it for a touchdown, we would have won the game. [UCLA won 17–15.] We shut them down. I mean we just hammered them. We played extremely well and I think that was the signature game that gave us the confidence that year. That game accentuated the fact that we were not a fluke.

At the end of that season, Mike [Reid] and I were elected co-captains. "Spaz" [Frank Spaziani] was our only senior, and we were juniors, although Mike actually was a senior but he had been redshirted. To be a co-captain at Penn State was the greatest honor I had in my college career because we had seven or eight guys who could have been co-captains, like Dennis Onkotz and Neal Smith. They were first-class people who were highly intelligent and well motivated.

We really had a great defense. Anybody can get beat physically, but we didn't get beat mentally. We had a bunch of guys who were really well coached and we played three years together. We had the experience and we weren't a bunch of dummies. The coaches could tell us what to do and how to do it and we did it. Nowadays the game is so sophisticated, with all the adjustments they do on offense prior to the snap, and defenses are changing on the fly. You didn't see much of that back in the '60s, but we were doing it. Denny would see a new offensive set and he would call out a color or a number, we'd change defense as they were lining up, and Neal Smith would coordinate the secondary.

Most people think we played our best defensive game against Missouri in the [1970] Orange Bowl. But I believe it was the game before, against North Carolina State. It was the last one in our regular season and it was televised. They didn't have a first down. We were beating them, like, 17–0, and I was hoping Joe would keep us in. Not until he took us out in the fourth quarter did they make some first downs and score. It was just lights out and we really hammered them. [The defense held NC State to 50 net yards while recovering two fumbles and intercepting three passes in the 33–8 victory.]

Of course, beating Missouri was great because they had a really, really great offensive football team. They had beaten Michigan that year by 20 or 30 points, and when I watched them on film, I figured that if we held them to 17 to 21 points we'd win the game. And we held them to three points and had an Orange Bowl record of seven interceptions [in a 10–3 victory]. It was just unbelievable.

I know there's been a lot of second-guessing because we voted to play in the Orange Bowl instead of playing Texas in the Cotton Bowl. But we never thought we'd have a chance to play for the national championship because Ohio State seemed to be a shoo-in to win again [until they lost to Michigan]. Sure, I have a little regret, but things just didn't turn out for us. I know we were better than Texas and I know we would have beaten them. Missouri was a better team than Texas. In my mind, we were the No. 1 team in the country. But it's over with. We had a tremendous career at Penn State and we really were student-athletes. Nobody can take that away from us.

Although overshadowed at defensive tackle by Mike Reid, Smear was a three-year starter who was a second-team All-American in his senior season. After playing for six years in the CFL for Montreal, Saskatchewan, and Toronto, Smear coached at the Naval Academy for a year and then became an insurance broker in Annapolis, where he and his wife, Diana, and family continue to make their home.

NEAL SMITH

DEFENSIVE BACK

1966–1969

I WAS A FRESHMAN ON JOE PATERNO'S FIRST TEAM, but he didn't know much about me because I was a walk-on. It was in September of 1966. I'm from Port Treverton, which is a real small town, and I went to Selinsgrove High School. I played tight end and linebacker and I wasn't big at about 170 pounds. So I didn't have big colleges looking at me. I talked to Lafayette and Bucknell, but they didn't have any financial aid for me

I went to Penn State to major in civil engineering and I wasn't even sure I was going walk on. George Keller was a neighbor of mine and he had graduated from Penn State. One of his fraternity brothers was Jay Livziey, a former player who coached Danville at the time and had coached Jack Curry. [Curry was a three-year starter at split end for Penn State from 1965 to 1967, and when he graduated he held most of the school's receiving records, including career yardage, career receptions, and most receptions in one game.] George Keller and Jay Livziey talked to me and convinced me to walk on.

I think I went to the first practice I could possibly go to but I really don't remember. I think the scholarship kids were already there and had been through a couple of practices. But freshmen weren't eligible, so there was no big preseason camp that freshmen could go to anyhow. They made me a wide receiver but we were basically cannon fodder. I think we played two freshmen games on Friday nights someplace and we were basically the foreign team for the varsity.

I didn't know the other freshmen because they knew each other through the recruiting process and everything. But it didn't take too long to make some friends and feel part of the team. George Kulka and I were civil engineering majors, so we hit it off pretty quick. I really wasn't that good of a wideout, and in the spring of my freshman year they moved me to cornerback. I earned a starting position for a short period of time but I broke my finger and couldn't play in the Blue-White game.

Neal Smith literally came out of nowhere to become an outstanding defensive back on what is considered by most historians to be Penn State's greatest defensive team of all-time in 1969. He also was a scholar-athlete who graduated with a 3.5 GPA in mechanical engineering.

I was on the second team to start the sophomore season. I can't remember whom I was playing behind. I played just a couple of minutes in the first game, which was against Navy, and we lost. I was a nervous wreck when I did get in.

Then for the second game we went down to Miami, and Paterno started inserting sophomores. I wasn't one of the sophomores he planned to insert but somebody got hurt, so I played maybe half of that game, the second half as I remember. We upset Miami, and people call that the turnaround game because the team did not have a good season in Joe's first year, but we started winning after that. In the spring of that year they moved me to safety, and for the rest of my career I was a starter there. [The week after the 1967 Miami game, the Nittany Lions lost by two points to No. 3 UCLA, and then went on a record-setting 31-game undefeated streak, including back-to-back Orange Bowl victories.]

We had a great defense, and many people think our defensive team in '68 and '69 was the best in Penn State history. I don't know about that but I think we had one of the best front eights that ever played college football. That front eight put so much pressure on the pass and stopped the run so well that it made the job easier for the rest of us.

I can't say enough about Mike Reid. [Reid, a defensive tackle, was a co-captain in both '68 and '69, and in his senior year won the Maxwell and Outland Trophies as the nation's best player and lineman, respectively.] He's one of the most fantastic persons I've ever met. He was a motivator, a leader, and just an unbelievable person. His overall ability was something to see, not just in playing football but in many things, like playing the piano and being part of the class plays. We had a lot of leaders like Mike, but he was just the most outstanding.

93

That front eight is the reason I became the interception leader. It's hard to believe I still hold the record for interceptions after nearly 40 years. [Smith had 19 career interceptions, and his 10 interceptions in 1969 is tied with Pete Harris (1978) for most in a season.] Quarterbacks were throwing from their backs half the time.

I remember when we beat Missouri in the [1970] Orange Bowl, I had two interceptions and might have had a third one but I ran into an official. We had seven interceptions. We had so much confidence at that point in our careers that it was fun.

I know we have been criticized for not playing Texas in the Cotton Bowl that year but things just didn't work out. We had our choice of the Orange

Bowl, the Sugar Bowl, or the Cotton Bowl. At the time we made our choice, Ohio State was ranked No. 1 and had been No. 1 the year before. We were ranked No. 2 and we couldn't play them because they were going to the Rose Bowl. So we narrowed the choice to the Cotton Bowl to play Texas or the Orange Bowl.

We decided to go to the Orange Bowl for a couple of reasons. We had a good time the year before, and we didn't have a shot at playing Ohio State. The black players preferred going to the Orange Bowl because they didn't want to go to Dallas, which was still having racial problems, and we kind of honored their request. I think in hindsight everybody would have chosen to go to the Cotton Bowl had they known how everything was going to turn out. But that's the way it went. [Michigan's upset of Ohio State after the bowl invitations had been accepted turned the Cotton Bowl into the mythical national championship game.]

Of course, I remember the Orange Bowl the year before when we beat Kansas [15–14], when they had 12 men on the field. I partially blocked a punt in the last minute or so of the game when we were behind. We had an 11-man rush on. We didn't practice this, as I recall, but we were in a situation where the coaches called an all-out rush, so I rushed from the extreme outside on the left. I was blocked a little bit and kind of rolled over the blocker and I got part of my hand on the ball. It rolled to the sideline and out of bounds, as I recall, about midfield. We scored a touchdown and then won on our second extra-points try after Kansas was penalized for having 12 guys on the field.

I also remember when we played Florida State in the Gator Bowl [in 1967] at the end of my sophomore year. Because they had a great passing attack, we shifted some people around. I actually played linebacker and did a lot of man coverage on the slot man. I remember intercepting a pass on a tipped ball but I don't remember what yard line it was on. What I remember most about that game is I had a legitimate sack on our blitz. [The game ended in a 17–17 tie.]

Another game I remember was when we went to Syracuse in '67. Larry Csonka was a senior, and I was playing cornerback. Tim Montgomery was the safety. I remember he had about 10 tackles on Csonka, one that broke Tim's face mask. We won [29–20], but it was a tough game because of Csonka.

I played with a lot of great players, and we had a lot of fun together. There's one story I tell a lot of people. Paterno always would throw us off the field in anger once in the spring and once in preseason. In my junior year, in preseason I think, Ted Kwalick took a big piece of cardboard and put blocks on it with times and dates, and then we all paid a dollar to predict when we would get thrown off that preseason. We all assumed that Joe found out about it because that's the only time he never did it. I think Kwalick kept the money.

I have wonderful memories of playing for Penn State and the pride of being part of those great teams. I think about the experience of playing for Paterno and respect him for how long he's stayed and what he's done for the university since I was there and the legacy he's built. I'm certainly glad I was part of the Paterno legacy at Penn State.

Neal Smith was a first-team All-American in 1969. He and Gregg Garrity are considered the two best walk-ons of the Paterno era. After a brief tryout in the NFL, Smith decided to forego a pro career and entered the highway construction business near his hometown. He married his high school sweetheart, Sharon, and they raised four children. Smith is now vice president of construction for Eastern Industries Inc., and lives in Selinsgrove, Pennsylvania.

The
SEVENTIES

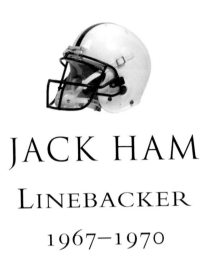

JACK HAM

LINEBACKER

1967–1970

IPLAYED LINEBACKER ON THE PITTSBURGH STEELERS' teams that won four Super Bowls in the 1970s. I was a part of the "Steel Curtain" defense that was one of the best of all time.

There was a parallel between my playing days with the Steelers and those at Penn State: I had a dominant defensive line in front of me with guys like Steve Smear and Mike Reid just like I later had with players like Joe Greene and L. C. Greenwood.

Steve Smear is actually a big reason why I ended up at Penn State. Or, should I say, why Penn State took a chance on a kid who weighed less than 180 pounds in high school and didn't even start until his senior year.

Steve and I went to high school together in Johnstown, Pennsylvania. I went to a military school for a year after high school and I was all set to go to Virginia Military Institute, but the more I experienced the military life, the more I didn't like it.

Steve was instrumental in telling Joe Paterno and the coaches up there about me. I think someone turned down a scholarship to Penn State, and in April or May I got it.

If I didn't have enough doubts about whether I could play at a level where there were All-State and All-American players coming in as freshmen, my first day I found myself in an elevator with Rich Buzin and Bill Lenkaitis,

Jack Ham is the only Penn State player in both the College and Pro Football Halls of Fame. He set a team record of three blocked kicks in 1968 and four blocked kicks in a career that was tied 20 years later by Andre Collins.

two offensive linemen who were going to be seniors. My father didn't even think the elevator was going to get off the ground, that's how big they were.

At that time I was probably about 200 or 205 pounds. I'm looking at these two guys, and you talk about having doubts. I think my father had more doubts than I did. He thought maybe this wasn't for me. Freshmen weren't eligible to play then and we were cannon fodder for the varsity.

I had to go up against Ted Kwalick, an All-American tight end, and I was lining up on him a lot as a freshman. You found out how tough you were very quickly being on the scout team. I gained more confidence my freshman year as I started feeling more comfortable.

Going into spring practice of 1968 Penn State had a lot of people coming back on defense, guys like Smear, Reid, Jim Kates, Dennis Onkotz, and Neal Smith. In my locker the first day of practice was a blue shirt, which meant first-team defense. I was shocked as we had some great, great players on that defense. All of the sudden I was in the huddle with these guys as an outside linebacker. Joe Paterno and the coaches showing that kind of confidence in me was a key to my career going on the upswing.

100

In 1968 we beat UCLA early on the road. I blocked a punt, and Jim Kates ran it in for a touchdown. We also beat Miami, which had Ted Hendricks at the time. They were two quality programs.

We ended up winning all of our games that season and beating Kansas 15–14 in the Orange Bowl. We had a dominant defense—talk about the joy of playing linebacker behind a front four like that. I didn't blitz all that much because those guys could get after the quarterback. I really learned to play the passing game, which later helped me a lot in the pros.

The next year we had the same guys, and the only team we really struggled with was Syracuse. We didn't play very well but we pulled it out in the fourth quarter. People will never realize to this day how good of a Missouri offense we faced in the Orange Bowl.

It was probably the biggest challenge we had during those two years—talk about a defensive statement. We held them to three points, and their quarterback threw seven interceptions. [Penn State kept Missouri's high-powered offense out of the end zone in a 10–3 win.] It was a fitting way for that defense to go out.

It really didn't bother me that we didn't win the national championship either of those two years. It's a much bigger deal today, being No. 1 in the country. I knew I'd played on one of the best defenses in the country both those years, but we had no control over the polls.

My senior year we struggled on both sides of the ball. We lost a tough game at Colorado, which snapped our unbeaten streak at 31 games. We lost to Wisconsin the following week and later lost to Syracuse on homecoming.

We ended up righting ourselves. John Hufnagel started moving the team at quarterback, and we started playing better defense, winning our last five games. It ended up being a 7–3 year, which paled in comparison to the previous two, but I take a lot of pride in the fact that we won our last five games.

Before Joe Paterno built the football program into a national power, too many people had been confusing it with the University of Pennsylvania. He tried to put this football team on the map, and I take a lot of pride in the way he did it and being a part of it and continuing that legacy of Penn State football. There's a pride factor to being a Nittany Lion that I have to this day.

I returned to Penn State football in a sense in 2000 when I started doing color commentary for radio broadcasts of the games. I'm not surprised Joe got the program turned around. I could see that the defense in 2004 was a quality defense, and the team just needed some skill players. He addressed that issue with players who were young but good. They were quick and they stretched defenses. He always felt they were very close, even when they were losing and he got the people he needed at the skill positions. I think he turned it around to the point where it's going to be a quality program and a winning program for a lot of years.

101

A three-year starter at outside linebacker for Penn State, Jack Ham was a consensus first-team All-American in 1970, when he had 91 tackles and four interceptions. A star on the Steelers' "Steel Curtain" defense, Ham played on four Super Bowl–winning teams with Pittsburgh and made the All-Pro team nine consecutive seasons. He was inducted into the Pro Football Hall of Fame in 1988. In addition to broadcasting, Ham, who lives in the Pittsburgh suburb of Sewickley, is the president of a drug-testing services company.

DAVE JOYNER

OFFENSIVE TACKLE

1967–1971

Having grown up in State College, my being a Nittany Lion goes even deeper than a lot of guys who came here. Orlando is the mouse. State College is the Lion. I was indoctrinated very early in just thinking about Penn State and the Nittany Lion. You're cognizant of those things from about 11 or 12 years old. It's all steeped in this mystique and this aura around here. We used to sneak over the chain link fence [at Beaver Stadium] for the football games. We wouldn't pay too much attention to the game, but we would run around and throw the footballs into the end zone. It's almost like it was part of my skin from the beginning.

Maybe I'm kind of unique [because] there weren't many [players here] older than I am that could have had that experience. There have been a number of kids from State College High School since then, but not very many, if any, could have jumped the chain link fence and run around in the end zone when they were 12 years old, when Hatch Rosdahl, Chuck Sieminski, and those guys were playing. Being a Nittany Lion is part of my skin. I feel that I am part Lion. I wrestled for Penn State, too, and I believe what I say can be applied to the Nittany Lion wrestling legacy as well.

It was a very unique bunch of people here early in Joe's tenure as head coach. I was in his first recruiting class. I redshirted a year because I had mononucleosis. So I ended up being in Franco Harris and Lydell Mitchell's class. But I was originally in Jack Ham's class when I graduated from high

Dave Joyner (No. 70), seen here congratulating Lydell Mitchell, was Penn State's first pure interior offensive lineman to be named a first team All-American (in 1971) and the only player to also be a two-time Eastern wrestling champion and a runner-up in the NCAA wrestling tournament.

school in 1967. From that point on, for the next six or seven years, Penn State was a very unique place. We were coming off two 5–5 seasons, and there wasn't a lot of respect for us nationally. We had respect for ourselves, and that was the kind of seed that grew into this great and unbelievable tree that's been around for the last 35 years. Some of the branches have broken every once in a while, but mostly it's a big, strong oak.

We were so blessed to have this catalyst occurring when all these great ingredients were sitting there. I'm talking about what may be a collection in one place of some of the greatest football players the country has ever known.

We had two of them on the All-Century Team—[Ted] Kwalick and [Mike] Reid—and we now have six players from this time in the College Football Hall of Fame, and a couple of them [Ham and Harris] in the Pro Football Hall of Fame. So if you look at that time frame—two years before me and two years after, running from Reid and Smear through John Cappelletti—it was incredible. I don't know if there are that many football programs around in that six- or seven-year span that can say that they have these two All-Century guys and all these people in the Hall of Fame.

Those guys had great talents, and not just physical talents. It was this mental thinking we had and because of the kind of coaches we had that gave us that. They treated us as adults. They made us look within ourselves to win football games. It wasn't outside stuff that won football games for us. You had to have a certain baseline talent. But it was just something special about how the coaches got us to believe in ourselves, and we believed in ourselves from the start. There was just this very unique thing that came together all at once with Joe and the coaches as the catalysts.

I mean the coaches were characters. They were old school and looked like boxers and literally played with leather helmets. What college coaching staff had J. T. White, who played in the Rose Bowl and won two national championships at two different [Big Ten] schools in the '40s? We had Frank Patrick, who was one of the greatest football players of all time, a two-time All-American who played in the NFL in the late '30s with guys like Bronko Nagurski when they hardly wore pads under their uniforms. We had Jim O'Hora, Bob Phillips, and Dan Radakovich. They all had crazy personalities, and it all mixed together. No matter how high you'd shave your ankles, the trainers would tape you above it, then Rad would come around when you couldn't get off the table and he'd pull all your hairs out of your legs. J.T. would hide in the bushes when we came out to the practice field. Kwalick would walk by and J.T. would jump on him, and they'd be rolling around, fur flying. That's old school, and you don't see that kind of thing anymore, and it was probably very unique back then.

What great college football program had this rapport between players and coaches but also had respect? It wasn't like we ever crossed those lines where we lost our respect for them as our superior or our mentor. But there was this connection that you could be loose and joke with them. It was this very unusual blend that made it very special, and that group of people and that energy had a 10-year influence on the program. And the dots kept going.

When my sons Andy and Matt were playing [in the 1990s], they told me Joe would get mad at the defense and scream, "Mike Reid, he weighed 250 pounds and he would kill all you guys." He would talk about Reid even 35 years later. Sometimes they'd wonder who Reid was, but the legend still connected all those dots. That's what's special, and I'm not sure that kind of thing exists but in a handful of places.

We were the players of Joe's Grand Experiment, this thing where you merge athletics with academics. What a novel concept. That's why I came here: I wanted good academics but I also wanted to play big-time sports. I thought this was the best place in the country to do this and I was right. The Grand Experiment worked and it's still working. I'm the first Paterno-era player who is a physician, but there are now a number of us who are doctors, dentists, lawyers, accountants, MBAs, and successes in multiple fields and facets.

Part of that reason is the way we were always taught. We certainly had no misconceptions that football was not big-time football here and winning a way of life. But we were always taught by Joe and the other coaches that athletics were part of academics, not a separate piece. I'm not saying that's not happening in other places, but that's a unique concept. A lot of people say it, but not all of them believe it. We live it. That attitude prevails from the top-down, and I mean from the [University] president and not just the athletics director and head coaches.

I might not have been as good a player if it had not been for Steve Suhey. The Suhey family and mine were family friends. Steve was one of those old Bronko Nagurski types. They were gladiators. [Suhey was an All-American on Penn State's undefeated 1948 Cotton Bowl team.] In my junior year, Steve dragged me off my living room couch and started showing me stuff. From then on he'd come over a couple times a week. He showed me and taught me things and what to do and how to do it. There again is that Penn State connection, the connection of all those dots. I'm connected to the greatest member of what is surely one of the greatest defenses that ever played college football.

There are two games in my senior year that really stand out. We played at Tennessee in our last game [of the regular season] and we were riding high. We had won 15 in a row and were already set to play in the Cotton Bowl. We beat up Tennessee pretty good and outgained them 400 yards to 100, but Tennessee did a great job with special teams, and we lost 31–11. Nothing seemed to go right. We had mistake after mistake and we were embarrassed. That gave everyone the excuse to criticize Penn State and belittle us about eastern football. They said we weren't good enough to play with the big guys, that we couldn't compete with the SEC, Big 8, and so forth. So everyone was saying Texas was going to kill us [in the Cotton Bowl].

So it was halftime in the Cotton Bowl, and we were behind 6–3. I was the captain, and Joe asked me if there was anything we should change. I said, "Don't do anything. We're fine. We got 'em where we want 'em." I could sense that we were beating them up and we were pounding them. He looked at me and just said, "Okay, keep it going, whatever you're doing." And we went out in the second half and just wiped them out. [Penn State won 30–6.] It was redemption for us because we beat a great Texas team in a defining fashion in a heavyweight title match.

We had great teams back then, and my only regret is that the press didn't understand how great those teams were. It was a mythical national championship, anyway. We should have been voted national champs in three out of six years. The two Orange Bowl teams were national champs and in Cappelletti's undefeated season they were national champs. And if there had been a playoff system of some sort, the team that lost at Tennessee in my senior year might have won the national championship because we were good enough to win. So as far as I'm concerned we were national champions. But heck, we're Nittany Lions. That's worth much more than a national championship.

106

Dave Joyner was a consensus All-American, an Academic All-American, and a National Football Foundation Scholar-Athlete in his senior year. In 1997 he was the recipient of the prestigious NCAA Silver Anniversary Award, honoring former students who have distinguished themselves in their profession. Today, Dr. Dave Joyner is an orthopedic surgeon and a physician for the United States Olympic team who also is active in various public service endeavors on a university, local, state, and international level and lives in State College.

LYDELL MITCHELL
RUNNING BACK
1968–1971

I F JOE PATERNO HAD NOT MADE ME MAD when he was recruiting me, I would have gone to Ohio State. And now because of Joe, because of Penn State, and because of my teammates, I am in the College Football Hall of Fame. When I was in school I never thought about the College Football Hall of Fame because we didn't have the media talking about it the way it does today. It's an extraordinary honor, and I'm truly grateful for it.

Would I be there if I had played for Ohio State? I don't know. I'm very proud to be from Penn State and representing Penn State in the Hall of Fame because Penn State's been good for me and helped me in many ways, not only in football. I got a really sound education and I'm more proud of that than playing football. Joe promised an education. That's what we got. Football took care of itself. If you were good enough to go to the next level, you went to the next level. But football doesn't last forever. When you get finished playing professionally, you're still a young man in your thirties. What do you do? That's what Joe and the coaches prepared us for.

I was just a country kid out of a small town in New Jersey but I had quite a few schools recruiting me. Back in those days, black players didn't go down south to play. So our choices were pretty much East Coast, Midwest, Big Ten, Syracuse, Maryland, and schools like that. George Welsh was recruiting me for Penn State, and I was a tough sell.

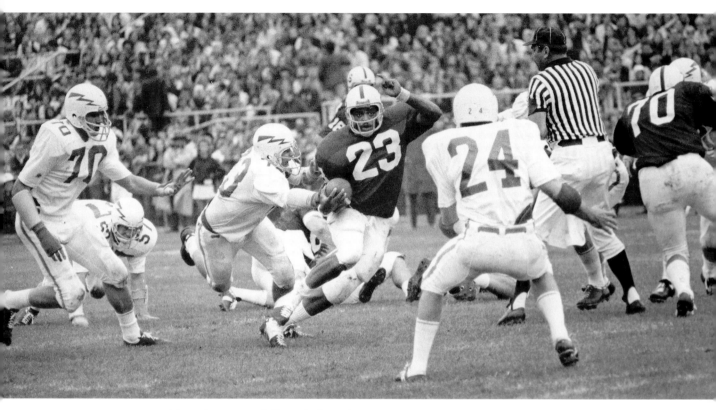

In his senior year, Lydell Mitchell set three NCAA scoring records—total touchdowns (29), rushing touchdowns (26), and most points for a season by touchdowns (174)—which are still team records. In addition to his running, he also was a standout on kickoff returns and is still among the team's career leaders.

I remember visiting Penn State, and Franco Harris was there the same weekend. We were both from New Jersey but we didn't know each other. It was wintertime. Football season was over and there wasn't a whole lot to do. We went to dinner with Joe at the Nittany Lion Inn and afterwards we hung out with a couple of the players who were freshmen. I remember distinctly that we went down to the pool hall and shot pool. That's how we spent our evening. I remember coming home, and the first thing I said to some folks was, "Heck, man, they don't even have a good radio station."

After that I had eliminated Penn State. I was a pretty good student in school but I always worked at the pool room in the evening to make a couple of dollars and I liked to hustle pool a little bit. George Welsh would still come around and would always catch me in the pool hall. We'd go out and have a quick hamburger and french fries, but I'd leave him and go back to the pool room. He never really got to talk to me about Penn State. He told Joe, "Franco is fine, but I just can't get Lydell to commit."

Finally, the day before signing, I walked out to the field with my high school coach and told him I was confused. I thought about going to Maryland because this girl I went to high school with was moving down there. Then I told him I was going to go to Ohio State because my grandparents lived in Columbus. I was familiar with the area because I used to visit them and it would be nice to be close to them. Penn State never came into the equation at all.

So when school was over, I had a phone call from the guidance office that someone was there to see me. I went down to the office and it was Coach Paterno. He was just checking to see what my thoughts were, and I said, "Coach, I'm not interested in going to Penn State. I'm going to Ohio State." He said to me, "Well, you're afraid to come to Penn State because Charlie Pittman is there and you can't play." He ticked me off a little bit and, within 10 seconds, I replied, "I'm coming to Penn State and I'm going to break all the records up there." That's exactly what I said to him, and with a lot of help from my teammates, I was fortunate enough to fulfill my promise. [By the end of his career, Mitchell had set three NCAA records of touchdowns, rushing touchdowns, and most points per season, as well as numerous Penn State records, including several that still remained at the end of the 2005 season.]

Even back then I think Joe knew how to get to me and motivate me and he didn't know me that well. If Joe didn't walk in the door that day, then I would not have gone to Penn State. As for Franco, we were close at Penn State and remain very close today. In fact, we are partners in a couple of businesses and talk several times a week.

We didn't play varsity football as freshmen, but we had a great freshman team. We'd go up against the second-team defense on the varsity, and we could beat them, but the first-team defense with Mike Reid and those guys was really tough. I was glad freshmen couldn't play varsity sports because we became well acclimated to college life and had a chance to really set our academic course.

I remember our first game as sophomores was against the Naval Academy. I scored a touchdown [of 39 yards], but I ran the length of the field with one shoe on. Of course, Joe has never liked to play first-year players. I didn't start and Franco didn't start, but we played. I had my first start against Kansas State out in Kansas. Charlie Pittman and Gary Deuel were both hurt, but I had a really good game and scored a long touchdown [of 58 yards]. After that I started and then Franco started. Joe just decided that he had to start us, and he did.

I also remember the Orange Bowl game against Missouri that year [1969] because I was quite disappointed going into the game. I didn't have any significant role in the offense because most of the running plays were designed for Charlie Pittman at halfback and Franco at fullback. But Joe put in this pass play for me and told me I was going to score on it if I practiced it.

In the beginning I wouldn't practice it. I was a stubborn young kid, and whenever we called the play I wouldn't run it. That's how mad I was. He said, "I put this play in purposely for you and I advise you to run it because you're going to score a touchdown." We had our little argument back and forth, and he said, "Hey, run the plays for you." So I ran it and practiced it and I scored the winning touchdown of the game on that play. [Mitchell's 24-yard touchdown on a pass from Chuck Burkhart came on the first play following the recovery of a fumbled kickoff by Missouri late in the first quarter. Penn State went on to win 10–3.] So, Joe does know a little bit.

Of course, my last game may have been my best, when we upset Texas in the [1972] Cotton Bowl. People didn't take us seriously. They didn't think we played good football up north. We were the laughingstock everywhere we went. It was very gratifying not only to play against a great Texas team, with all the tradition they have from year to year, but to go out there and just completely dominate them. The score was 30–6, and that was the very first time they had never scored a touchdown with their wishbone. So it was a good feeling knowing that we really accomplished something as a team. No one thought we could pull it off besides Joe, the coaching staff, and ourselves. [After rushing for 146 yards and a touchdown on 27 carries, Mitchell was named the Offensive Player of the Game and in 2004 was inducted into the Cotton Bowl Hall of Fame.]

When I'm asked what Penn State means to me, my answer is pride, and it is more than football. It's about getting a first-class education. It's about the kind of relationships we build, the guys we meet, and things we learn from Coach Paterno that are everlasting throughout the rest of life.

I often remember those meetings on Sundays after the game when we would sit around and Joe would bestow his philosophy on us, just basically about life itself—about standing up and being a man, about making decisions, and about once you make a decision you go with it. If it's wrong, you admit that it's wrong. If you're right about it, you don't have to gloat and show off or embarrass anybody. Back then you'd kind of sit back and say, "Oh, I have to listen to this again." But once you get away from there and you have a chance to reflect, you say, "You know what? The guy knew what he was talking about."

We learned a tremendous amount from Coach Paterno. That's the way I conducted my life, and those are the things that I believe in. I wouldn't trade that for the world and I would do it all over again the same way.

Lydell Mitchell was inducted into the College Football Hall of Fame in 2004. In his senior year he was the country's leading scorer and finished fifth in the Heisman Trophy voting. He still holds the Penn State records for scoring in a season (174 points in 1974), most touchdowns in a season (29) and career (41). Mitchell retired from the NFL in 1981 after an All-Pro career with Baltimore, San Diego, and Los Angeles, and is now involved in sales and marketing in several businesses, including Super Bakery, a nutritional baking company. He and his wife, Jeanette, have three daughters and they live in Baltimore.

JOHN CAPPELLETTI
TAILBACK/DEFENSIVE BACK
1970–1973

WINNING THE HEISMAN TROPHY puts me in a different category from a lot of other players, but I'm really not that much different from my teammates or anyone else who played football at Penn State. You go back 35 years, when I was recruited in 1970, and we were just a family with five kids, growing up in a suburb of Philadelphia, barely paying the bills. That was our life, and we had a lot of relatives around and a lot of fun. Sure, life is different today. I live in California now, but my values are still the same as they were when I was growing up and going to Penn State.

I'm not naïve. I've been told that outside of Coach Paterno I may be the most recognized figure connected with Penn State football, and I have a sense of that. But there is more to it than just being the football player who won the Heisman. I'm sure it goes back to my speech when I won the Heisman and dedicated the trophy to my brother Joey, who was sick and dying of leukemia. I was fortunate that I was sensitive enough to the situation and mature enough to try and deal with it. I wanted to tell people about it, as hard as it was.

Then the movie [*Something for Joey*] and the book came out, and it's been an ongoing thing. So I think people identify with me in a different way than they do other players, not just with football and Penn State, but in a broader sense. I think they realize that what happened to our family could possibly happen to them or they have already had a similar experience. When I meet people today, one of the first things they bring up is my speech. You can't believe it, but I still get letters each week.

I'll get a package of letters from 30 or 40 kids from schools around the world—Japan, Mexico, Canada—from kids who are just reading the book at this particular time, and the teacher says, "Well, you kids all write a letter and tell Mr. Cappelletti what you thought of the book and we'll package it up and send it to him."

Reading the letters can get pretty emotional. Obviously, the letters have to be somewhat similar, but there's still so many different things that the kids write about: what was important to them and why it meant something to them, whether it was because they had a family member that had the same disease, whether it was a grandmother who just passed away of natural causes, or whether they were constantly fighting with their brother or sister and they don't want to do that anymore. And this is 30 years after the fact. I never dreamed Joey and I would have this legacy.

I also think it's ironic because I was recruited primarily to play defense, not to run the ball. I was a running back, defensive back, and linebacker in my senior year in high school. George Welsh recruited me for Penn State. I also remember visiting Ohio State, Miami, and Virginia Tech, which was then Virginia Polytechnic Institution. My father could only make the Penn State visit, so he was the only one who came up with me. He had a good feeling for the people and the University when he was there. Even though it was not an easy place to get to, it was easier than other places, as far as distance, for my parents. They had to be able to see games without getting on a plane because, with Joey being sick, there was not much of an option for them.

I don't know how high up I was on Penn State's recruiting list. But Joe makes an impact. He came in and had a lot of things in common with my parents, just naturally being Italian and being Catholic. I remember Joey was sick at that particular time, and Joe showed a genuine interest in his health. He and George ate dinner there. So it was one of those familiar kinds of visits from somebody that you had a lot in common with before you even met him.

What I remember most about my freshman season was that I failed psychology in my first semester and pretty much thought that was the end of my life. I didn't want to go home with an F. And number two, I remember it was a three-game season for us, and I couldn't even tell you the teams we played except one was Pitt. I remember playing more linebacker than anything else, and I think I returned some kickoffs, but the freshman season was more dedicated to just being the scout team for the varsity.

I was looking forward to trying out and playing running back in my sophomore year. Joe came to me in the spring and said they were going to be loaded on offense with Lydell and Franco still there and probably a little bit thinner on defense, and would I mind going to the defensive side of the ball with the intention that I would try and come back to the offensive side as a junior. Since there was a chance that I could play on defense, that was fine.

So I was a starting defensive back in '71 and ran back punts and kickoffs. They put me and Eddie O'Neil back to return punts and kickoffs the first couple of times, and I don't remember ever practicing punts and kickoffs an awful lot. I think I fumbled a time or two and some of the guys started calling me "Fumbelletti." But I continued running back punts and kickoffs, and I had a pretty decent career by average and the amount of returns. I remember when I was a junior returning one punt at West Virginia for about 50–60 yards, down to near the goal line. [Cappelletti's return was for 68 yards to the WVU 2-yard line.] And I wasn't the guy with the breakaway speed, either.

114

We lost the last game of my sophomore year and the first game of my junior year to the same team, Tennessee, which was disappointing, although we upset Texas in the [1972] Cotton Bowl. They switched me back to running back in my junior year, and it wasn't an easy transition. There were three of us at running back—me, Gary Hayman, and Tommy Donchez. We were going back and forth in the first three games, and they were so-so games for me. The breakout game for me was at Illinois in the fourth game of the season. I think I had over 100 yards for the first time. [Cappelletti rushed for 124 yards and a 53-yard touchdown on 21 carries.] After that it was just one game better than the next, game after game. That was the turning point.

We didn't lose another game until the Sugar Bowl [against Oklahoma], and that was disappointing. I woke up in the middle of the night [on game day], and everything just started coming out from everywhere. It was some kind of virus or flu or food poisoning, and it just hit me at that moment in time. By game time I could hardly lift myself up. If the game had been 24 hours later, I would have got it all out and they'd have had a chance to pump me full of fluids. [Without Cappelletti, the Penn State offense was stymied, and Oklahoma won 14–0.]

I had a lot of confidence going into my senior year. I stayed healthy for as much as I ran the ball, even though I missed the Syracuse game because of a

In 1973 John Cappelletti gave one of the most emotional acceptance speeches in the history of the Heisman Trophy award, bringing tears to the hundreds of people in the room as he honored his dying brother, Joey, suffering from leukemia, who was in the audience.

partial shoulder separation against Army the week before. We had a great team, and I was having a good year, and about halfway through the season Joe sat down with me and said the Heisman was being talked about. He said to just continue to do what we were doing as a team and as individuals. You know what Joe always says, if you take care of the little things, the big things take care of themselves. He said if we practiced well, focused on winning the game, and had a good season as a team, individuals would get attention. Of course, that's what happened.

Our toughest game was against North Carolina State late in the season. Lou Holtz was the coach, and NC State had a very good football team. I don't think we realized how good they were. They thought they were going to come up here and knock us off. It was just one of those games where we scored, they scored, we scored, they scored. We won the game 35–29. That was probably the most satisfying game to win because, once we got into the fight, we reacted to it. It also was my best game, and I had the most carries and yards in a single game. [Cappelletti's 220 yards, three touchdowns, and 41 carries all set team records for a single game at the time.]

I was disappointed we couldn't play for the national championship. We were the only team to go 12–0 after beating LSU [16–9] in the Orange Bowl, but there wasn't anything else we could do. We did what we had to do, as players, as a team, as coaches. I think Penn State always has to do more than its fair share to get the national recognition that other teams get. But you can't sit here and cry about that.

I've often been asked where I was when I found out I won the Heisman Trophy. I was in New York for the Bob Hope All-American [TV] special that he did every year. We had done our thing, and I was sitting in the stands watching the other guys do their taping. A representative for the Downtown Athletic Club came by and announced to the group that I had won it. I really felt good because I was sitting there with all these guys who were really good players, including the guys who finished second, third, fourth, and fifth in the Heisman balloting. I really felt like we won something. The guys congratulated me, and the next thing I knew I was in a limo to the Downtown Athletic Club with Bob Hope. That was one of those numbing experiences in itself. We just did the taping of the show, and now I'm in the back seat of the limo with Bob Hope.

As I look back, I think winning the Heisman Trophy took some of the edge off not winning the national championship. I mean that for the team, too, because without my teammates, I would have never won the trophy, and I will always be grateful to them and to the coaches.

Joe and the coaches drove us to become the best we could be. In my freshman year, Joe was only in his fifth year as head coach and he wanted to build a program. Joe wanted to go to the next level and still try and make it an experience where we were still college students and still student-athletes but yet we could still play at the highest level. Without Joe for our four years, we probably don't achieve what we all achieved as a team and as individuals. Joe had a vision and a plan to accomplish it.

Joe was a good teacher, a good mentor. You look back at him and you look at what he's still doing and the sayings that he has and it's still the same. Don't get me wrong, every once in a while when you're out on the practice field and you're day to day to day with Joe, you want to go up and just grab him and want to shake him and say, "Hey, enough." But you still find yourself hearing what he told you years ago and using the same sayings every once in a while. Joe was a good person to have in your life for those four years, whether it was on or off the field. I look forward to going back for reunions with my teammates, seeing people who have been with the program for many, many years, and participating in events. I am happy to say I'm a Nittany Lion forever.

117

John Cappelletti is Penn State's most celebrated football player and the school's only Heisman Trophy winner. He was inducted into the College Football Hall of Fame in 1993, and in 2006 he was inducted into the Orange Bowl Hall of Honor. Following a nine-year All-Pro career with the Los Angeles Rams and San Diego Chargers, Cappelletti became a businessman in California. He and his wife, Betty, have four sons and live in Laguna Niguel, California.

MARK MARKOVICH

OFFENSIVE GUARD

1970–1973

Moments after Penn State lost to Michigan last season [2005] on the last play of the game, something happened that exemplifies what being a Nittany Lion is all about. Joe was cornered by reporters, and you could see how crushed he was with his eyes. As he was being questioned over and over again about the devastating loss and how he and his team would respond, he stated something like, "Come on, guys, we're going to wake up tomorrow and it's another day. We lost a game and that's all." While that may be insignificant to most people, to me that typifies Penn State, the attitude and the mentality and the maturity of being a Nittany Lion.

Penn State means pride and poise, and there's an aura and class about being a Nittany Lion that transcends any other college. As players, we knew we were always better prepared than our competition and knew we were always better coached. Joe used to say that you have to decide when you are going to perspire. Are you going to perspire during your preparation or during your presentation? At Penn State, hard work during your preparation always provided a cool, calm, confidence while performing.

People would ask us what did Joe and the coaches say when it was a tight, tough game and how did he get us enthused, riled up, and ready to go? We'd look at each other and say, "Really, nothing." You made some adjustments if needed, but, regardless, you knew that if you believed in the game plan—

if you believed in the process and if you believed in the program—you knew you were better prepared than your opponent and in the end you would prevail.

I frequently tell the men and women who work for me in my company about an event that happened during my freshman year. Study hall was mandatory five days a week, an hour and a half each day. One night in the winter we were finishing dinner in West Halls and, as we got up to go to study hall, a non-player asked us why we went to study hall and what they would do if we didn't go. We all looked at each other and said, "We don't know. No one's ever missed." You bought into the program, so you did what the program asked you to do, and it worked. That's the kind of respect there was for the program and for the style and the system that made you a Nittany Lion. I strive for the same in my business.

It's also those intangibles. I earned my first start my sophomore year in mid-season at Syracuse. We were in the old Archbold Stadium, and several of us were sitting on the floor in the shower room a few minutes before the game. I was obviously nervous, and Dave "Hippo" Joyner, our captain, must have seen me. Hippo came over and sat down. He didn't say anything, he just started humming. What he was humming was the song, "Jeremiah Was a Bullfrog." He had performed that song the prior spring in a skit during Spring Week, which was a major event on campus back then. Hippo was humming the song and then he started singing it, and without even thinking about it, I started singing along with him. And then, as unannounced as his arrival, he departed. The quiet ease that "Jeremiah" brought me was exactly what I needed. And even to this day when I go into a meeting that is crucial to my business, I find myself humming that silly song!

119

We won the Syracuse game [31–0], and I started the rest of my career. We lost only three games and beat Texas in the 1972 Cotton Bowl [30–6], and LSU in the 1974 Orange Bowl [16–9]. Many fans thought we should have been No. 1 in '73. We were the only team to go 12–0, but for some reason the media was not impressed, even though Cap [John Cappelletti] won the Heisman Trophy. I don't remember anybody involved with Penn State talking about us getting screwed or us getting a raw deal. I'm not going to say that not being No. 1 wasn't important because that would not be correct—everyone wants to be recognized as the best. We beat everybody that we had an opportunity to play, and, in our hearts and in our minds, that's all we

Mark Markovich was the leader of the offensive line that led the way for John Cappelletti to win the Heisman Trophy in 1973. As he told sportswriters at the time, "We knock people down at the line, and Cappy comes through and knocks them down again."

needed. Joe made a presentation after the [Orange Bowl] game and declared us No. 1 and found a way to provide us with national championship rings. I wear that ring proudly.

The '73 undefeated and championship team had a reunion in 1998 and again in 2003, and we're not bitter about what happened 30 years ago. Joe always said you couldn't judge a team or a class until 20 years after they graduated. We proved we were the best on the field and proved we're the best over the last 30 years by the type of responsible family/business people we became. We have doctors, company presidents, sales executives, guys with MBAs and CPAs, you name it. Being a Nittany Lion transcends any disappointment we might have felt about not winning a national championship.

Besides, how many people can say they blocked for a Heisman Trophy winner? Cap was one of us and he never did anything in any way, shape, or form that would have suggested he wasn't. But to be honest, it was no different blocking for John than it was blocking for Bobby Nagle, Tom Donchez, Walt Addie, or anyone else running the ball.

Obviously, I had more time with Cap than any of the others, and on the sweeps and counters we ran, I had the opportunity to provide the lead block. He was great setting me up for those blocks, and I never had to worry about running off course. When Cap won the Heisman, nothing changed. He was still the shy, awkward hick from the wrong side of the state that he is today! Remember, he was the guy who played defense for two years; we called him "Fumbelletti" because he had to learn how to not fumble punts as a sophomore and to hold on to the ball at the start of his junior year. John and I are very close friends, and the special relationship was there before he was the Heisman winner and it continues today.

But I have to tell you I never thought I would be the lead blocker for a Heisman Trophy winner. I was a tight end and defensive end at Greensburg Central Catholic High School in Greensburg, Pennsylvania, and was recruited as a tight end by most of the schools on the East Coast. One old coach from a school that I won't mention actually handwrote a contract guaranteeing me I'd be their starting tight end my sophomore year. When I visited Penn State, Joe said, "You're too slow and don't have the hands to be a tight end. If you come to Penn State, you will be an offensive lineman." When I looked in the mirror, I knew he was right. I didn't have the speed and had marginal hands at best. Joe was the first person to be honest regarding my future potential. On the way home I told my parents that I was tired of all the hoopla and stated that this was the first honest presentation I had. Penn State was where I was going to go.

I coasted through high school and never considered pushing to achieve my best in the classroom. That changed at Penn State, as we had a very unique freshman class. We had some geniuses, starting with Buddy Ellis, who were very serious about their studies and not only went to but actually worked hard at study hall. I also went to study hall and learned not to miss a class. At the end of the first quarter, 12 out of the 22 of us on scholarship were on the high honor roll of 3.5 or above.

If you were foolish enough to schedule a Saturday class, thinking that you might not have to go because you had a home game, you'd be dead wrong. I remember skipping my first class on a Saturday of a home game. The class was taught by Bob Mitinger, who had been an All-American [end] at Penn State in 1959. On Monday morning, Bob and Pat [assistant coach Frank Patrick] informed me in no uncertain terms that if I thought I was getting preferential treatment because I was a player that I was sadly mistaken, and that if I missed another class again, I would be a very unhappy young man. Again, this goes back to Joe and what happens on the field. Joe would tell us that if there were two guys whose performance on the field was equal, he would choose the one living up to his potential in the classroom. And we saw that happen more than once.

What does it mean to be a Nittany Lion? It's the structure—that discipline, that honor, that pride, and that commitment to developing to be the best you can be. Seldom does a day go by that there isn't something I find myself doing or saying that, when I think about it, doesn't come back to my days of growing and maturing and earning the right to be a Nittany Lion. And no one can ever take that away from me.

Mark Markovich was a second-team All-American and co-captain of the unde-feated 1973 team. He also was a first-team Academic All-American and win-ner of an NCAA postgraduate scholarship and a National Football Foundation Hall of Fame Scholar-Athlete Award. After playing six years in the NFL with San Diego and Detroit and earning an MBA, he entered private business. He now owns his own machine and tool company in Peoria, Illinois, where he lives with his wife, Mary, and three children, Kevin, Emily, and Jack.

GREG MURPHY
DEFENSIVE END
1971–1974

I DON'T THINK THERE'S EVER BEEN ANOTHER player from Brooklyn who played for Joe. Joe was always nice to me, and I guess that Brooklyn connection helped out. I was one of the most recruited athletes in the country at the time. I was the first freshman captain of my school and was a high school Parade All-American in my senior year. But Penn State was not my original first choice. In fact, I wouldn't have thought about Penn State if it weren't for Joe's brother, George Paterno, who was coaching at Michigan State.

In those days you could take a lot of visits, and I made, like, 15 trips in my senior year. It was a great experience, and I had a lot of fun. I went to Tilden High School in Brooklyn. My coach and guidance counselor was Vinnie O'Connor, who's still coaching but is now at St. Francis Prep. He had players who went to Notre Dame, like Gerry and Larry DiNardo. So Ara Parseghian was the first guy who called me. Coach Ara came to the house, and when I took the trip to Notre Dame, I really had a good time. So I signed the letter of intent to go to Notre Dame.

Then I took a trip to Michigan State. George Paterno was recruiting me. In those days you could sign a letter of intent with each conference. It was such a great trip and I was ready to sign a letter of intent, since it was Big Ten and Notre Dame was independent. But the next week, Bo Schembechler came to my school and said he'd like to get me to Michigan. I also had taken a trip to Ohio State, and Woody Hayes had come to my house. When I took my trip to Michigan, there was a major blizzard that night. I came into the hotel and there must have been five feet of snow. I walked through this pane glass window, right into the middle of the lobby. I didn't get a scratch and I went right up to my room. I said, "Boy, that's a good sign. It's the place for me." So, now, I was going to sign with Michigan.

I talked to George Paterno on the phone, and he said, "Look, you can't go to Michigan because you're going to have to beat Michigan State, so do me a favor and go see my brother up at Penn State." Bo was very angry that I was even talking to George, since I had decided on Michigan, and he put a little pressure on me. I kept talking to George, and he sent [assistant coach] John Rosenberg and a man from my area, Art Gladstone, to recruit me. Art convinced me to take a trip to Penn State.

I took my aunt with me, and the person I stayed with was Franco Harris. My aunt is about the same age as Franco, and she fell in love with him. She said, "I want to see Franco again. So you have to pick Penn State." Then Joe came to the house, and we went to eat at a famous place in downtown Brooklyn. My father didn't eat that night because he didn't think it was right that I was going to go to Michigan and Joe was buying us a meal. After Joe left, he sent my mom flowers. Nobody else had sent my mom flowers, and she thought that was very, very nice. The guys from Michigan State came, and Woody came and Ara came, and Joe was the only one who sent her flowers. She said, "I want you to go to Penn State." My aunt was really happy because she loved Franco, and that's how I ended up at Penn State.

124

I was an All-American linebacker in high school, so I thought I was going to be another linebacker for "Linebacker U," and that's where I played my freshman year. In those days you had to get your schooling together and go to study hall and just play a freshman schedule. We played three games, and Mike Hartenstine, who [later] played for the Chicago Bears for 13 years, was the other inside linebacker.

I definitely had to work at my studies because it was a culture shock coming from New York, which was all black, and going to State College, which was almost an all-Caucasian school at the time. I think maybe out of 20,000 people there were maybe 1,000 black people all together at the school, and 500 of those flunked out after their freshmen year. I think there were only five of us [blacks] on the team.

I had a friend who went up there with me named Glen Ford, who was a highly recruited defensive tackle. Glen had gone to Boys High School, which

Greg Murphy's sense of humor continues to make him one of the most popular of Penn State's players, but on the field he was usually all business. He was the first player for Paterno who came from the venerable coach's hometown of Brooklyn.

was all black. My school, Tilden, was all Caucasian. Because of bussing in those days, the students from the black neighborhoods like me were bused to the Caucasian school, so I had one up because I had had the exposure from bussing. Glen Ford was one of the people who left school because he couldn't adjust to it.

I was in the division of undergraduate studies because I wasn't exactly sure what I wanted to do, so I had a lot of time to study. I did enough to get by, but it was a tough school for me. I excelled in high school, but being away from home, and in study hall, I really felt I needed that freshman year to get acclimated to State College.

In the spring of my freshman year, they moved me to defensive end and Mike Hartenstine to defensive tackle because there was just no room for us. We had such great linebackers. Eddie O'Neil and Greg Buttle became All-Americans. We also had Jim Laslavic. They all went on to play in the pros.

When I got transferred to end, J. T. White became my coach and I became one of J.T.'s "knuckleheads." I had a really great experience with J.T. You could have a lot of fun with J.T., but we always respected him as a coach. I remember in a meeting once before a game J.T. was giving us the spiel about what we should do on different situations and the formations. He was talking about a passing formation called "Trips" when they have three guys outside. I got up and said, "Well, what the heck do we do if 'Trips' come out? Do we rush the passer? What do we do on 'Trips?'" And in that growling, raspy voice of his, J.T. said, "Murphy, it's none of your business what I do on trips!" Because he was the recruiting coach, he thought I was asking him what he does at night on recruiting trips. And everybody just fell on the floor *laughing*. It was hilarious. He did many, many things like that, and it was just natural.

I was slated to start [at defensive end] my sophomore year but I sprained my ankle. So Dave Graf started for me on that side and Bruce Bannon was the starter on the other side. I had to play second team behind Bruce. We lost our first game at Tennessee [28–21] and then won the rest and played Oklahoma in the Sugar Bowl. It was such a great experience. There was a big controversy that Joe was supposed to leave to coach New England. After the game, the reporters came in and asked me, "What do you think? You came here and you thought Joe was going to be here." I said to the reporters, "I don't know about Joe, but I want that Bannon to leave." I didn't realize it was going to be as big a deal as it was, and they put it in the headlines on the front page, Hotdog Murphy Speaks Frankly, saying that, "he doesn't know about Joe going, he just wants Bruce Bannon to leave." Joe gave me a raised eyebrow over that.

I started the rest of my career. When I was at Penn State we only lost five games by about five points, and we won the Orange Bowl against LSU [16–9] and the Cotton Bowl against Baylor [41–20]. We had a great team in 1973. We went 12–0 and we had the Heisman Trophy winner. The whole defensive team played in the pros. But we didn't get much respect and couldn't win the national championship. I have many, many, many regrets over that.

I was told that my recruiting class was the biggest recruiting class ever. I think there were like 70 players that came in and only 22 played. But those other players got an education, and they're doing very well. They're doctors and lawyers now, and they add to the community. That's what Penn State is all about. It's awful hard work playing college football, and without graduating I think maybe you get cheated because you don't have anything to take with you. We all got degrees.

There's a big network of players out there, and we all like to go back. It was a wonderful experience and we are very, very proud of the school.

Greg Murphy was a second-team All-American in 1974 and graduated with a degree in rehabilitation education. Although he was in the NFL for six years, he never played a game because of a severe groin and pelvis injury. He is now in the construction business in New York City and has been involved in such projects as the Airtrain at Kennedy Airport and Battery Park City. He and his wife, Brenda, live in his hometown of Brooklyn Heights, not far from the Brooklyn Bridge.

CHRIS BAHR
PLACE-KICKER/PUNTER
1971–1975

ENJOYED GOING TO SCHOOL AT PENN STATE. In terms of football, it means coming from a program that was well respected, and the longer you're away from school the more you appreciate what went on there. We did get an education and we were forced to go to class. Nothing was given to us. I'm proud to have been associated with a program like that because there are a lot of programs that aren't that above board. Some schools don't really care about the students that they have and they're not student-athletes, and I heard all the stories in the NFL. I'm sure they have their problems, like any other program, but I think they run it as cleanly as possible and I think what you find is that most of the Penn State players who go on after college and play professional football, generally, know how to carry themselves as a group. They were generally fairly classy kids and knew how to do things the right way. They are a well-respected group in the league.

But I'm not a huge alumnus. I still go to the games, but I don't live or die with whether the football team beats Michigan. I'd like to see them win, but I've moved on in my life. I'm glad I went to a school like this and not some others. The football program generally is genuinely concerned how you do after and they follow you. I know that Sue Paterno knows what every one of us did. I'm sure she knows better what we're doing now than Joe does.

I was originally recruited for soccer, but in the context of being recruited for soccer I wanted to make sure that I would have the opportunity to try to

Chris Bahr was known for the distance of his field-goal attempts and he still holds the Penn State records for the most field goals of 50 yards or more (7) and the longest field goals with three for 55 yards in 1975 against Temple, Ohio State, and Syracuse.

kick for the football team as well, and I wanted to go to a school that would allow me to do both. I was a kicker at Neshaminy High School. I practiced football for 15 minutes a week. I only went to practice once a week and went to the games on Friday nights.

At the time, my dad was the soccer coach at Temple. [Walter Bahr coached at Temple from 1971 to 1973, then coached at Penn State from 1974 to 1987, taking the Lions to 12 straight NCAA postseason tournaments.] He was teaching at Frankford High School and coaching at Temple, and I just wasn't going to go to a school in downtown Philadelphia. He never really asked me to go either. There weren't a lot of people recruiting for soccer back then. The only schools that really contacted me were Ivy League schools.

As for football, I had fairly good notoriety as a kicker, but nobody back then recruited kickers that I can remember. Most of the kickers were straight-on guys. So football recruiters knew about me, but I don't remember talking to too many football people. I just wanted to make sure I could do both. I really don't remember how Penn State came about except that [Penn State's soccer coach] Herb Schmidt recruited me for soccer. Quite frankly, this was the only scholarship offer I had. My last term, I was actually on a football scholarship, though, because my soccer scholarship had expired after my four years. I left to play professional soccer for a summer and then came back in the fall and football picked up the cost.

I wasn't even planning on kicking the football the first two years. They had a kid named Al Vitiello, and I didn't even go to spring practice. I was just in the background. I think I went to spring practice my sophomore year. I played soccer my first two years, so they considered one of those a redshirt year, and I became the first-team kicker in football in my junior year. But I almost didn't kick here at all. I almost went to Temple after my sophomore year. Before the fall, I looked at the schedules and saw that there were four conflicts, four soccer games and football games at the same time. I said, "Well, I guess that's not going to work." My dad was still at Temple, and I talked to him and knew [Temple football coach] Wayne Hardin would work around it. So I was going to go to Temple. I heard the Penn State football coaches thought Temple had tampered somehow. So I came up here to just straighten it all out, and when I got up here for the meeting I saw that there was only one conflict left on the schedule. So I stayed at Penn State.

More than once I played soccer on Friday night and then caught a plane for the football game. I particularly remember the Iowa game [early in 1974]. I actually got hurt, a real deep thigh bruise, playing soccer Friday night. My dad drove me to the Pittsburgh airport after we played. Sitting in the car and sitting in the plane and the whole bit in trying to get to Iowa, my bruise just got worse and worse. I woke up in the morning and I just couldn't kick. I could not place any weight on my plant foot because of the thigh injury. [Penn State won 27–0.] That didn't fit very well with the coaches, and John Reihner kicked for a while. I was still kicking some of the longer field goals, but it wasn't until the last game at Pitt that they let me kick everything. I think I kicked four goals, and that was actually the first game where I started to get some notice in terms of [pro football] agents. It was a national TV game, and that's where it all sort of started to snowball.

The kick that sticks in my mind the most is the first field goal I ever tried. It was against Stanford in '73. Here I am, a wide-eyed kid, and it was national television out at Stanford. It was from 42 yards or something and it was on the hash. I lined up as if it was a 20-yard kick, so my angle was a little off. To kick your first one was very nerve-racking. I didn't come close. I hit it good but I hit it as if it was a 20-yard field goal in terms of angle, and the hashes were wider back then. So it was immediately wide.

Another game that sticks out was that [1974] Navy game in the rain and the cold, which we lost 7–6. I had to hit a field goal at the end of the game. I still remember the series of pictures in the paper. I knew I made it as soon as I hit it, and it was dead center. It was a 40-yarder or something, and in the last 15 yards, it blew 15 yards to the right. I mean it literally just took a right turn because of the wind.

I'm told I still hold the Penn State record for longest field goals. [Bahr kicked three 55-yard field goals and one of 52 yards in 1975.] That's just because we tried a lot of long field goals because of the rules back then. If you missed, the ball went to the 20. So even if you punted inside the 10, to give up 10 yards for the chance of points seemed to make sense.

I always felt pressure kicking for Penn State and when I played in the NFL, but I was never scared. Kicking's not real complicated. It's mental. I've been telling guys for years they should just let the kicker go out and kick rather than call timeout at the end of a game because he's known for 20 minutes to a half hour that it's coming down to a kick. So you think that extra minute is going to bug him? It allows you to get your head together a little bit more. It actually allows you to relax a little bit being out there because you've been waiting for this the entire time.

The worst thing I ever went through was playing [golf] at Cypress Point and Pebble Beach in the [1981 Bing] Crosby celebrity tournament. Teeing off the 1st hole at Cypress Point the first day was the hardest thing I ever did in my life, athletically. They announced my name on the 1st tee, and you could literally see my hand shaking. The next day I had a putt at Pebble Beach that was about a foot and a half on the 8th hole, which is the number one handicap hole, and I had 15 minutes to think about a foot-and-a-half putt straight uphill. There's nothing but people on one side and the ocean on the other, and I'm thinking, "You know, if you miss this you're going to really look pretty stupid." If I had walked up, pulled the flag out, and tapped it in right away, it would have been okay. That's the difference. Kicking is what I did for a living. Kicking for Penn State was fun and I'm proud to have gone there.

Chris Bahr was an All-American in soccer (1972, 1973, 1974) and football (1975) at Penn State. In a 14-year NFL career, he kicked for the Bengals, Raiders, and Chargers, earning All-Pro status and playing in two Super Bowls. He earned a law degree while playing in Cincinnati, and since 1992 he has been a financial advisor living in State College with wife, Eva, and sons, C.J. and Dieter.

GREG BUTTLE

LINEBACKER

1972−1975

EDITORS' NOTE: Greg Buttle is one of the all-time "characters" and great players of the Paterno era. He agreed to be included in this book if he could literally write his own chapter and have approval of all edits. Against our better judgment, we agreed. Triumph Books thinks we are crazy, so the reader should know the publisher is not responsible for the content, punctuation, or anything else associated with this chapter. It is certainly different but we think readers will be happy with the result.

★ ★ ★

"We Are…Penn State!" and "I'm Proud to be a Nittany Lion!" may sound trite to many, but they ring true for the vast hundreds of thousands of Penn State alums and especially Nittany Lions football players. Why? Because it is true.

I have never heard "We Are…Ohio State!" or "We Are…Notre Dame!" being shouted or even whispered. Loyalists are driven to use the vernacular of their sports teams as in, "How 'bout them Dawgs!" or "Hook 'em Horns!" Certainly these are colorful metaphors and useful at sporting events, but pretty thin when it comes to defining one's university. All of the aforementioned and others have their loyalists. But if I hear another "Fight On" by the

USC marching band after a simple first down by the Trojans (someone, please kill the horse), I think I'll just throw up!

You see, what I and a great amount of other Penn Staters believe is that the defining characteristics of the Pennsylvania State University are simply more than a football team. Sure, football has a role and place at PSU, but that's it! A place just like wrestling, women's lacrosse, gymnastics, et al. The football program, on the other hand, places first when it comes to money. After that, the football team is just like the rest of the student body, only a tad larger in physical size.

I and all the other players before me experienced a number of things at Penn State—playing on TV in front of millions of people, running into Beaver Stadium in front of the screaming hometown crowd, signing our first autographs at Picture Day during our sophomore year. Fans. They always showed their appreciation by patting you on the back as you ran from the field after a win or a loss. There were the wins, of course. There were the losses, too! And there were special times, like the undefeated season of '73 and, hell, we even won the Heisman Trophy that year! Actually, Cappy won it, but he made us all feel like we did.

There were many other football-related challenges, experiences, and stories that maybe only players can appreciate. One of those challenges was tight-roping a fine line with Joe Paterno and coming out unscathed, particularly on Game Day. To Paterno, game day was serious stuff. To us, game day was serious fun. Practice was serious stuff.

Okay, it's Game Day. Get your game face on and don't take a team for granted. My great friend and roomie, Jim [Rosie] Rosecrans and I did get serious but only at kickoff. But with Joe, you never, ever took a team for granted: "Any team could beat you on any given day, so always be ready, be serious, yadda, yadda, yadda." So everyone, sans a few, was serious!

Jim and I decided this one game to be ourselves, with caution, mind you. In those days we rode over to the stadium in those ugly, blue "only at Penn State" school buses. The "Very Serious Defense" and coaches were always on bus No. 1, "Serious Offense" and coaches on bus No. 2, "Mildly Serious Backups" on bus No. 3, and the rest of the team and the "Not Quite Really Serious At All Guys" on bus No. 4. Now, bus No. 4, affectionately known by us all as the "Mops Bus," was a perfect hiding place for the not-so-serious-until-kickoff-but-ready-to-play guys. That would be Rosie and me!

Regarded in the Nittany Lions' record books as "Mr. Tackle," linebacker Greg Buttle was one of the true "characters" in the history of Penn State football, with his antics off the field. But on the field he was an intense competitor who relished hitting and punishing an opposing player.

Jim and I were really expressing our confidence in preparation. I, of course, the one of disciplined preparedness, and Rosie, the one of undisciplined readiness. *He* was crazy!

Now, we're on the way to the stadium. We're in the last seats at the back of the bus really yukking it up. We're making fun of the "Very Serious" stiffs on buses No. 1 and 2 and laughing with the "Mops" about Joe, when suddenly the bus comes to a halt because of pedestrian traffic. We're sitting there, right outside of the stadium, when Rosie looks out the window and notices a couple of our friends, the Spencer sisters, walking near the bus. "Hey Butts, look, it's the Spencers," Rosie says. We slide down the windows, lean our heads out, and begin waving and screaming, "Go State, Go State, Go State!" The crowd around starts screaming with us, and now we're halfway out of the windows, going crazy and having loads of fun.

All of a sudden we hear that recognizable shriek coming from the front of the bus, and sure enough, it's Joe. He got on bus No. 4, not bus No. 2. I quickly slide back through the window, but Rosie has his shoulder pads hung up and can't get back in the bus. Joe is screaming towards the back of the bus, "What's going on? Who's that back there? We have a game to play!" To this day, we want to thank the "Mops" who stood up in the back of the bus to ensure that Joe didn't recognize who it was! Now that's what it means to be a Nittany Lion! By the way, we manhandled Kentucky that Saturday afternoon by a score of 10–3!

In 1972 I was 17 years old, a punk kid from Linwood, New Jersey, and was being recruited by hundreds of schools. My parents were really interested with the Penn State "thing" early on in the recruiting process, so I make my last visit to good old PSU. Two feet of snow had engulfed the Penn State campus. Roadways are covered with ice. The wind and frigid temperatures are depressive, and here I am on a recruiting visit. It's not easy to impress a recruit and his family from the beaches of the Jersey shore. Little did I know how different the University and recruiting process at PSU would be compared to the other universities.

We checked into the Nittany Lion Inn Friday night. We met the coaches, and I said hi to my recruiter, George Welsh, and to Joe Paterno. Together with the other recruits' parents, Sue and Joe entertained my mom and dad. I went with my special player host for the weekend, Alex Wasilov (aka "the Waz"). He said, "Let's have a few laughs," and I agreed. We trudged up one hill and down another, through the snow and felt the wind chill (it had to be zero degrees) on our walk. We walked past the Pattee Library, where Waz said, "Remember this joint. You'll be here for study hall every night of your first year!" We moved on to the famous Creamery and met a few babes. Then we visited three different sororities (sororities were all located on certain floors of different dormitories) and met some more babes that knew the Waz.

135

Already I was learning something. Nothing about the football program, just the Greek alphabet!

Finally, we visited a fraternity house party. There were a few Nittany Lion players having some laughs, but the overwhelming amount of partygoers were Penn State students. I was surprised to find that nobody was screaming and yelling in a drunken tirade. Isn't that what happens at all college parties? Waz introduced me to a few players—Hufnagel, Skorupan, O'Neil, Laslavic, and some guy named Cappelletti. Not one spoke of Penn State football. They spoke of two things only—the Penn State that they knew and me, whom they didn't know. We started out as two loners and wound up with 30 people, five of whom were players, and became a "party waiting to happen."

Saturday night came fast! There was a basketball game where all the recruits, parents, and coaches got together. Meet a few other recruits, see a "big-time" college basketball game and check out the cheerleaders. It was the first time my parents and I really got to hear the cheer, "We Are…Penn State!"

After the game, my parents went back to Paterno's house for a little get-together and were entertained by the "*famous*" Italian Tenor, JoePa-Terno. My mom fit right in. She ended up playing the piano with everyone listening to the Caruso wanna-be. But what really struck her fancy was Joe's wit and sense of humor. Many times during other recruiting visits there had been gratuitous offerings. Not so here! You got what you saw. My parents saw and got two things that weekend—a special up-close and personal, inside look at a unique individual, Joe Paterno, and a place out of time, Penn State. It was a place unlike any other we had visited. It was a place that was uniquely tied to its football coach. I would find out later what it was like to be a Nittany Lion!

What it means to be a Nittany Lion becomes apparent only after graduation and playing in the NFL. In my final analysis, one has to take a good look at what it means over time. Penn State is, and I hope always will be, the same old place in a different time. I compare it to the Broadway musical *Brigadoon*. Brigadoon, as Penn State, is a wonderful place out of time! Brigadoon appears for one day every 100 years, and yet it appears as it always has been.

Penn State is a place out of time. The town, the people, the school, the businessmen, and the professors all have relatively remained the same. Since 1966, the Penn State football program has remained the same. Same philosophy.

Same coach. Same results. Just a different time. Players have come and players have gone, each with their own experiences of what it means to be a Nittany Lion. What began as some wacky experiment, started by the "Nutty Professor" doesn't seem as wacky now! It takes time to reflect on something that is so special to so many for so many reasons. What an experiment!

Sure, there are others that work hard but none with as authentic a work ethic as the Nittany Lion. Sure, there are others that unfortunately straddle the line, many that talk the line, fewer that even walk the line, but none that walks the straight-and-narrow line of principle as walks the Nittany Lion. There are many proud and rich traditions that deserve merit, but none are so steeped in the merits of character and discipline as the Nittany Lion. And, finally, none have Joe Paterno.

What began at PSU, in 1966, as "the Grand Experiment" will surely be Paterno's legacy founded on what I call the "Paterno Principle":

> A principle of design ignited with experiment consistent of line and of purpose, class, and dignity, and one which chooses not the easiest paths in its eternal pursuit of excellence.
>
> —G. Buttle

What it means to be a Nittany Lion begins and ends with Joe Paterno, the Grand Experiment, and the Penn State experience. I, for one, am proud to be a Nittany Lion! "WE ARE...PENN STATE!"

Greg Buttle was a consensus All-American in 1975 and in 2005 still held the team record for tackles in one season (165 in 1974) and career (343). He spent nine years with the New York Jets, earning All-Pro status in '79 and '80, helping further Penn State's reputation as "Linebacker U." Buttle is now a sports marketing specialist. He and his wife, Rita, raised three children: Christina, a member of Penn State's women's lacrosse team, Gregory, and Allegra. They live in East Meadow, New York.

JIMMY CEFALO
WIDE RECEIVER
1974–1977

EDITORS' NOTE: As with the other chapters in this book, this chapter was put together from an interview with Jimmy Cefalo and was not written by Cefalo.

★   ★   ★

I grew up in Pittston, Pennsylvania, a small coal-mining town centered between Wilkes-Barre and Scranton. I played my high school football at a stadium called Charley Trippi Stadium. Charley had played for Georgia, was a runner-up for the Heisman Trophy in 1946, a member of the Pro Football Hall of Fame, and was from my hometown. Charley recruited me to go to Georgia, and Georgia has one of the great journalism schools in America, so I decided to go there.

I flew home from my recruiting visit ready to tell my parents that's where I was going. When I walked into the house, Joe Paterno was sitting at the kitchen table. My father was pouring him a glass of his homemade wine and my mother was putting sauce over his spaghetti. Joe ignored me and looked at my mother and said, "Mrs. Cefalo, this pasta is better than Mrs. Cappelletti's." If Joe's not in my kitchen that day, I am absolutely a Georgia Bulldog.

Jimmy Cefalo was at his best in the clutch as a wideout. In his senior season he also ran back punts, setting a team record by scoring two touchdowns, one for 75 yards against Kentucky and another for 57 yards against West Virginia.

My father actually wanted me to go to King's College, a small college in Wilkes-Barre, so he'd be able to see me all the time. Penn State was the compromise, being two-and-a-half hours away. Sever Toretti, an assistant coach who recruited me, was maybe the biggest reason I went to Penn State. He was every uncle I had—this kind, wonderful Italian man who had his priorities straight.

I was the first freshman to start for Joe. He started me against Wake Forest in 1974, the fifth game of the season, and I scored a couple of touchdowns.

I had a very good freshman year and I didn't turn 18 until October 6, about a week after my first collegiate start. The publicity was extraordinary. TV crews from an NBC affiliate came up and followed me around for a day or two. That kind of stuff came with being so young and being the first freshman to start for Joe. Joe tried to protect me from that in a lot of ways and he was successful for the most part. When he let Derrick Williams, Justin King, and some other true freshmen [from the 2005 season] talk to reporters, he said, "I haven't let freshmen talk to the media since Jimmy Cefalo."

We changed offenses after my freshman year. I had been playing a wingback [a combination running back/wide receiver] and Joe wanted me to play tailback. He wanted me to bulk up to 202 pounds, and I had been playing at 175 pounds. I gained all of that weight, and I did it with a lot of weight-lifting, but I lost a little quickness.

I broke a thumb and badly sprained an ankle and I kind of fell out of favor with everybody my sophomore year. It was the most unpleasant 12 months of my life. I blamed myself for all of it, for not having the kind of year that I wanted. Now that I'm older, I look back and think I might have been a little too hard on myself because there were so many factors involved.

Right after my sophomore year, I was at a function with Charley Trippi and said, "Charley, do you think it's too late for me to transfer?" He said, "Jimmy, stay where you are. I would love for you to go to Georgia, but I think you should stay where you are."

I lost the weight and got put at wide receiver; the first time I played pure wide receiver was as a junior. Going into my senior year in 1977, the expectations for the team were not very big. We ended up with the same record as Notre Dame and Texas [11–1]. Yet we didn't play for the national championship because, I think, before the season Joe was saying we weren't going to be any good. Outside of two quarters in a torrential downpour against Kentucky that took us out of our game, we would have been undefeated and played for the national championship.

We were up big on Kentucky early and then the skies opened up. It wasn't a rainstorm, it was a deluge, and it just changed the complexion of the game. You couldn't throw the ball, and they had a big quarterback who was able to run the option and control things. We lost the game 24–20.

I ended up leading the nation in punt returning. That set up a trick play that helped us beat Pitt. When I touched the football, I drew a bit of a crowd so we ran the reverse to Mike Guman, which was unheard of, and that set up the winning touchdown. A reverse on a punt return at Penn State? You've got to be kidding me.

What I remember about the game is that Pitt scored with no time left on the clock and they trailed by two. Brooms had to be brought out to brush off the goal line because it was snowing so hard. Bruce Clark and Matt Millen made a stop at the goal line, and we won 15–13. We played seven games my senior year in rain or snow storms. It was brutal.

We were in line to go to the Orange Bowl, but in the last minute it fell through. I don't know why they would do that to Penn State, so we ended up going to the Fiesta Bowl. At the time, it was not a major bowl and it was played on Christmas Day. We beat the dog out of Arizona State [42–30] in their stadium, and part of it was because we felt as a class of seniors that no one respected what we had accomplished, stood for, and represented.

Football was actually the smallest part of my Penn State experience. I was the president of my fraternity. I was the co-chairman of the Dance Marathon, the largest fund-raiser on campus. When I think of Penn State, I think of the Carnegie Building, the Dance Marathon, my fraternity, and my wonderful teammates I was so close to.

If I had to do it over again, would I go to Penn State? That's something I ask myself a lot. The experience I had there with the education was terrific. The friendships I wouldn't trade for anything, so I guess in my heart of hearts the answer is yes.

I love Penn State and I wish my experience had been different in some ways. But had I gone to Notre Dame or Stanford or Princeton or wherever I'm sure there would have been circumstances that would have been difficult. And I don't know that I would have found success in my chosen field or taken the path I have taken to get here had I not gone to Penn State.

Jimmy Cefalo's 67-yard punt return in the 1977 Fiesta Bowl is still a Penn State bowl record and he returned two punts for touchdowns that season as well. A third-round pick by Miami in 1977, he played seven seasons for the Dolphins before retiring. In 1984 he caught the pass that allowed Dan Marino to set the NFL's single-season record for touchdown passes. Cefalo is the radio play-by-play voice of the Dolphins, as well as the sports director at a Miami TV station. A five-time winner of Florida Sportscaster of the Year, Cefalo and his wife, Janice, have three daughters.

MATT BAHR

KICKER

1974–1978

Y OU WALK INTO A LOT OF TRADITIONS when you first go to Penn State. You're slowly made aware of them in all the academics, in all the history of the school, and in all the sports. There are certain traditions that you're really unaware of until you get there and you slowly grow into them, and by the time you finish, you feel you're part of a storied history. That never leaves, even years and years after you're gone. Most of my best friends are Penn Staters.

The stadium itself is part of that tradition. It's the same stadium, having been moved around the campus over the years, taken down, rebuilt, taken down, rebuilt, and finally it's in its permanent location because they cemented it in. It's pretty much the same stadium they played in years ago, they just keep adding on to it. I remember before I started at Penn State I was at one of the bowls with my brother and I met the Cappellettis, and that brought the traditions home with the Heisman talk, saying [to me that] you're now a part of that.

It's not just in football either. Take soccer. It's called Jeffrey Field. I didn't know what that meant until I got there. Then you find the tie-in between Bill Jeffrey, my father, the World Cup, the historic victory over England. [Penn State's head soccer coach, Bill Jeffrey, coached the championship U.S. World Cup team in 1950 that included Walter Bahr of Temple.] When I got

Matt Bahr followed his brother Chris as Penn State's kicker and was more prolific. In 1978 he set a team record that still remains for most field goals in one season, making 22 on 27 attempts. He also has the mark for most field goals in a half, with four against SMU in 1978.

143

to Penn State, I discovered more of my father's history, more of Bill Jeffrey's history, and said, "Hey, this is not just a soccer program I'm coming into play for a couple of years. It's got a great, great past and, hopefully, a great future."

It's a little ironic because I almost went to the Naval Academy. [Football coach] George Welsh had been an assistant at Penn State. He and Glen Warner, the soccer coach, both recruited me to go to the Academy. My oldest brother, Casey, had gone to the Academy, and it seemed like a good opportunity. Then about a week before plebe summer, when I was supposed to report, they were getting another soccer coach. I couldn't find out who that was going to be and so I said, "Well, I think I'll accept the Penn State offer."

Freshmen were eligible, but I was redshirted that year. One of my first memories was spring practice when we were getting ready for the Blue-White game. This was where the traditions come in, and it's also some of the weaning process where the upperclassmen accept the freshmen and things of that nature. Greg Buttle grabbed me in the locker room before the game or a couple practices before. He just kind of grabbed me by the shirt and the shoulder and said, "We're going to win this game and this is why." And he started shaking me. It was just the Blue-White game, but it was neat. You were treated as part of a team. That really is a fond memory.

Like my brother, I also played soccer Friday night and then would drive or fly to our football game. Yeah, Joe didn't like that so much. We'd have soccer games, like at Army, where you'd just get the tar beat out of you, and then you'd drive all night or all evening to get back to school. Then Saturday morning, if the game was away, they'd fly me to wherever the team was playing, and, understandably, Joe didn't care for it because sometimes we were really beat up and sore, and here I was trying to kick competently for a team that was in the hunt.

144

Every day I would have soccer and football practice. I would start out at football practice. I'd kick with the center and the holder and we'd move around the field. One of the coaches, or a distracter, would more or less throw things at you or run in front of the ball to try to mess you up, but it just made you concentrate better. I would then jog to soccer practice, and if Joe had field-goal practice scheduled, he'd schedule them at the end so that I could make it back after soccer practice ended. I'd jog back and get in pads and kick with the team. It was a little awkward, and my grades were not as good as I would have liked. My major was electrical engineering, and the hardest time was in the spring, oddly enough. There were no games for either sport, but football practice would be in the afternoon and soccer practice in the evening. So instead of more or less doing one long practice, two practices would be as much as five or six hours out of your day, which really became a little awkward.

But all the practicing was worth it. I learned that from my father and Joe Paterno. Just do as well as you can on each day, in each game and each practice. Practice to get better. That was the type of attitude that we got up there.

Quality practicing always translated into the games. You can't go onto the field the same way you come off the field, so you might as well practice to get better. If you're not practicing to get better, most certainly you're getting worse. You cannot stay the same.

I kicked a lot of field goals at Penn State and in the NFL, but I can't remember many of them. I remember the ones that were more challenging. There was a game at Pitt [in 1977] where the field was just a sheet of ice, and you had to kind of chip the ice before you could do anything. You try to chip your steps out so that you don't slide getting to the ball, and I think we made three kicks. It was a very difficult day to kick, but we won. [Bahr kicked field goals of 34, 31, and 20 yards in a 15–13 victory.]

I remember that it was always windy at Beaver Stadium, and Joe apparently was aware of where the more favorable locations were on the field. He knew them better than I did, that kicking from the left hash going into the closed end was better than hitting from the right hash into the open end. It was open then. He knew based on where the wind was outside what it was like in the stadium, and those little things do help.

I understand I still hold the record for kicking four field goals in the most games. I guess I did it four times. [Bahr set the record in 1978 against Rutgers, Ohio State, Southern Methodist, and North Carolina State.] You remember them because it was a good season and we just moved the ball up and down the field constantly. That was just a fun team. I had Bobby Bassett holding and Draz [Andy Drazenovich] snapping. That year, even the ones I missed, I wish I had another chance at them because I really felt I had a good opportunity at making them. It was disappointing to lose the national championship to Alabama in the Sugar Bowl, but if the better team always won, they wouldn't play the game. I really felt we were the better team. However, on that day, Alabama beat us. They played really well. We had a lot of great players on that team: Matt Millen, Matt Suhey, Bruce Clark. Just go down the list. They're all guys who probably will be in the College Football Hall of Fame.

Without question, playing for Penn State helped me have a long career in the NFL. The average lifetime in the NFL is 3.2 years and a kicker's average life is less, and I played 17 seasons. Penn State players were looked upon by the pros as team players. They were always good to have on the team because they were some of the core players that you need to have for a successful team

145

and a successful season. That's, without question, due to Joe in that he always made guys look to the future, telling us that very few would go on to play pro football, so what you had to do was get a good education while you were there. And if you are lucky enough to go play pro football, because of your education, you know you don't need football to earn a living. So, consequently, they can play a little longer because the pressure isn't there to say, "God, I really need this job." I think that's a big part of it. I think that's a credit to not only Joe but to Penn State, the institution itself where the teachers, the faculty, and the staff at Penn State treated all the students as students. Just because they happened to be athletes didn't change their attitude toward them, and the athletes knew that. They knew they had to buckle down and perform in the classroom. They were there to get decent grades and succeed, not just to play soccer and football. I am proud to be part of the ongoing Penn State tradition.

Matt Bahr was an All-American in 1978 and at one time owned the NCAA record for career field-goal accuracy. He kicked for six NFL teams over 17 years, including Super Bowl Champions at Pittsburgh and New York. Bahr earned an MBA and is now involved with several businesses from his home base in suburban Pittsburgh.

TOM BRADLEY

DEFENSIVE BACK

1974–1978

I THINK EVERYBODY WHO HAS PLAYED AT PENN STATE remembers the first time Joe Paterno yelled at them. Mine came at a meeting when I was a freshman. I wasn't late to it, but with Coach Paterno, 10 minutes early can be five minutes late. I came in and it was four minutes before the meeting had started and he started on me, "You're two minutes late! There's 100 guys, that's 200 minutes. You're not worth three hours of anybody's time!"

I couldn't get any lower in that seat. It's one of those moments in your life that you'll never forget. Since then, if he calls a meeting at 4:00, I'm there at about a quarter to 8:00. He always gets somebody every year, and I just sit there and chuckle. That was not the only time I got blistered my freshman season.

The first day we put on pads no one wanted to be the tight end, so I figured I'd just jump in. I'm thinking, "What the heck, it's just a drill." I came across the middle, and Jim Rosecrans lit me up like a Christmas tree and he said, "Welcome to college football." The other mistake I made: one day I was the scout-team tailback. I did a good job and I ended up staying there. There's nothing worse than being the scout-team tailback because of these famous words by the defensive coaches: "Run it again." I'd think, "Ahh, not again. What are you doing to me?"

One day I got into two fights in practice on the same day and got thrown off the field for one of them, so that's how the nickname "Scrap" started. I

147

don't know how it took off. I never tell my players what happened. I let the story get bigger and bigger and keep them guessing. I started thinking about coaching when I realized I wasn't good enough to play. I enjoy being around the game and being a part of it.

No question playing is great, but as a coach you do a lot of things that have an impact on a young man's life. A former player came up to me not long after the 2005 season and said, "Hey, I was a walk-on here, and the day you told me what an influence I had on my teammates and how hard I worked had a big impact on me." That's nice to hear and sometimes it's the smallest things.

If someone had told me I'd go into coaching right after I was done playing and never leave Penn State, I'd have thought, "Coach Paterno has lost his marbles." I told him one day, "Gee, Coach, you have 350-some victories. If I hadn't played here, you'd have 360, if I hadn't coached here, it would be, like, 370." He stuck his head into the doorway of my office a little bit later and said it was 380.

I get a kick out of all these recruiting services that say "He's a three-star. He's a four-star," because of a guy like Shane Conlan and his amazing story. I get this film less than two weeks before signing period in 1982, and it's an 8-millimeter home film from Frewsburg, New York. Now, I'm not kidding, pick any three people at work and any car of girls going down the road and we can beat this team. I liked the film, but it's Class D football in New York, and that's about as small as it gets.

I call the coach and say, "Well, who's recruiting this guy?" He says, "Nobody, Edinboro [a Division II school in Pennsylvania] turned him down." Now I'm thinking, "I like this kid. Maybe he'll walk on." His coach says, "You've got to see him play basketball. You've got to come tomorrow because it's his last game."

At this time I'm recruiting a lot of other players and doing a lot of other things. I had a Honda and I went up Route 219, which is also called the Buffalo-Pittsburgh Highway, and anybody familiar with 219 knows what I'm talking about. I'm making the tracks in the snow, and I'm thinking to myself, "You are a blankety-blank idiot. This is so stupid."

I knew I was in Frewsburg when I saw a barn that said, "Welcome to Frewsburg." So I get there and I watch Shane's team warm up, and here's a guy who's 6'3", 190 pounds, maybe. I'm thinking, "At halftime, I'm outta here. I'll say the weather's bad, I've gotta go." First play of the game, one of his teammates lobs it up to him and Shane throws it down.

The intensity and motivation as a player made Tom Bradley (seen here with assistant coach Larry Johnson) an overachiever, and when he became captain of special teams on the unbeaten 1978 team, it was named "the Scrap Pack" after his nickname "Scrap." That same intensity and motivation has never wavered throughout Bradley's coaching career.

So I start watching and he fouls out in the third quarter because he's Shane Conlan and he's so aggressive. I talk to him after the game and I say, "Shane would you like to visit Penn State?" He says, "Yes," and I say, "Well, it would have to be this weekend." So I set the visit up and I go back and tell the same story to our coaching staff. They look at me like I'm out of my mind.

His visit comes up, and we go through the whole weekend not sure if we want him. Joe says, "Tommy, you've got to coach him. If you think he's that good, you better be right." I'm like, "What am I doing?" I called him a couple of days before signing day and Shane is a man of few words. I said, "Shane, would you like to come to Penn State?" He said, "Yeah, I'd love to."

I said, "I really haven't been to your house yet. Do you want me to come up and meet with your parents?" He goes, "That's stupid. I just saw you." End of conversation. Tuesday I called him and said, "Look Shane, Signing Day is Wednesday and we're allowed to pick up these letters of intent. I can come over and get it." He goes, "I thought you guys were supposed to be smart at Penn State. I'll just mail it in." That's my best recruiting story just the way it happened. [From such humble beginnings, Conlan became a two-time first-team All-American and helped Penn State win the 1986 national championship.] That's why I laugh about these people with these ratings. A couple of years ago they couldn't even pronounce Paul Posluszny's name.

I kind of chuckled when Joe got criticized [during a stretch of four losing seasons in five years]. If people think criticism bothers Joe, they don't know him very well. I knew where we were and where we were heading. We just had to show it and convince some recruits, "Hey, we're on the right path." In 2003 we were a good football team, we just couldn't come up with a play when we had to make a play. We were just one play off.

In 2004 the kids played such great defense, but after the goal-line stand at Indiana, they had a whole different swagger about themselves. They knew they were good, but that stand, it carried right through to the winter program and the spring, and they had a whole different walk about them, a whole different attitude about the way they did things. I knew we'd be okay coming into the year and I thought we'd be pretty darn good on defense. When quarterback Michael Robinson made the big play on offense against Northwestern, we took off from there. It's what Joe had said from the year before, "We just need a play. Hang in there. Hang in there."

I think everybody in our profession aspires to be a head coach. There hasn't been the right situation for me, and I think that's the thing about Penn State that's so endearing to so many of us. When they say, "We Are…Penn State!" it's a family atmosphere. There's a feeling about that place that's different. It's like with Paul Posluszny. He's got it. I don't what it is, but he's got it, and Penn State is like that. You feel it about the place and with the people. I've had opportunities and there have been places with more money involved. But it's not always about money.

Tom Bradley lettered in 1977–1978 and established himself as a special-teams terror. His brothers, Jim, who is now the orthopedic surgeon for the Pittsburgh Steelers, and Matt, also played for Penn State. After earning a degree in business, Bradley joined the Penn State coaching staff as a graduate assistant and never left. He has been in charge of the defense since 2000. In 2004 Penn State was the only Division I-A team in the country not to give up more than 21 points in a game. In 2005 the Nittany Lions defense finished in the top 10 among Division I-A teams in rushing and scoring and produced consensus All-Americans Tamba Hali and Paul Posluszny. Bradley lives in State College.

KEITH DORNEY

TACKLE

1975–1978

THE BALL COULDN'T HAVE BEEN ANY CLOSER to the goal line. It was fourth down. Penn State was down by seven in the fourth quarter, but the momentum had changed. All we had to do was move the football one inch. Just one inch!

We huddled. Chuck Fusina called the play, a handoff to Mike Guman up the gut, with fullback Matt Suhey leading the way. I jogged to the line of scrimmage. The thick and humid bayou air, superheated inside the enclosed dome by the throng of 76,824 screaming fans, hung from the rafters like molasses.

I hugged the line of scrimmage so the top of my helmet was just behind the ball, leaned forward with my all my weight on my down right hand, and crouched just inches from the green blades of artificial grass in an attempt to get lower than the Alabama defensive lineman lined up on my inside gap. As the noise, exacerbated by the confines of the dome, reached its crescendo, I strained my neck awkwardly towards Fusina, who was barking out signals as loud as he could, in an attempt to hear the cadence. Coiled like a tightly wound spring, I exploded off the ball on cue, ramming my head into the crimson helmet attempting to cross my path—straining, pushing, clawing forward.

I found myself flat on my stomach, trapped under a pile of bodies, unable to move. The crowd noise gave no indication of our success or failure. It was just a deafening and constant roar. Those excruciating seconds seemed like an eternity. When we finally untangled, my heart sank. The Crimson Tide defensive players were celebrating wildly. Penn State had come up short.

That Sugar Bowl, played in what was then a brand-spanking-new Louisiana Superdome, has been called the greatest bowl game ever played. It was a rare, pre-BCS matchup between the No. 1 and No. 2 teams in the country. Penn State was riding a 19-game winning streak and had an undisputed No. 1 ranking going into the game.

Winning that football game, my last as a collegian, was the most important thing in the world to me. I was prepared to play the best football game of my life, to play those 60 minutes as hard as possible, and to be able to say I'd expended every ounce of energy, put every bit of my heart and soul into each and every play. I'd walk off that field as part of a national championship team. Losing was not an option.

To lose like that—to be that close and then be denied—was devastating. How could it have slipped away? Walking off the field that day, I had no sense of pride. There was no honor, no satisfaction, no sense of legacy. All I felt was pain and dread.

Is this what it meant to be a Nittany Lion? At that very moment, I didn't know and I didn't care. It would take me years—decades—to shed the bad memories of that last damn game to uncover the true answer to this question.

The feelings from that day stuck with me longer than most, I suppose. Actually, they're still there, but continue to be diluted by the years. It still hurts when I think about it. I can't help it. It's my nature.

That was my advantage, my leg up on my opponents. I'd work harder in practice than they would during game week. I'd dwell on my assignments at night, going through them over and over in my mind, again and again, until I had visualized those intricate movements hundreds of times before it mattered for real. On game day, I'd focus on one thing and one thing only: what did I need to do to best my opponent and help my team win? Then I'd add all the passion and emotion I could muster and attempt to play harder than I ever had before.

The upside to this strategy was when we won. To know you played as hard as you possibly could, to have left every ounce of energy out there on the field, and then to win, well…there's no better feeling in the world. The downside? Testing the deep dark waters of despair is something I don't miss,

A consensus All-American in 1978 and Penn State's first pure offensive lineman inducted into the College Football Hall of Fame, Keith Dorney was outstanding in the classroom as well as the football field and was selected an Academic All-American in his senior year. *Photo courtesy of Keith Dorney.*

and I never felt it more after a loss than after that damn Sugar Bowl. And this is from a guy who endured another 83 losses as a pro.

It wasn't until recently I started to gain some perspective on that football game. After all, we were 22–2 my junior and senior years, from 1977 to that fateful New Year's Day in New Orleans in 1979. We also played in four major bowls during my four years. That's pretty good!

I gained more understanding on a recent visit back to Happy Valley. It was an unseasonably warm and sunny Friday afternoon in November, and I decided to go for a walk. From downtown, I strode up the mall. The elm trees, guarding the grand pathway like timeless sentinels, were at the peak of their autumn splendor. I took time to relish the sublime colors of the leaves, the timeless 19th-century architecture of the surrounding buildings, and the ubiquitous gray squirrels I had loved to watch as a student.

Up past the Lawn, Old Main, Pattee Library, and then west to the Lion Shrine, Rec Hall, and through Waring Commons I walked. Penn State has seen changes—dramatic changes—since my four years there, but a whole lot has stayed exactly the same.

Memories of my magical four years came roaring to life as I stood in the upper West Hall quad and gazed up at the window of my old dorm room. How many young men and women had lived, studied, and socialized within those walls? I continued my saunter.

I ended up at Atherton Hall. That's where my mom lived during her four years at Penn State. I recognized an archway from a photograph I have of her. She was standing there in her radiant youthful beauty, her wavy hair done up, a big smile on her face. I stood in that same stone archway where she stood 60 years ago and felt the cold gray stone with the palms of my hands. A tear rolled down my cheek.

The answer to the question, posed on that fateful day so long ago, was changing. I was starting to understand.

Dick Anderson was my offensive line coach when I played at Penn State, and he was still the offensive line coach 27 years later. He asked me to stop by that Friday, the day before their game against Wisconsin, to meet the Nittany Lions' current offensive linemen. As I walked toward the football facilities, I became disoriented. The east end of campus had changed considerably.

After finding the Lasch Building Sports Complex and interrupting the offensive line's meeting, I was a bit embarrassed. It was the day before a very important game—Penn State would be playing Wisconsin for the 2005 Big Ten title the following afternoon—and I wondered why these young men would want to meet some old has-been from the '70s. But Coach Anderson talked of tradition and legacy, of how we all were a part of the same thing, of how what I had accomplished was part of them, and how what they would do tomorrow would be a part of me. I saw determination and pride in their young faces. I also saw respect and admiration for what had been accomplished before them.

The next day Penn State came out focused, prepared, and ready to play football. And they played *hard*. The effort level shown by the Nittany Lions squad that afternoon was awe-inspiring and inspirational, and it resulted in a resounding victory. [Penn State won 35–14.] Perhaps I had forgotten the intensity level needed to be a successful Division I football player? Or perhaps time had eroded my own memories, my own victorious moments of glory and victory, and left only the taste of that last, bitter defeat.

Later that same year, I was humbled to be inducted into the College Football Hall of Fame. The events associated with that honor were great, but they were overshadowed by my old teammates who came out of the woodwork.

Kurt Allerman, aka "Clark Kent," was my host when I first visited Penn State as a 17-year-old high school senior. Years later, he spent a few years as my teammate with the Detroit Lions. I coined that nickname for him because he was unassuming, friendly, and shy off the field, then would turn into a superhuman hitting machine on game day.

Frank "Gonzo" Case flew in from Colorado. We'd been through so much together. After a slow start at Penn State, he went on to receive MVP honors in the 1980 Fiesta Bowl and earn multiple undergraduate and graduate degrees, as well as play pro ball. He's currently still on the line, this time on the front line of education, teaching high school English.

The "Kipster" missed his son's football game [Kip Vernaglia's son, Anthony, was playing football for the University of Notre Dame that weekend] to visit, coming all the way from California. I got to return the favor later that year when we met Kip and his family at the 2006 Fiesta Bowl to watch Anthony's team play.

I could go on and on. Old stories were recalled, updates on our kids exchanged, and good times relived.

It was then that my epiphany hit me like a 300-hundred-pound defensive lineman. Only then could I finally answer that question posed so long ago. Only then had the bitter memories from that last game finally fallen away to reveal the obvious.

It's Chuck and Matt and Mike. It's Coach Anderson and his current crop of young studs. It's Kurt, Frank, and Kip. It's JoePa and all the players who have come both before and after me. It's the national championships and the losing seasons. It's the kids living in Jordan and Atherton Halls, and the young scholars cramming for an exam at Pattee Library. It's the squirrels and the 200-year-old elm trees. It's the old sturdy buildings and the shiny new ones. It's my mom.

We are Penn State.

Keith Dorney was a two-time All-American and the number one draft choice of the Detroit Lions in 1979. After a 10-year All-Pro career he went into the time-management business in Southern California but later moved to Sebastopol, California, where he became a teacher and earned a master's degree in education. He now teaches English at Cardinal Newman High School in Santa Rosa while also coaching the offensive line of the school football team. His first book, *Black and Honolulu Blue: In the Trenches of the NFL*, was published by Triumph Books in 2004. Dorney continues to write in his spare time and expects to have a novel about professional football published in the near future. He and his wife, Katherine, have two children, a son, Clayton, and a daughter, Alea, neither of whom is an offensive lineman.

CHUCK FUSINA

QUARTERBACK

1975–1978

BEING A NITTANY LION MEANS to be part of a unique tradition, unlike few others across the country. We were put on a standard where we always felt that we had to meet expectations, not only on the field but in the class-room as well. We always felt that we were a little different than the other teams, not that we were better or anything like that. When I went up there and while I was there, I wanted to be part of it.

When I played pro football, all the other players respected the program and respected what Joe had done. They'd ask what it really was like up there. "Is it really as much fun as you say it is? Do you guys really graduate?" Yes, I would tell them. Many of the schools they went to were different and many didn't graduate. I'm not saying we're the cleanest, the nicest, or we had all goody-two-shoes guys. But it was a unique place. Our standards were very high, and we can say, with our heads up, that we went there.

Looking back, I'm still disappointed our team [in 1978] didn't accomplish what we really set out to do. We always thought we had a good combination with our senior and junior classes. We had a very successful '77 season, and we were so close to getting to the national championship game. [In 1977 no major college team finished undefeated, and Penn State was among five teams that finished 11–1, losing in an early season upset to Kentucky, 24–20.] We knew we were coming back in '78 with an experienced, good team and we

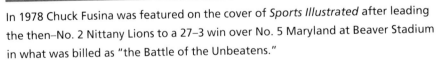

In 1978 Chuck Fusina was featured on the cover of *Sports Illustrated* after leading the then–No. 2 Nittany Lions to a 27–3 win over No. 5 Maryland at Beaver Stadium in what was billed as "the Battle of the Unbeatens."

were confident. We felt that we could play with anyone, and on any given day we'd win that game. We were a fun team, a very together team, and it was just a really fun season until the end. [Penn State finished No. 1 in the polls at the end of the regular season but lost the national championship to Alabama in the Sugar Bowl, 14–7.]

I know I didn't play my best game against Alabama, and I have never watched tapes of the game. Initially, it was awfully tough. For the first few years it bothered me. But you come to realize that those things happen and that Alabama had a pretty good team. It was two awfully good teams, and it could have gone either way. But getting older and wiser now, I realize that we took a lot for granted, and it's not easy to be 11–1 two years in a row. We came up a little bit short, but that will not erase what we accomplished. There was a bias back then against eastern teams. We were the first Penn State team to get to No. 1 and we showed that Penn State deserved to be there. I think people should have realized it quicker with some of the players who came out of Penn State who played professionally and some of the teams they had. But getting into the national championship game put a little different light on us for people, and I think that made things a little bit easier for the teams that went on to win the national championships [in '82 and '86].

Sometimes we're called Penn State's forgotten team, and I understand. Everybody remembers the winner but not the loser; I don't care what it is. Does anyone remember who came in second three Super Bowls ago? That's sort of what hit us and, unfortunately, that's just the way it is. People think, yeah, they were a pretty good team but they didn't win it all, which is too bad because I think the people who were there knew we were better than just a pretty good team.

I don't think too many people remember I was second in the Heisman that year, too, but it's not something that I think about. I've moved on with my life. [In what was the closest margin in 14 years, Fusina actually had more first-place ballots but lost by 87 votes to Billy Sims.] Back then, there weren't any ceremonies or television spots with the announcement. The papers had mentioned me [as a possible winner], but I had not given it much thought. My roommate, Tony Petruccio, and I were getting ready to go out for breakfast at The Diner when I got a telephone call about finishing second. We joked around about it and then went out to eat. I was sort of surprised because I did not have a very good year statistically. But our team did well,

159

and a lot of times a quarterback gets a little more recognition because the team is doing well. Since we were playing for the national championship, I felt that had a lot to do with it

Many Penn State fans occasionally remind me about being on the cover of *Sports Illustrated* that year. I didn't know it was going to happen. It was after we beat Maryland. They were undefeated and so were we. I remember it was really a beautiful day, a nice, clear, crisp day, and our defense dictated the game just as they had most of the year. Our defense got us the ball in really good position a number of times. When you have a defense like that, it makes it so much easier for the offense, particularly the quarterback. We won [27–3], and the *Sports Illustrated* cover was nice for the team because we were starting to get a little recognition. We became No. 1 the next week after beating North Carolina State, and sometimes that's what it takes. Some people see that and they recognize that team may not be too bad out there. So they were paying attention to us after that.

It may seem hard to believe, but when I was a freshman I wasn't sure I was good enough to play at Penn State. I was recruited by Bob Phillips, who had been the coach of my high school rival, Montour. I went to McKees Rocks. In all honesty, I wasn't a blue chip–type of recruit. I was really recruited late by a lot of people, maybe because I was hurt a lot my senior year. Initially, Penn State didn't recruit me, and I had to cancel a trip to Cincinnati to go to Penn State. I visited five schools: Notre Dame, Michigan State, Pitt, West Virginia, and Penn State. It really came down to Penn State and West Virginia, with Pitt also in my final three. I remember going up to Penn State after they got back from the [1975] Cotton Bowl. There were no other recruits. I stayed with Ron Coder and the Nittany Lion mascot. There were no other students on campus, so they really couldn't show me too much of a time. I remember going over to the coach's house for dinner. Coach Bob was one of the big reasons I chose Penn State, and, of course, Coach Paterno, and it was one of the best decisions I ever made.

I got hurt right away in my freshman year. I sprained an ankle really bad and I spent a lot of time at the beginning on crutches and watching and wondering if I'd ever be good enough to play there because there was a lot of talent there. A couple of guys could really throw the ball, and I said, "Man, I wonder if I'll ever be able to step on the field here." When you're young and you get a lot of those kind of thoughts in your head, you're maybe not as confident as you should be. But once you get out there and see that you can play with people, you get excited and you get confidence in yourself and you feel like you belong. I did get some action at the end of the ['75] season in the Pitt game. That was really exciting because that was my hometown.

I remember in my sophomore year starting my first game against Army after John Andress got hurt [in the fourth game of the season], and I started the rest of my career. We had a lot of success, and that goes back to Joe and the coaching staff. Obviously, Joe's techniques and his philosophy have been very successful. I can still hear that strange voice of his rippling across the practice field when he saw something he didn't like. He didn't play favorites. He'd throw me off the field as well as the next guy. You had to have thick skin. You knew there was a reason—it wasn't for lack of effort but he didn't like silly mistakes. I think the players felt a little bit better when he got in their face because we sort of knew there was a reason for it, that he expected more from us.

It still gives me much pride to be from Penn State. It's an accomplishment to have been part of that program and it's helped me a lot in life. It was just a great experience and one I wouldn't give up for anything. Once you're a Nittany Lion, you're a Nittany Lion forever.

Chuck Fusina won the Maxwell Club Award as college football's outstanding player in 1978 when he was a consensus All-American. He played eight years in the NFL and USFL, leading the Philadelphia Stars to three championships. Fusina earned his MBA while playing pro football and since retiring in 1987 has been in medical sales. He and his wife, Jackie, have two children and they live in suburban Pittsburgh.

MATT MILLEN

Defensive Lineman/ Linebacker

1976–1979

COACH PATERNO ACTUALLY HAD TO HAVE a letter of intent flown to me because my sister had thrown away the one he had sent earlier. She wanted me to go to Colorado, and the truth is, so did I. Ohio State, Michigan, Penn State, and Florida State were some of the schools I visited. I took a bunch of recruiting trips because back then there wasn't a limit on how many visits you took.

I went to a Penn State game against Kentucky during my senior year of high school in 1975. After the game Coach Paterno asked me what I thought. I didn't say it as a boast or with any arrogance, I just said matter-of-factly, "Coach, if I can't start here right now, don't even recruit me."

Even though I lived near Allentown in eastern Pennsylvania, I committed to Colorado and signed a conference letter of intent. When the time came to sign the national letter of intent with Colorado, my dad thought I was getting involved with some stuff I shouldn't get involved with out there. I was only 17 and he wouldn't sign the letter of intent. Penn State [assistant coach] John Chuckran came in and said, "Why don't you just come here?" and that's how I ended up at Penn State.

The first live drill we had, I went up against [future NFL player] Brad Benson. It was a simple dive drill where it's just the running back, the lineman,

Matt Millen burst onto the scene in his first collegiate start in 1976 with a 14-tackle, one-interception performance. He and Bruce Clark went on to form Penn State's famed and feared "Salt and Pepper" combination at defensive tackle. Millen later won four Super Bowl rings during a distinguished NFL career.

and the linebacker. You take on the lineman, get rid of him, and make the tackle. I didn't know who Brad Benson was, so I hit him, threw him aside, made the tackle, and went to the back of the line. John Chuckran comes up to me and says, "Do you know who that was? That was our starting offensive tackle." I said, "We're not going to be very good this year."

I started seven or eight games my freshman year. [Millen had 14 tackles and an interception in his first career start.] I think after the third game Bruce Clark and I started in the middle of the defense.

My sophomore year [1977] I thought we were as good as any team in the country. We got beat by Kentucky on a bad-weather day. Derrick Ramsey was the quarterback, and they had a good team. We were probably better than they were and that was the only loss we had all season.

That was the year when we started believing we could be really good. Chuck Fusina had a good year at quarterback and he was only a junior, and [offensive lineman] Keith Dorney had an excellent year. We had a bunch of young players who were going to turn out to be good college players and good pro players as well.

When I came back as a junior, we thought we were pretty good and thought we had a chance to win the national championship, which we did, as it turned out. Maryland was ranked pretty high when we played them, and Mike Tice, I think, was their quarterback. They weren't very good, and we handled them pretty easily. [Penn State's 27–3 win over No. 5 Maryland eventually led to the No. 1 ranking.] It was an exciting time because Penn State had never been ranked No. 1.

I don't really think much about our 14–7 loss to Alabama in the Sugar Bowl. I've never seen a replay of it. It will come on every now and again on some ESPN show, and every time it's played, one of my kids will call and say, "Hey, Dad, I saw you miss a tackle," or something like that. All I know is I thought we were the better football team. I've talked to Alabama defensive lineman Marty Lyons and other guys about it, and they'll say, "You guys were better than us."

I remember I left right after the game. I never took a shower, I just changed and walked back to the hotel. I was disgusted, but as you look back on it, they had some really good players. Future Pro Football Hall of Famer Dwight Stephenson was the center, and Bruce and I alternated back and forth over him. Jeff Rutledge was the quarterback and Tony Nathan was the running back.

The tone for my senior season was set before we played a game. We had to make two half-mile runs in a certain time during preseason practice, and I didn't do it. I thought they were dumb then and I think they are dumb now. [Paterno stripped Millen of his captaincy after that incident.]

I have always thought this and will always think that you go back to the Ty Cobb theory of sport: if you're going to play a sport, you practice the sport. I'm all for conditioning, and nobody would lift harder and do all of the running stuff. But I was 270 pounds, and I've got to run two half-miles? I said after I didn't make it, "If I have to chase a guy for half a mile, he's going to score."

I was probably wrong. I was a captain and if I had given it more thought I would have made those times because you are setting an example for the rest of the team. I hurt my back in the second game of the season against

Texas A&M and I played in parts of only three other games. It was a different year, but that's the way it goes.

My relationship with Joe really hasn't changed over the years. If I was playing at Penn State now I'd probably approach it the same way and Joe would still yell at me. The difference is, being on this side, as president of the Detroit Lions, I understand what he's trying to get out of his guys. As a player, I think you have a tendency to take everything personally because it's directed at you. You're not mature enough where you understand the big picture—while he's correcting you, he's correcting a lot of people at your position.

Joe will give you a good, sound base. You'll always maintain discipline, you'll know your assignment, and you'll play with the fundamentals of the game. You'll take a guy who has good skills like Curt Warner, who should be in the Pro Football Hall of Fame, and Mike Munchak, who is in the Hall of Fame, and this Paul Posluszny kid, who I am watching now, and go all the way back to Denny Onkotz.

All the guys Joe coached from 1966 on—and you're talking about a bunch of different players who played a bunch of different positions—had varying degrees of success. But they understood the fundamentals, and their skills took them to another level. I can take players from certain schools like Penn State, Michigan, Notre Dame, USC, Miami, and Florida State and know they're going to have good fundamentals, they're going to play hard, they're going to be smart, and they're going to have a certain level of skill.

Had I gone to five different schools, then maybe I'd be able to say which one of them was the best. All I know is I went to one school, played for a great coach, and had a great experience. Would I go to Penn State again? Sure, I'll take a great experience every time.

Matt Millen was a first-team All-American in 1978, and his 22 career sacks and 36 tackles for losses still rank among the best in Penn State history. A second-round pick of the Oakland Raiders in the 1980 NFL draft, Millen won four Super Bowl rings during a pro career that spanned more than a decade. He distinguished himself as a broadcaster before joining the Lions organization as a top executive. Millen is married to former Penn State gymnast Patty Spisak, and they have four children.

MATT SUHEY

TAILBACK/FULLBACK

1976–1979

MY FAMILY HAS A UNIQUE PLACE IN THE HISTORY and tradition of Penn State. My grandfather, Bob Higgins, played there and was an All-American [in 1915 and 1919] and then coached the team for almost 20 years [from 1931 to 1948]. He's in the College Football Hall of Fame, as is my dad, Steve Suhey, who played for my grandfather on the undefeated Cotton Bowl team in 1947. My father went on to marry his coach's daughter, my mother, Ginger. My uncle Jim [Dooley] played for Rip Engle and married my mother's sister, Nancy. My brothers, Larry and Paul, and I played for Joe Paterno, who lived with my parents when he was an assistant coach. Now I have a nephew Kevin, Paul's son, who plays there. There's also my aunt Mary Ann's husband, Tip Lyford. He was in the Blue Band. And, perhaps, the best of all, my mother has been going to Penn State games longer than anybody. She started going to games back in the '30s. So there's a lot that goes back a while. It's a pretty special tradition and one that we hold very dear. Beyond that, Penn State is a special place in the way they do things and how they do things and the class in which they do it, and it all adds to that tradition.

I remember my father taking my grandfather to the Penn State games up in the press box. My brother Paul and I would somehow find our way up to the press box and sit next to him and eat the brownies. I was more excited to eat the brownies than to watch the game. I used to go over to my grandfather's

Matt Suhey was never more than an honorable mention All-American, but he is rated as one of Penn State's toughest and best runners after playing tailback and fullback. His 2,818 career rushing yards (with 26 touchdowns) is eighth in Nittany Lions' history.

apartment and play checkers with him a lot. At that time he had been paralyzed on his left side by a stroke. I also remember Uncle Joe—that's what we
called Joe Paterno when we were growing up—and Uncle Red—Red Moore
who played on the '47 team with my dad and then with the Steelers. We had a
lot of guys who came around. Everything was Blue and White. Everything
was Penn State. I didn't really know anything different.

We went up to Beaver Stadium many, many times for the scrimmages,
from the fifth and sixth grades through high school. We used to run around
the stadium and screw around but also watch the scrimmages. A lot of the
times, Joe would sit in the stands at the 50-yard line and watch the scrimmage. During the season we would park cars at the stadium, sell programs,
and scalp tickets all through junior high and high school. It was a great way
of making money.

Penn State was all I knew. I think I played basically in the same offense
from when I started playing football in high school until the time I finished
college. Same plays, same defenses, same everything. Jim Williams, who went
to Penn State, was our high school coach. He was a great guy and a great
coach. He wound up joining the Penn State staff my sophomore year, and it
was all the same, just a natural progression. It was all very familiar and it was
a family tradition.

But I almost went to Ohio State. I felt it might be interesting to seriously
look elsewhere. Alex Gibbs, who ended up in the pros, was at West Virginia,
and he started recruiting me in my junior year. I wasn't interested in West
Virginia, but the next year he was at Ohio State. He told me from the very
beginning that I would play fullback in that particular offense. I was intrigued
by that and by the opportunity to play for Woody Hayes, so I went out there
and had a great time.

Brian Baschnagel and Jeff Logan showed me around, and Brian actually
ended up being my roommate for a year when I was with the Bears. I was
pretty close to committing, and I think I told Alex and Coach Hayes that I'd
like to go to Ohio State. There's a story that my dad encouraged me to go to
Ohio State because he didn't like the way Joe handled my brother Larry.
While there was a disagreement between my father and Joe, I don't think
either my father or Joe would have let that affect my decision. I had to do
what was right for me. Larry's senior year was my freshman year, so we over-
lapped for one season. And the irony is, I ended up replacing Larry when he
got hurt in preseason.

I told my mom and my father that I thought I was leaning toward Ohio State. In fact, I thought that might be a good choice for me to get away from home after being born and raised in State College, living in the same house, the same environment. The next morning, Joe was in my high school waiting for me. He's very difficult to say no to. He's very convincing. I folded like a house of cards. The more difficult phone call was the one I had to make to Alex Gibbs and Coach Hayes.

I was fortunate to be able to play with my brothers, although Larry missed most of his senior season because of his injury. But Paul and I played together for three years, and we had two great seasons in my sophomore and junior years. We might have played for the national championship in '77 except for that [upset] loss against Kentucky, 24–20, early in the year. Then in '78 we had that great year until the end. We had such an overpowering defense, kind of the way it was when I was with the Bears [in '85] when we won the Super Bowl. I remember when we beat North Carolina State [19–10 at Beaver Stadium] and were ranked No. 1 in the polls for the first time. We were ahead 12–10, and I returned a punt for a touchdown that clinched the game. I don't think it was even 50 yards. [It was 43 yards.] That was pretty exciting. But then the offense played so poorly in the Sugar Bowl.

Everybody seems to remember Mike Guman and me not scoring on Alabama's goal-line stand, but we turned the ball over too much. We kind of got away from what we had done so successfully all season—running the football. We didn't turn the ball over. I can't remember because it was quite a long time ago, but in the Sugar Bowl we just kind of got out of playing our game. I don't think we scored but seven points, but we had some opportunities to score a bunch. No question, it was one of the most disappointing games in Penn State history.

The irony of that is, seven years later, [in January of '86], I scored a touchdown in that same end zone in the Super Bowl, the first touchdown that helped Chicago become world champions. Was that any more important than winning a national championship? I don't know because Penn State never clearly won a national championship at that point, and Chicago hadn't won a Super Bowl until '86.

My senior year was a difficult one. A lot of guys got hurt. We had a lot of great players in my class who went on to play in the pros like Bruce Clark, Matt Millen, and Mike Guman, but it was a tough year. You come in with a lot of great expectations and you want to play well, especially going out as a senior, but it was a transition year. We struggled against every team we played that year. I was playing with a bunch of young guys who ended up being great, like Mike Munchak, Curt Warner, and Sean Farrell.

I remember looking around in my first year with the Chicago Bears and thinking we had a better offensive line and better defensive players at Penn State. Seriously. Chicago had some good players and a couple of great ones, like Walter Payton. But at Penn State we had Munchak and Farrell and Keith Dorney and Irv Pankey, Millen and Clark, and I knew how good those guys were. And I'm thinking, "Jesus, we really had a good team at Penn State, talent-wise." You just look at the talent, the physical talent, and how they play the game and the consistency and the preparation they got at Penn State. I had pro scouts tell me, "You look at a Penn State kid and you know exactly what you're going to get. You get a first-class kid. He's going to be respectful. He's going to be smart. He's going to work his tail off. He's not going to make mistakes. You know exactly what you're going to get. You know coming out of Penn State, out of Paterno, and out of the Penn State coaching staff that that's what you're going to get."

That's how everyone looks at Penn State. It's very positive, consistent, smart, and classy. Being a Penn State football player carries instant respect and a positive reputation. It's a tradition that goes back a long way in my family, and I'm very proud of that.

Unlike their grandfather, Bob Higgins, an end, and father, Steve Suhey, a guard/linebacker, Matt Suhey and his oldest brother, Larry, were running backs at Penn State. Middle brother Paul, defensive captain of the '78 team, was a linebacker. Matt is still among the Nittany Lions all-time career rushers. He also was a standout fullback for the Chicago Bears until retiring in 1991 and still lives in Chicago with his wife, Donna, and children, Joe, Allison, and Scott, where Matt is now involved in several businesses. His brothers live in State College. Larry is a sales manager for a nationwide ring company, and Paul is an orthopedic surgeon and a member of Penn State's Board of Trustees.

The
EIGHTIES

LEO WISNIEWSKI
DEFENSIVE TACKLE
1978–1981

I WAS RECRUITED BY A LOT OF PROGRAMS, and I narrowed my finalists to Penn State, Michigan, Notre Dame, and Stanford. I think Coach Paterno had an awful lot to do with me committing to Penn State. Your parents spent a lot of time with Coach Paterno during the recruiting weekend, and he and Sue really do a great job of winning the parents over. They're very genuine, and Joe's desire is to really impact young men from the standpoint of character development and making sure academic commitment is a big priority. Those things resonate with most parents.

I almost went to Stanford. It's a gorgeous campus. Bill Walsh was the coach, and the school has a great academic reputation. I really thought my parents were going to be living in Pittsburgh, but by the time I graduated from Fox Chapel High School in 1978, my dad had taken a job in Houston. Had I known about the move before I committed to Penn State, things might have turned out differently. A huge part of the attraction for me at Penn State was that my family was going to get to see all of my games.

One of my very first impressions when I got to Penn State was meeting Sean Farrell. He was this thick-necked, big, strong kid from Long Island. We were in the weight room, and Sean was a man at 18 years old. He was just banging reps on the bench press with 315 pounds. I got three reps and I'm thinking, "My God, what am I in for?"

Leo Wisniewski was a fan favorite at the turn of the 1980s because he always appeared to be playing his heart out. In 1981 when he was co-captain, Wisniewski won the Ridge Riley Award given to a senior for "sportsmanship, scholarship, leadership, and friendship."

I got in the two-deep mix very early and got to play second-team line-backer behind Lance Mehl. Getting in there boosted my confidence tremendously. We played Ohio State the first game, and Woody Hayes promised that Art Schlichter would start for him as a true freshman and he did. We beat up on him pretty good, and I got to play most of the fourth quarter at the Horseshoe.

It was a dream-come-true season, getting to play as much as I did and then getting to go to New Orleans and play in the Superdome. I was a wide-eyed freshman on Bourbon Street; I had never seen anything like that. I remember a businessman from Alabama offered me $500 a ticket for any tickets I was willing to sell. I started adding that up pretty quickly—I had 12 tickets for my family, and that was $6,000. I thought for a couple of minutes if I could swing that one, but I didn't.

One of the big memories I have from that game was walking into the locker room afterward. [No. 1 Penn State lost to No. 2 Alabama 14–7.] We were pretty crushed because we wanted to be the team that gave Coach Paterno his first national championship. He said, "Men, I'm proud to have walked this entire year with you and to have fought the good fight together. We have an awful lot to be thankful for." He then led us in the Lord's Prayer. It really clarified for me that he wasn't any less of a coach for not having won that national championship and we weren't any less of a team for not having scored more points that day.

In preseason practice you had to pass a conditioning test where you ran a half mile and then after a rest interval, two or two-and-a-half minutes, you had to run a second half mile. It was unbelievable. For the linemen, you had to run a three-minute half mile and then after the rest interval you got an additional 15 seconds to run the second half mile in.

Matt Millen ran the first one and he was just spent. During the second one, he just cramped up and kind of collapsed. Sure enough, Joe was chasing him down the track, saying in that high voice, "Millen, what are you doing! You're a quitter!" Matt gets interviewed about his conditioning test and he says, "Ah, it's a stupid test. If I ever have to run a half mile to catch a running back or a quarterback, they're always going to win. As far as I know the field is only 100 yards long." Joe stripped him of his captaincy and that kind of set the tone for the season.

There were high expectations for that season, defensively anyway. We were starting over at quarterback and offensively we had some real obstacles, but defensively we should have been very, very good. A couple of games into the season Matt hurt his back and he was out most of the year.

That was really my breakthrough because I had eaten myself out of line-backer and I was backing up Matt at defensive tackle. We ended the regular season at 7–4 and went to the Liberty Bowl where we won an ugly ballgame there, 9–6, over Tulane. We go 8–4 and you would have thought the bottom just dropped out of the program.

It was just a really, really tough three weeks of practice for that bowl game, and Joe used it almost like spring practice. We were in full pads for all but about three of those practices and we were really banging hard. He wasn't pleased at all with the year we had. I tore meniscus cartilage in my knee and missed spring ball. But we turned things around and had a pretty solid season in 1980.

In 1981 we lost two games and went into the regular-season finale against No. 1 Pitt an underdog. Jerry Sandusky's game plan had us rushing two guys or, at most, three. They were throwing the ball a ton and they had a very good offensive line, and I was one of those guys rushing their quarterback, future Pro Football Hall of Famer Dan Marino.

I was thinking, "If I beat Jimbo Covert, he's got plenty of help." We were down 14–0, and I was thinking, "Oh my gosh, aren't we going to change anything? We're just going to sit back and let him pick this nine-man zone apart?" I was really thinking we were in trouble and then we got the big interception from Mark Robinson.

Our secondary really changed the whole momentum of the game, not only the interception but also how physical they were and how they pounded Pitt's receivers. For those of us who played our high school ball in Pittsburgh, the win made it that much sweeter.

What it meant to be a Nittany Lion is playing at the very highest level. It also meant getting an education and growing up to be a man of character and recognizing you were a part of a legacy of greatness.

An honorable mention All-American selection in 1981 and defensive MVP of the '82 Fiesta Bowl, Leo Wisniewski got selected with the first pick in the second round of the 1982 NFL draft by the Baltimore Colts. He made the NFL's All-Rookie team in '82, but had to retire in 1985 because of a knee injury. Wisniewski earned a master's degree from Trinity Episcopal Seminary and is a part owner of an integrated media business. He and his wife, Cindy, have two children and live in the Pittsburgh suburb of Bridgeville.

SEAN FARRELL
OFFENSIVE GUARD
1979–1981

WHEN I LOOK BACK AT PENN STATE and the experiences I had there, there's a sense of pride that is not all that easy to describe. It was part of something that was very, very special. It was very special because of the leadership qualities that were exhibited by the folks who ran the program and who nurtured all the young people. They had the ability to identify a) good people from good families, and b) talented people, in that order. Looking back, that's exactly the way they made their choices, and I think that's why they've been so successful for so many years.

I was out of West Haven Beach on Long Island. We had about 700 kids in high school and about 160 kids in my graduating class. Although my high school was small, I was fortunate enough to have a nice career. Back then there were very few choices if you really wanted a good academic experience as well as a real quality athletic experience. You couldn't find that many places that could offer both. I believed that I had enough ability, that I might be able to get to the next level. So I really had to plan for that coming out of high school.

I had pretty much narrowed down my choices to Stanford and Penn State. Franny Ganter recruited me. Franny was one of the best recruiters I've ever seen. The guy never let me down in the whole time I was at Penn State. Bill Walsh was the coach out at Stanford. You could make six visits at the time, and I had taken five visits to Stanford, Syracuse, Wake Forest, Miami, and

Virginia. I still had not visited Penn State. I knew very well that's where I ultimately might go, but when you're 17 years old and you have these visits and opportunities, you think about other things. So I had a visit scheduled to the University of Alabama, but it was more of a party than anything else. They had tickets on the court for an SEC basketball game and all sorts of things. It just sounded like a terrific weekend. It was the last weekend for visits, and I decided I was going to go down there and enjoy myself. Then I got a call from Joe, who said, "You can't do that. You can't make a decision without seeing us." I said, "No, I'm very confident. I'm pretty certain where I'm going to go." Of course, he talked me out of it, and so I missed that great weekend. Then Joe said, "Why don't you come on up to Penn State?" So I went up on a Sunday night. I got my $7 for bowling and I sat with Matt Suhey and Doc [Mark] Latsko in their dorm room for the night, and that's the way I was recruited by Penn State. No question, it was the worst visit anybody had ever had in his life.

Freshmen were eligible but, as you know, Joe didn't like to play freshmen. You're 18 years old and you're thinking, "Joe just doesn't get it. We all should be playing." That was in '78, when the team went undefeated until the Sugar Bowl. We'd get in the games where we were up 25 points, so I had a fair amount of time that year.

Going into my sophomore year there were two guard positions open and there were three people vying for the positions—me, Mike Munchak, and Irv Pankey. [All three would later have long careers in the NFL.] So we had some pretty good people looking for the same slot. I knew at the time that we were all having a good camp. It wasn't that much of a difference and I felt pretty confident that I was doing pretty well. Then they moved Irv to tackle and Mike and I were the starting guards.

I started for three years, and there are games that I can remember and really enjoyed. I enjoyed going to places that were really hostile environments. West Virginia was a great place to go. I enjoyed going out to Nebraska [in '79 and '81]. That was really special. When you went out to Nebraska, you saw nothing but red and it was as loud as it could get. We beat them up pretty good one year [30–24 in '81]. Those were exciting things. On an individual level, there were points that season where I know that my personal development had come to a level where I could compete with anyone.

My last game in a Penn State uniform was quite a game. It was at Pittsburgh, and they were undefeated and No. 1 in the nation. We were definitely

177

underdogs. We had gone into that game very confident that we were going to win, and we made an awful lot of noise about it. That's pretty unusual for a Penn State team to be shooting off that way, but we felt like we could back it up. Before you know it, we're down in a hurry. [At the end of the first quarter, Pitt led 14–0 and was inside Penn State's 20-yard line.] We were down by two scores within about a blink of an eye, and I remember sitting on the bench, and Joe walked over and said, "Okay, that's enough. Just calm down. It's all going to be fine. You're going to go out there and you're going to take care of business." He said, "Just keep your head about you. It's all going to work out. It's no big deal." At the time, I looked at him and I thought, "You know what, you're right. You're absolutely right." And that's really all it took, for everybody to say, "Okay, no big deal. We're down two scores. We'll get that back and we'll work from there." And it wasn't like we had that kind of offense where we could score 40 or 50 points. It was a more methodical type of offense, but after listening to Joe, we were sure we could go out and get two scores and work from there. We turned it around and won by several touchdowns [48–14].

In my junior year I was named a first-team All-American and I was thrilled. It was something that I had not expected. After something like that has happened for you, it's likely that it repeats the following year. So as great as it was [to be selected] again in my senior year, and as proud as I am of that, I probably was more excited and even on a bigger high about it when I was a junior.

If I have any regrets, it's missing out on the national championship. We might have won it in '81 if things had worked out, and then they won it the next year when I was playing for Tampa. The regret is that I truly believe that the group of people that we had on our last team was a very capable group and, talent-wise, may well have been one of the best teams I've seen in college football for many, many years. Unfortunately for us, it didn't all come together at the same time. Amazingly, a lot of those people were gone after the '81 season, and Penn State went ahead and won a national championship without them. That was incredible.

It's very much a team concept at Penn State. It really is not about the individual or making stars of people. If they're fortunate enough to go on and be successful and be stars that's great, but it's not about that. There's a greater issue and that's what makes the place special. Once you're in the league [NFL], it's a completely different ballgame. And that's when you start to

Sean Farrell was a three-year starter at guard and Penn State's first offensive interior lineman to become a two-time All-American. At the end of his career, Joe Paterno said "there wasn't a better guard in the country. He's Superman."

understand the difference, the difference in people and the differences of what you came from versus what someone else came from. That's when it was glaring to me, in my first year or my second year in the league, the differences in the character and the quality of the people, what was expected of people, how they carried themselves, and how they'd been taught. It was significant. I know it prepared all of us for much better things.

When you're 18 to 22 years old, you think you have every answer, and you look at Joe and you look at anybody in a position of authority and you have the natural tendency to discount everything they say. Then about the time you hit 23 and 24, you look back and realize everything they told you was true. They weren't trying to kid you. They weren't trying to pull a fast one on you. I find myself doing so many things, and my life is very reflective of a lot of the things I was taught by Joe or by the way Joe acted. Everybody that I knew in my time at Penn State were just great people, people who you loved being involved with and you could count on. That's one of the reasons why I'm really proud to be a part of it.

Joe Paterno once said of Sean Farrell, "If there's a better guard in the country, he's Superman." Farrell was a finalist for the Outland and Lombardi Awards in his senior year when he was co-captain of the 10–2 team that finished third in the country. After an injury-plagued but All-Pro career with Tampa, New England, and Denver, he retired in 1992. He is now a financial management executive for Merrill Lynch in New York, where he lives with his wife, Rene, and their daughter, Ashley.

MIKE MUNCHAK

OFFENSIVE GUARD

1978–1981

WHEN I WAS IN HIGH SCHOOL at Scranton Central, I really never thought about playing college ball until my senior year. I wasn't one of those highly recruited guys, but I had narrowed it down to Syracuse, Maryland, NC State, the University of Miami, and Penn State. I was about 6′3″, 230 pounds. I played defensive end and fullback, but I was more like a lead blocker. I thought I'd play defensive end or the standup outside linebacker in college.

I figured if I wanted to go to a school that played big-time football, I'd go to Penn State since it was in our state and two-and-a-half hours away. But I felt I would fit in quicker and play sooner somewhere else. Before the signing date I called Jim Williams, who was recruiting me, and told him I wasn't going to Penn State. Coach Williams was surprised, and Coach Paterno came on the phone. He said he'd like to see me one more time and to ask my parents if it's okay to come tomorrow for dinner.

Obviously, you don't say no to Coach Paterno. When he came to my house, it was like the whole city block just froze for about three hours. People were peeking out their windows just to see the guy. He came and was just himself, very personable. He had dinner with us, and we sat around and talked about what my opportunity was there and what they were offering me. There was no hard sell.

During his Penn State career, Mike Munchak was in the shadow of his guardmate, All-American Sean Farrell, but he blossomed in the NFL, where he became a leader for the Houston Oilers during the heyday of running back Earl Campbell.

That night changed my way of thinking. When he left, I knew it was a challenge to go there. I knew that if I had the talent in me, Penn State would bring it out. I also thought having a degree from Penn State meant a lot, especially in Pennsylvania. Joe brought back the good feeling I had when I visited there. If Coach Paterno had not come that night, I probably would have made a big mistake.

They didn't know what to do with me at first and they moved me around so fast I thought I *had* made a mistake. The first day, they moved me from defense to tight end and the next day they moved me back to the defensive line. A few days later, Sean Farrell and I were called in by Joe and told we were moving to the offensive line because they needed depth there. Sean was playing nose tackle and he was going through some of the same identity crisis I was. Joe said he'd give us the opportunity to go back to defense in the spring.

I remember calling home and telling Mom and Dad I didn't know if this was the right place for me. Dad said, "Well, I'm glad it's going so good, son, we'll talk to you soon. Keep up the good work." He didn't hear what I said or didn't want to hear because he probably anticipated me being this way.

From that point on, I became an offensive lineman for the scout team. Now, I was going up against Bruce Clark and Matt Millen, who were All-Americans, and [linebackers] Paul Suhey and Lance Mehl and guys like that. I was playing tackle and I had to get them ready to play. They forced me to learn what I was doing or otherwise I'd get killed in practice. Those guys were pretty good to me during that season and were a big part of my development.

I was on the special teams and I traveled to all the games. That year we went undefeated, and it was just great to be part of that, to be around these guys and get to know them and see what it was like to play on a big-time level against the teams we were playing. Even though I was a lowly freshman, I was competing against some of the best players in the country.

I didn't work out with the offense, but on game day I'd be with the offensive line and I'd pair up with Keith Dorney, who was an All-American. I'd be the defensive lineman getting him ready to play. Seeing his intensity had a big impact on me.

They never did ask me in the spring what I wanted to do. Thanks to Dan Riley and my strength training, I was up to about 250 and they put me at

183

center. I was running second team in spring ball, and they moved me to guard on the first team. I was shocked because I had never played the position before. But as I practiced, it felt natural playing the position and I liked it. Playing offensive guard was like what I had been doing at fullback. I was blocking.

When we came back for my sophomore year, Dick Anderson called in me, Sean, and Irv Pankey and told us we would play equally in practice and the best two would start. Before the first game they made me the starter at the strong-side guard, with Sean and Irv splitting time at the weak side. After two games they moved Pankey to tackle, and the three of us ended up starting the whole year. All three of us ended up playing 12 years or so in the NFL.

When I saw Irv get drafted in the second round [by the Los Angeles Rams] after that season, that's when it first hit me that I had a chance to get drafted and play in the NFL. When Joe first talks to all freshmen, he says, "Very few of you will play pro football and this is the end of it." I believed him until I started seeing the guys drafted.

I had to sit out my junior year because of a knee injury I got at the end of the Liberty Bowl [in 1979]. We had a good season my senior year, and after the Fiesta Bowl, I talked to Joe and made the decision to come out. I had my degree and wondered what would be the reasons for me to come back. I also figured I hurt my knee before and I could get hurt again.

I thought I might be a third-round or maybe a second-round pick, and then after the combine, I heard I might be a late first-round offensive lineman. I was shocked on draft day when I was picked eighth [overall]. I played 12 years with Houston until my knee wore itself out. I loved my career. The first five years we were rebuilding, and then we went to the playoffs seven straight times.

By coming out with eligibility left, I missed being part of the [1982] national championship team. Even though I went on to the NFL, I still feel part of that national championship team. I had my chance in my freshman year to win a national championship on the 1978 team. That team was so good and I thought no one was going to beat us. Then we lost to Alabama [14–7] in the Sugar Bowl, and it was hard to watch those guys lose after what a great year they had.

My last year was the same way. We had a great team with great players, but we just couldn't get it done. We were No. 1 for about seven or eight weeks.

I remember we went out to Nebraska early, and we knew how hard it was to go there and win, and we beat them [30–24]. Curt Warner had a big game [238 yards rushing], and it was a great feeling as a lineman being part of that.

Then we went down to Miami. We played in the rain and were down something like 17–0 in the fourth quarter. We fought back to 17–14 and had a chance near the end of the game to tie or win it, but we lost. We lost again at Alabama but then finished strong by beating Notre Dame [24–21] and then beating Pitt when Pitt became No. 1. We went out there on Thanksgiving weekend and hammered them 48–14. To beat them and knock them out gave us a little satisfaction because the Pitt–Penn State game was a huge rivalry back then.

Then we played USC with Marcus Allen, who was the Heisman Trophy winner, and our defense shut him down [with 85 yards and no touchdowns]. Curt had another huge day [with 145 yards and two touchdowns]. So to finish, beating three big-time teams like that the way we did was a nice way to end our senior year.

Even before I went there I looked at Penn State as something different. In my hometown, everyone's a Penn State fan. But you really don't completely understand it until you're there. You really get to enjoy college life. You don't live in football dorms and you get a chance to meet a lot of kids other than football players.

185

Then you're with Joe and you start playing and you see the fans, the way things are done, the whole package, and you start to realize you're part of this tradition. I'll always remember the first time I was on the bus going to an away game. In those days we had to drive two hours to Harrisburg to fly. I'm a fifth-team tackle and I'm thinking I'm part of this. Here's a team that could be one of the best in the country, we're wearing our suits and ties, and I'm going to contribute in some small way. It felt right that I was there.

Then you start learning the other traditions. We are different because of the way we do things, like the uniforms. They're very simple. Everyone knows this is Penn State. We have the white helmet and we have no names on the jerseys because it's about team, it's not about individual names.

You start listening to Coach Paterno when he talks to you before a game, like on Sunday after the game, and he'd talk about life, tying whatever happened in a game to something's that going to happen to you in life. And slowly the whole thing just sinks in.

I think you appreciate Penn State even more after you leave. When I went into the pros and said I was from Penn State, people turned their heads. It just carries such a respect factor, and that continues to this day. They respect us for all the things we were taught at Penn State. When anyone from Penn State comes up in the draft, they know certain things come with a Penn State guy, that Joe recruits certain type of personalities and certain types of people. They're great people and they're going to be ready to play.

There's a pride you feel that you went there, not just the athletes but other students as well. You're proud of what you accomplished when you were there and you're proud of the way our school handles itself. I love everything I did at Penn State and I love to tell people I went to Penn State. The "We Are...Penn State!" thing is *absolutely true.*

Mike Munchak was a second-team All-American in his senior year at Penn State, and in 2001 Munchak became the sixth Penn State player and the first pure offensive lineman to be inducted into the Pro Football Hall of Fame. After an All-Pro career with the Houston Oilers, he went into coaching and for the past nine years has been the offensive line coach of his old team, now known as the Tennessee Titans. He met his wife, Marci, at Penn State, and they have two daughters, Alexandria and Julie. The Munchaks live in Brentwood, Tennessee.

CHET PARLAVECCHIO
LINEBACKER
1978–1981

COMING OUT OF NORTHERN NEW JERSEY, I had the opportunity to go to pretty much any school I wanted to. But my heart was pretty much set on going to Penn State from the time I played youth football. I'm an Italian-American and Joe Paterno is a famous Italian-American. And it was close to home. It was "Linebacker U," and I was a linebacker. It just seemed like everything was a match.

I remember my parents taking me to Penn State for training camp and my mother and father walking me into the old weight room. As we walked in, there were two gentlemen with a glistening sweat and their bodies just so well defined. It was Bruce Clark and Irv Pankey. My mother started to cry and she said, "I'm not leaving you here." I was getting nervous, looking at these two guys and going, "Am I out of my mind? I can't play here." Then I was on the scout team and holding bags. Here I was, thinking, "I'm the number two–rated linebacker in the nation, I'm not supposed to be doing this." Well, guess what? Everybody that was there was the best from where they came from and they could give two craps who you used to be.

I got thrown off the field my first week-and-a-half five times. I even had a fight with [kicker] Matt Bahr. At first, my relationship with defensive coordinator Jerry Sandusky was rough. Jerry was very much a methodical, fundamental coach who wanted guys to think a certain way. This was the man who developed "Linebacker U," and I was a little different.

At first I rubbed Jerry the wrong way. As time went on and he understood me and I understood him, I think both of us found you can't have one without the other. One of the biggest compliments I received in my life was when Jerry was going to take the Temple job and he asked me if I'd be his linebackers coach. I later found myself so much like Jerry, obsessed with fundamentals, when I coached. Isn't that funny? I have nothing but the greatest respect in the world for Coach Sandusky.

When you play at Penn State's level, you want to be a two-year starter. I got to training camp my junior year in 1980, and Walker Lee Ashley was in front of me, and I didn't know where this had come from. Jerry liked Ashley. He liked speed, he liked strength, and I don't think he had that much respect at that time for intangibles, and that's all I was.

By the third game it got to me. I lost my cool during practice and I walked off the field and said, "This is it, it's time to move on." I had a meeting with Joe and Jerry and the two captains. I was leaving. Joe convinced me to stick it out, that things would be okay. I remember my best friends, Rich D'Amico, Leo Wisniewski, Sean Farrell, and Mike Munchak, all came to get me and said, "Chet, don't leave." It was close. I felt Jerry and I were clashing, and then I finally got to start against Maryland. I had 16 tackles and intercepted a pass and ran it back 50 yards to set up the game-winning touchdown. From there, I never looked back.

188

The game that defined my career came at the end of my senior year when we played top-ranked Pitt in our regular season finale. At that point we were 8–2, but we had played six or seven top-20 teams. Pitt was 10–0 but hadn't played anybody. We heard all week how great they were. Todd Blackledge and I were on Stan Savran's talk show, trying to be as politically correct as possible. People were calling in, saying, "Do you guys really think you have a chance?" I was sitting there thinking, *You know something? It's time to get this thing going a little bit.* Then Stan asked me what I thought, and I said, "You know what I think, Stan? I think we're going to beat 'em 48–0." He said, "Chet, do you really?" I said, "Who have they played? Do they play Thiel next week?" Man, the switchboard lit up.

Why the name "Thiel"? Earlier in the week Rich D'Amico's buddy was up from Pittsburgh and he played for Thiel. I actually got a letter from the head coach at Thiel. I didn't mean anything by it, so right away I wrote a letter back to him apologizing if he took it wrong.

One of the most aggressive and outspoken of Paterno's linebackers, Chet Parlavecchio didn't back down from anyone, and in 1981 he challenged Pitt coach Jackie Sherrill face-to-face in front of the Panthers bench during the major Pitt–Penn State showdown at Pitt Stadium.

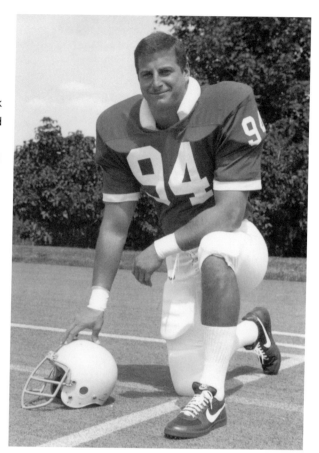

189

I said what I said and I wasn't going to back off it. I believed in us. Here we came out for the game and, my gosh, Pitt's quarterback, Dan Marino, was on fire. He was throwing lasers all over the field and it was on national television. Before we knew it, it was 14–0. They were just ripping us apart. All I could think of in that huddle was, "Oh, you look like an ass." I will say this: when I hit Julius Dawkins out of bounds—I nailed him, and he was almost getting a drink of water—I knew what I did and exactly why I did it.

We needed something to get our butts going and when the opportunity arose, I took it. I remember Walker and D'Amico came in to get me, and [Pitt coach] Jackie Sherrill and I had some words. I won't tell what was said, forget about it. Roger Jackson intercepted a pass in the end zone and from there we ran off 48 straight points. We won 48–14.

I got lucky because my ploy worked. The focus got on me real quick with a lot of those linemen and I got knocked on my butt a few times and broke my nose in that game. But that's what you need to do sometimes, just get them off their focus because they were in a zone. Marino was just killing us.

As for that brash prediction, this will surprise a lot of people, but Joe never said a word to me about it. Years later, Fran Ganter and I were out and he said, "You know something, Chet? One of the things that blew us away during that whole thing with that Pitt game was Joe never said a word. You should be very complimented by that." It was almost like he had faith that I knew what I was doing.

We were not your vintage Penn State team. We had an attitude, we had an anger about us. We were not the best football players in the world, we were just some of the toughest men in the world. Joe knew that. That's what made him a great coach. It was a different group, but it took that arrogance to go into Nebraska and beat Nebraska. It took that arrogance to go into Missouri and beat Missouri.

We went to the Fiesta Bowl and gave USC a good spanking. That was important for us because they were very smug the whole week prior to the game, it was the Rose Bowl or nothing for them. We knew it was an important game for legitimizing eastern football.

By the end of the season, we were the best team in the country, no doubt. We were battle-tested. We played Nebraska with Roger Craig. We played Miami with Jim Kelly. We played Pitt with Dan Marino. We played Southern Cal with Marcus Allen. You're talking about four Hall of Famers we played against.

After the Fiesta Bowl, I flew to California to play in the East-West Shrine game and guess who the East head coach was? Jackie Sherrill. After the Fiesta Bowl, I was talking to a reporter and he said, "Do you know who the coach is?" I said, "Yeah, yeah." And he said, "Well, what do you think is going to happen?" I said, "I've been working on my extra-point holding all week because I think that's all I'm going to do."

As soon as I got off the plane, he was at the airport. He grabbed me and said, "What happened in Pittsburgh happened. Let's have a fresh start here." I said, "Coach, you've got it. Those rivalries get heated and our emotions sometimes get the better of us." He said, "Those things happen. I just want to make sure you get everything out of this week that you can." We had a great week. At the end of the game, the funniest thing happened. We were walking off the field and he said, "Hey, Chet, Paterno never got you an MVP. I did." I just started laughing and he started laughing.

The best time of my life for me as a man was Penn State. I made my best friends, my best memories, and I was young. I felt young. Mike Munchak does a benefit for the Leukemia Foundation, and Leo Wisniewski, Rich D'Amico, Pete Speros, Dan Biondi, and I have been going for 18 years. We golf, we play cards, and we raise money for leukemia research. Through the years we've gotten very close with Bruce Matthews. Bruce will be a first ballot Hall of Famer with Munchak and he's one of the all-time greats to play his position. One of the years we went out to dinner after golf. Bruce, Ricky, and I were talking, and Bruce said, "You know, I envy you guys. I don't talk to anyone from Southern Cal. You guys act like you're still in the dorm together." I said, "You know what, Bruce? We always felt that's what made Penn State different from most places." He goes, "Well, take it from me, a Trojan, it does."

I have some regrets in my career, things that I could have done differently, but one was not where I went to college. If I had to live my life all over again, I'd go to Penn State.

Chet Parlavecchio led Penn State in tackles in 1980–1981 and earned second-team All-America honors in 1981. He played three seasons in the NFL before knee injuries cut short his playing career. He has been an assistant college coach and a head high school coach. He and his family live in Floram Park, New Jersey, where he teaches physical education.

TODD BLACKLEDGE

QUARTERBACK

1979–1982

J EFF HOSTETLER AND I WERE IN THE SAME recruiting class. I knew he was from western Pennsylvania, but it's not like today where you know about everybody with the Internet and all the recruiting services. When I got to Penn State, I met Jeff and saw that he was a tremendous athlete and had a big, strong arm.

Obviously, it was a competitive situation, but we both understood that was just part of the deal. Ironically, by the time my second year rolled around, I had become a born-again Christian and involved in Bible study with other guys on the football team. Jeff's older brother, Doug, who had played at Penn State earlier and was still in the State College area, was actually kind of our chaplain and Bible study leader, so Jeff and I were involved in that together. I think it was a healthy relationship.

I ended up redshirting that first year in 1979, and Jeff and I battled for the starting job in the spring and all through the summer of 1980. Joe made a decision probably the Friday before our first game that he was going to start Jeff. I was going to play some, and he wanted to make sure I didn't get discouraged. We opened with Colgate and then played Texas A&M down in College Station. The third game was against Nebraska at home. We lost that game 21–7, and I ended up playing most of the second half. I became the starter the next week.

In 1982 Todd Blackledge won the Davey O'Brien Award as the nation's best quarterback as he led the Nittany Lions to their first national championship. His early–fourth quarter touchdown pass to Gregg Garrity in the Sugar Bowl national title game helped make him the Outstanding Player of the Game.

The first day back from the Missouri game, I had a light blue jersey in my locker and that was the first time that I'd had that. It signified I was the starter and it pretty much went that way the rest of my career. At the end of that year Jeff transferred to West Virginia.

I knew we had a really good team going into 1981. We were still going to be a run-oriented team, and I think my job that year was to manage the game and not put our defense in bad situations.

One game that stands out is the first loss we had against Miami in the Orange Bowl. Curt Warner got hurt in the first quarter, and it really affected our running game. This was about 10 years before Miami got really good, but they got after us pretty well. It was probably my most prolific day as a quarterback at Penn State, and yet we lost 17–14, so it was one of those bittersweet-type deals. The loss really hurt, especially since we were No. 1 and fell to a team we didn't think was as strong as we were but outplayed us that day.

The Pitt game later that season was ugly early. I think we had minus one yard of total offense in the first quarter, and they were just stuffing us. We couldn't stop them, and they were going in to score again when the game changed—Roger Jackson made his hit and got the interception.

We were able to tie the game at halftime when it very easily could have been 21–0 Pitt early on. Once we drew even, it was a whole new deal. I don't think they respected our ability to throw the football very much, and we ended up getting big plays on them. [Penn State beat Pitt 48–14.] It was a great feeling individually, it was a great feeling as a team. It really kind of showed that we were one of the premier teams in the country that day.

People ask me this all the time, and I think the '81 team was probably more talented than the '82 team, but in some sense we underachieved. Still, we beat Pitt when they were No. 1. We beat USC with Marcus Allen in the Fiesta Bowl and finished No. 3.

Going into the '82 season, we kind of had an idea that we were going to throw the ball more. We had lost guys like Sean Farrell, Mike Munchak, and Jim Romano. We were young on the offensive line. We had more speed in our skill positions with Kenny Jackson, Kevin Baugh, and Gregg Garrity than we had had before, and I think Joe trusted me with throwing the football and with making some checks at the line of scrimmage.

The Nebraska game is one of those reasons why you go to a place like Penn State. I do remember that we should have really blown them out because in the first half we had a couple of touchdowns called back because of penalties. We had three missed field goals, I think, and we could have gone in at halftime up a significant amount. That would have really put pressure on them because they were more of an option-run team.

To their credit, they stayed in it, and when we went down with about a minute-and-a-half to play, that was the first time we trailed in the game. I don't know that any of our guys really felt we were going to lose the game.

We had played too well and controlled the game for too much of it to see it slip away.

Before Kirk Bowman's game-winning touchdown catch, Mike McCloskey was probably out of bounds when he and I connected at Nebraska's 2-yard line. Obviously, it would have made a little difference yardage-wise, but I still think we would have found a way to win.

The next week at Alabama, we got behind and I threw four interceptions. That wasn't a great Alabama team, but they were certainly a good team and had a lot of pride and were accustomed to playing in big games. We kind of fought and clawed our way back and at one point the score was 24–21, and it really felt like the momentum was starting to change.

We got stuffed on a short-yardage play and then had to punt. That's when we got the blocked punt—or blocked our own punt, I should say—and things kind of got out of hand after that. Had we made the first down on that third-and-one I think we could have turned the game around, but we didn't play well enough to win. [Penn State lost 42–21.]

The thing that game did, which ended up being a really positive thing for us, was it forced us to go back and say, "Hey, we've got to run the football better. We just can't rely on throwing it." The next game against Syracuse we didn't throw the ball much—I might have thrown 12 passes—and we really got back to running the football.

We were on our way after that because, by the time we finished the season, we were a very difficult team to defend. We got our running game back and we had a lot of weapons in the passing game. The game that typified that more than anything was the Boston College game. We beat them 52–17, but the remarkable thing was we gained exactly 352 yards passing and 352 yards rushing.

We had climbed to No. 2 in the rankings by the end of the regular season and accepted an invitation to the Sugar Bowl. Georgia was No. 1 and had Herschel Walker, but we knew we were capable of playing with them.

When the game was kind of on the line there, when we needed that last touchdown, it was set up by the run. Between Curt, Jon Williams, and Skeeter Nichols or whoever was in there, we ran the sprint draw, I think, six times in a row. And then we ran the play-action pass off it. Gregg was a lot faster than people gave him credit for and he was able to get behind the defender and make a great catch. He made another catch that was just as important.

In our last offensive possession, we needed a first down before we punted, and it was a third down and three or four, and Joe let me throw it. He let me check to it [audible] on the line of scrimmage. It was just a little quick out, and Gregg made the catch and got us a first down. We were able to take the clock pretty much all the way down before punting. [Penn State beat Georgia 27–23.]

The reaction we got back in Pennsylvania after we won the national championship was shocking. I had my car in Harrisburg, so I wasn't on the bus that took the team back to State College after we flew in from New Orleans. Curt and another kid from the team were with me, so we drove back ahead of the bus and there were people lined up all over the place.

Joe, Curt, and I went up to New York to be on *Good Morning America* with David Hartman. We flew up in a university plane, and it was a whole different feel to Joe that day. It wasn't so much like the coach-to-player thing. It was much more personal and friendly and relaxed. I think Curt and I both got to see a side of him that we had never seen before.

I was close to returning to Penn State for my fifth year because there were certain things I did not do that I would like to have done, even though we had won a championship. I had never been a captain. I had never really been considered a senior. If I didn't think for sure I was going to be a first-round pick in the NFL draft, I wouldn't have come out.

I am very proud to have played football for Penn State and especially proud and honored to have been the quarterback of Joe Paterno's first national championship team. Being a part of the Penn State football legacy is very special to me because I truly believe that we do it the right way. We win, we compete for championships, we graduate, and we display class and character on and off the field. We Are…Penn State!

196

The 22 touchdown passes Todd Blackledge threw in 1982 are still a school record, and his 41 career touchdown passes are tied for first. A Phi Beta Beta, he is a member of the GTE Academic All-America Hall of Fame. The sixth overall pick of the 1983 NFL draft, he played with the Kansas City Chiefs and Pittsburgh Steelers from 1983 to 1990 before going into broadcasting full-time. Blackledge is now the lead analyst for ESPN's coverage of college football. He and his wife, Cherie, have four sons and live in Canton, Ohio.

GREGG GARRITY
WIDE RECEIVER
1979–1982

M Y ROOMMATES IN MY FRATERNITY came up one night and they said, "Guess who's on the cover of *Sports Illustrated*?" I said, "Todd? I don't know?" They pulled it out and it was me.

Maybe I was just shocked, but I didn't even call my parents. I look at it now and it's cooler than it was at the time. I bet I still get at least one or more a month to sign. I feel like I've signed them all, over the years, but they just keep coming. It's pretty funny.

I made the cover of *SI* after making the touchdown catch that proved to be the difference in Penn State's 27–23 win over Georgia in the Sugar Bowl. Capping my career with a national championship and that catch was fulfilling, especially since most schools—and myself, to a degree—thought I was too small to play Division I-A football.

My father played at Penn State, but I didn't have a burning desire to play there only because I looked at them and figured there was no way. I was always a small, skinny kid, so I knew size would be a big issue.

A lot of smaller schools around the Pittsburgh area recruited me coming out of high school, but Penn State didn't, which was fine. I was really leaning toward Clarion or Kent State. Kent State decided they didn't want me, which was pretty funny because the head coach back then was Ron Blackledge, Todd's dad. If they hadn't said "no" to me I probably would have gone there.

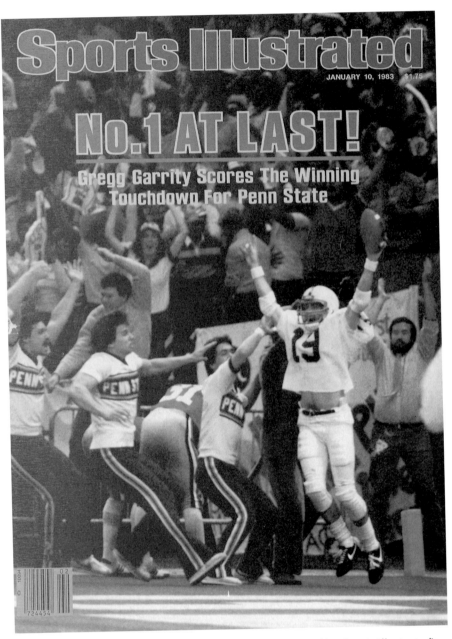

Penn State's 1982 national championship was immortalized by *Sports Illustrated*'s cover, featuring Gregg Garrity and his teammates celebrating in the end zone just moments after Garrity made a diving catch in the fourth quarter of the 1983 Sugar Bowl win over Georgia.

I talked to Clarion and the coach, Al Jacks, was also a good friend of my dad's and had gone to Penn State. I met with him a couple of times, and he was probably the second biggest reason I went to Penn State, my dad obviously being the first.

He saw all the film and basically said, "Go up there and give it a try. If it doesn't work out, there will be something back here for you."

When I did go up there and visit with my dad, Joe was showing us around and he was showing me the weight room and I was 140 pounds probably and there were two guys in the weight room, Matt Millen and Bruce Clark. He introduced me to them and I'm going, "You've got to be kidding me!" Their legs were bigger than me.

But I kind of got that out of my head, and when the freshmen went up the four days before everyone else, it was cool because they treated me just like I was on scholarship. Most of the guys, probably until my second year, didn't even know I was a walk-on. I did everything they did, except I had to pay for everything.

Joe said if I proved myself to him and the other coaches they'd give me a scholarship and give me every opportunity to play. I did well in drills and was pretty high on the depth chart when the older guys came in, so I was like, "Wow, he's putting me ahead of almost all of the scholarship guys." Going up there, almost everyone is an All-American, and these guys in my class were huge.

199

My freshman year I played on a lot of special teams. I was to the point, too, where I was a second-string safety, mainly because Pete Harris had academic problems and so did Karl McCoy. They had vacancies I think they weren't counting on, so they didn't recruit a lot of defensive backs.

I was a running back and defensive back in high school, but after the 1979 season we graduated a lot of receivers, so they said, "We're going to try you out at receiver in spring ball and see how it works. If it doesn't work, we'll send you back to defensive back." I was a little bummed, a little upset. It was tough because you finally got the feel of the calls and what everything meant because they throw all this stuff at you. I was used to defense and they flopped me over.

It was a big adjustment, especially since I had never played it before, but I had a good spring. I was also thinking realistically that unless I got a whole lot bigger, which I never really did, I'd be pretty undersized as a defensive back. I was living out a dream, more or less, and proving people wrong who had kind of discouraged me during the recruiting, the West Virginias and the Syracuses.

I talked to a lot of those schools, but when they came to visit me and when they saw my size, they weren't real pleasant, the things that they said. Even though they liked the film and stuff, they kind of discouraged me, and that hurt. I felt I was good enough to play at maybe one of those types of schools that, at the time, was not at the caliber of Penn State.

Growing up outside of Pittsburgh made the 48–14 win over top-ranked Pitt my junior year even sweeter. Dan Marino was on fire and they went up 14–zip. I said, "Oh man, here we go." Actually they were driving for a third score and Roger Jackson laid Julius Dawkins out, and I don't think he was the same for the rest of his career there.

For the rest of that game those guys were so afraid to do anything. Their arms were, like, two inches long and they didn't want to stretch out and get anything after Roger's hit. We just seemed to flow right after that. The momentum changed, and we just rolled right over them. My junior year I thought we were the best team in the country. I thought we were better than in my senior year; we just blew that one game in Miami.

The next season the Nebraska game was the first big, big test. We were losing with less than two minutes to go and we had a long drive but we had been driving almost at will. One catch was questionable—Mike McCloskey's on the sideline—but the touchdown was a touchdown. I felt McCloskey was definitely out, but the referees called him in.

After that game, I think we realized that we had something special because Nebraska had a great team. We felt good after that game and then we went to Alabama. It was almost a comedy of errors: the punter kicked the ball off his personal protector. I still think we played pretty well, even though the score doesn't indicate that. [Penn State lost 42–21 in Tuscaloosa.] Everything we did wrong was huge and they capitalized on it.

We dipped down pretty far in the rankings. My roommates and I would look at what was going on and say these teams all have to lose before the end of the season for us to move. We'd look at the schedule and say, "There's no way these guys are going to lose to these guys," and they did. It was weird how it all fell into place.

We were pretty confident going into the Sugar Bowl, but not as confident as Georgia and their fans. You'd be walking down the street in New Orleans, and we're poor college kids so we had to wear all of our bowl presents—the sweats and stuff—and they'd come and bark in your face.

Most of their players were pretty good guys, but the one that stands out to me was Tony Flack, a defensive back. He was talking trash all week that he was going to shut down Kenny Jackson and me. He was just going on and on and on. Kenny and I didn't say anything, and Joe pretty much kept us under wraps anyhow.

We were leading 20–17 in the third quarter when Kenny and I ran streaks down the sideline, McCloskey ran a streak down the hash, and Curt ran a streak down the other hash. We ran it almost every game, and I never got it all year. I was open a bunch of times during the regular season, but so was someone else. Todd would look in at the hashes first and work his way out. The defense they had was perfect for the play. Flack was out on me and I just juked him and went around him.

If you look at the cover of *Sports Illustrated*, he's the one who's bent over behind the cheerleaders because he knew he was the one who got beat.

Gregg Garrity lived another dream when his hometown Pittsburgh Steelers selected him in the fifth round of the NFL draft. He played parts of two seasons with the Steelers and eight overall in the NFL. Garrity owns his own business in the Pittsburgh area, and he and his family live in the suburb of Bradford Woods.

CURT WARNER

TAILBACK

1979–1982

I HAVE JOKED WITH TIM CURLEY on numerous occasions that if it weren't for me, he wouldn't be the athletics director right now. My English teacher in high school and a very close friend of the family, Libby McKinney, sent a handwritten, two-page letter along with clippings to Joe Paterno, and Joe passed that along to Tim Curley, who was his recruiting coordinator at the time.

He and Joe came down to Pineville, West Virginia, to watch me play basketball, and Jackie Sherrill from Pitt and some other coaches, including one from Nebraska, were there. It was probably as cold at it's ever been down there. They took a small commuter plane in, and Joe told Tim, "He better be worth it, Curley." I'd like to think I was, since Tim and I are still very close friends to this day.

Going into my senior year of high school, I wasn't really paying attention to Penn State or anyone else. I actually had a couple of scholarship offers for basketball, including one from West Virginia. Even though I had been first-team All-State in football as a junior, I was thinking more basketball than football at the time. Once football season began and I started racking up yardage, it pretty much put basketball on the back burner.

In a five-week time frame, schools went from interested to being *really* interested. I was scheduled to visit Nebraska and Notre Dame, but I got snowed in both times. I respected Nebraska's program and Coach Tom

Curt Warner is considered by most fans and media that saw him to be the overall best tailback in Penn State history. Besides his skill at tailback, he also was an exceptional kickoff returner and holds the team record for return touchdowns (3) and is second in career return yardage (28.8 average on 32 returns).

Osborne, who even came to my house in the tiny town of Wyoming [West Virginia]. But it was too far away, and being kind of a mama's boy, I really didn't want to be that far away from home.

I picked Penn State not knowing much about its history and tradition. Once I got there, it didn't take long to figure out what it was all about. There are always doubts when you are a freshman about whether you can play at the next level, especially when you're practicing against guys named Matt Millen and Bruce Clark. I figured if I could play against Matt and Bruce, then I could play at the major college level.

As I started gaining confidence, I told my freshman roommate during training camp, Mark Battaglia, "You know what, Batman? I'm going to be the man." He's a sophomore and he's got to be thinking, "This guy is full of himself." He reminds me of that every time we talk. Still, I had pretty much told my parents that I wasn't going to see much action and not to expect it to be like high school. Well, I actually played a lot in the first game. [Warner scored three touchdowns in Penn State's 1979 season opener against Temple.]

I was on the kickoff-return team and had almost broken a long return on the first play of the game. I guess about the third or fourth series, running backs coach Fran Ganter said, "You're up next series." I'm just sitting on the bench, minding my own business. I was kind of looking around the stands because the stadium was huge, especially to someone who had played in front of 3,000 fans maximum in high school. There are people screaming and cheering and I'm like, "Wow, this is big-time college football." When Fran said that, I was thinking, "He must be talking to somebody else," and I actually looked around. He said, "No, *you're* up." I grabbed my helmet, and the rest is kind of history.

I didn't think we were a very good football team that year, although we had a couple of All-Americans sitting out for various reasons. [Penn State went 8–4 in 1979.] Going into my sophomore year, there were a lot of guys competing at the tailback position, so nothing was a given at the time. That was my thinking, especially with guys like Booker Moore, Joel Coles, Skeeter Nichols, and Jon Williams battling for the tailback position along with me. Booker had shared the tailback job with Mike Guman—I played behind them—in 1979, but at the beginning of spring practice he moved to fullback.

We had a good football team in 1980 and had the potential to go all the way. But we lost to Nebraska and Pitt that season, and they were also pretty good football teams. In my junior year, I believed we could contend for a national championship because we had a wealth of talent, both offensively and defensively.

Midway through the season we were ranked No. 1 in the country, but then we went down to Miami and got beat 17–14. We missed five field goals and lost by three points. Sometimes you're just not going to win. We had everything going against us that day. Every time Brian Franco tried to kick the ball, the wind would kick up or something else would happen. We shouldn't have lost that game.

We lost to Alabama [31–16] later in the season and played at No. 1 Pitt in the final game. Even when we got down 14–0 early, nobody really panicked. We were just like, "Okay, let's go out there and play our game." We got an interception and, from that point on, everything just kind of changed. [Penn State beat Pitt 48–14.]

Going into my senior season, Joe talked about how we were going to throw the football. Being that I had heard him say that the previous three years, I probably didn't take him as seriously as I should have. I was surprised when we did throw that first game because we took pride in pounding people on the ground. After the game I was upset about not getting the ball, and I kind of expressed that in the press. Joe reprimanded me pretty good, individually and in front of the team.

205

Our quarterback, Todd Blackledge, was my best friend and roommate, and so I had to readjust my thinking and not let my frustration affect our friendship. It was a tough stretch for me for about three or four weeks. There was never any animosity between us because we were such good friends. He'd say, "Hey, Curt, I'm sorry." I'd say, "Todd, don't worry about it. Keep throwing the ball. I don't like it. I'd like to run the ball more, but we're winning and that's the most important thing."

Looking back, that was probably one of the better decisions Joe made because I don't think we would have won the national championship just by running the football. By the time we got the running game going again, people had to respect our ability to throw the ball. We started 4–0 and beat Nebraska on a late drive, but we lost at Alabama the following week [42–21]. It was a lot closer than what the scoreboard indicated. We just fell apart after one of our own players backed into Ralph Giacomarro as he was punting. I can't explain to this day what happened in that particular game.

After that game, we started emphasizing the run more, and that made us a more balanced offense. Against Boston College the passing and rushing yardage were exactly the same [352]. To me that was the epitome of balance.

Late in the season we were in a tough game at South Bend. Notre Dame had a 14–13 lead against us early in the fourth quarter when I lined up as a slot receiver. The play wasn't designed to go to me, but for whatever reason they didn't have anybody covering me. I looked at Todd and he just looked at me.

It was one of those things where we were really good friends, had a real good rapport, and there was an opportunity. I took off down the field and turned around, and the ball was right there. I scored a touchdown and we won that game 24–14. We needed a play like that to get us going, and that goes back to balance that we had due to the fact that Joe had changed his philosophy during the early part of the season. We then beat Pitt to set us up against No. 1 Georgia in the Sugar Bowl.

Georgia had Herschel Walker, who had won the Heisman Trophy, and I was back in a familiar role. The year before I was the other running back when we played Marcus Allen and USC in the Fiesta Bowl, and it's always a motivating factor when you're going up against a Heisman Trophy winner. I respected Herschel Walker's game, but I felt confident about my ability to run as well.

The one thing I remember when we were down in New Orleans was the spirit of the Georgia fans. We heard, "How 'bout them 'Dawgs!" over and over in the week leading up to the game. By the end of the week, we were determined to shut them up and shut them down.

If you give our defensive coordinator, Jerry Sandusky, a month to get ready for a game, it's a given that he will come up with a plan to shut down the opposing team's offense. We did it to Marcus Allen in the Fiesta Bowl the previous year and we were able to shut Herschel Walker down as well [Penn State held Walker to 103 yards on 28 carries], and more importantly, we did win the game [27–23]. It's a great feeling to know you're the undisputed champion. There's no BCS. It's the two best teams on the field and winner takes all.

What I'm most proud of is the fact that we had a bunch of guys who were in it together, played together, and had an opportunity to win it all and did it. It's amazing the number of people who remember the '82 season. It's a humbling experience to know that you still have that kind of impact more than 20 years after the fact.

I got a chance to get back for homecoming in 2005. I took my 12-year-old son, Jonathan, to show him what Penn State football is all about. While we were there, he got an opportunity to meet Coach Paterno. I got to talk with Joe and I told him, "Joe, I consider it an honor and a privilege to have played for you." You can't fully appreciate what he's trying to do when you're a 19- or 20-year-old kid.

If I had to do it again, I'd without a doubt pick Penn State, and I would have stayed there longer because it's a great place to be. I got the whole college experience, from being a part of the student body to being held accountable for my classwork and being a part of a group of guys who were committed to Penn State's winning tradition.

A two-time first-team All-American, Curt Warner is Penn State's all-time leading rusher with 3,398 yards. He also has the most 100-yard games in school history (18) and his 462 rushing yards in bowl games is also tops at Penn State. The third overall pick of the 1983 NFL draft by the Seattle Seahawks, Warner held the organization's all-time rushing record until Shaun Alexander broke it in 2005. In eight NFL seasons (all but one with the Seahawks), Warner rushed for 6,844 yards, scored 63 touchdowns, and made the Pro Bowl three times. Warner, his wife, Ana, and their three children live in Camas, Washington, and he owns a car dealership.

MARK ROBINSON

DEFENSIVE BACK

1980–1983

THE FIRST THING THAT COMES TO ME when I look back on my career at Penn State is pride. When you're out in the community and you say you played at Penn State, there's a difference. You're thought of as being special, and that's the way I've always felt about being a Nittany Lion. When I was coming out of high school [in Silver Spring, Maryland], I didn't know the magnitude of my decision to go to Penn State.

I was recruited by 100 schools, including Ivy League schools, but I wanted to stay pretty close to home. I visited Ohio State because Coach Earle Bruce was there, and he was the best man to my high school coach at his wedding. I went to North Carolina because my soon-to-be wife was going there. I went to Indiana University because my brother was playing at Indiana State University, which was close by. I had a high school buddy who was a fullback at the University of Virginia, and I visited Maryland because they were the local school.

The choices weren't even close. There was no comparison as far as being a Nittany Lion and being at Penn State and showing the pride that that organization and Coach Paterno spearheaded from the beginning. I learned so much and have so much admiration for Coach Paterno and the things he taught me over the years. A lot of people say, "I'm at school but they should be honored that I'm playing for them." I look at it totally different. It's an honor to have worn the blue and white.

Mark Robinson had an instinct for getting to the ball quickly. In the 1983 Sugar Bowl game for the national championship, Robinson made several one-on-one-tackles against Georgia's Herschel Walker, while intercepting two passes and deflecting another.

I played in my freshman year and didn't redshirt. Matt Bradley was the "hero" back at the time. He was a senior, and we actually split time in the Maryland game out there. It was five games into the season and I remember the coaches telling me, "Go out there and play. You've earned it." I got an opportunity to play half a game, and that was a big thrill. So I started splitting time as we went. In my sophomore year, I was the starter and actually moved back to free safety at that time, and Harry Hamilton moved to strong safety. Harry ended up playing with me with the Tampa Bay Buccaneers, so we got to know each other really well.

I've been told that the Pitt game that year was one of greatest in Penn State history. Pitt was our biggest rival, and the game was always the last of the season. Pitt was No. 1 and no one gave us much of a chance, although we had only lost two games. It had started out 14–0, and [at the end of the first quarter] they were driving down on us. Our backs were nearly in the end zone, and I remember thinking, "We're not going to be able to come back from 21 points." [Defensive coordinator] Jerry Sandusky, the nicest man I've ever met in my life, kept us composed. He was saying, "Hey guys, we're going to get back in. We just gotta make a play, gotta make a play." Julius Dawkins was Pitt's slot receiver. Dan Marino threw a pass in the end zone, and I remember hitting Dawkins and Roger Jackson intercepted it in the end zone. It stopped them and then we started making our comeback. Our offense went 80 yards for a touchdown, but Pitt came right back and we were on our heels again. This time Marino threw a pass to Dawkins at the goal line, and Roger Jackson hit him. The ball popped up and I caught it and ran it back to about the 20-yard line. The rest is history.

I remember making another interception when we were way ahead in the middle of the fourth quarter [41–14] and Pitt was driving again. I knew Dan liked to throw those little quick slants, and I remember Dawkins making that break. I remember seeing Dan Marino's eyes and he was looking right at me. I was thinking, "He can't throw that ball."

I was literally in better position to catch the football than Dawkins, but Dan felt he could throw that football and he didn't care where the defensive back was. He forced it a little bit, and I got the interception. I started running, and Dan dove down to get me and took my shoe off. I ran the length of the field with my sock coming off. [Robinson's 91-yard interception is still the second-longest in Penn State history and capped a historic 48–14 upset.]

I also remember we played Nebraska every year. Nebraska was a big foe. They had Irving Fryar and Roger Craig, and they were such big games out there. There was a lot of trash-talking going on in a heated game. I remember Irving Fryar caught a couple of passes early in the '81 game. He would spin the ball in front of me and say, "Thirty-two, you're nothing." He was just talking and talking and that just burned me up. I'm not a real big talker, but it was just eating me up inside, and I just wanted to hit him so hard his kids would laugh at him. All of a sudden Irving Fryar came down, he ran a slant, and I just hit him in his mouth. He fell down and I remember looking down at him. I stood over him after I hit him and I told him to "stay down." His eyes kind of rolled up into his head. He jumped up and said, "I'm not hurt." And then he collapsed. He was out for like eight weeks or something like that and he never came back and played that year.

Obviously, I remember the national championship game against Georgia in the [1983] Sugar Bowl. It was an honor to win the [school's] first national championship. We had been so close so many years. I remember 1978, watching the games on TV and seeing them lose to Alabama in the Sugar Bowl, and then for us to do it, it was special. I remember Coach Paterno coming up to us before the game and saying, "We're going to bounce Herschel out." He said, "Robbie, I want you to come up and just clean him up." And the first play from scrimmage, they pitched the ball to Herschel Walker, everyone in the Sugar Bowl knew who the ball was going to. Herschel went around the end and he was coming up and I just took a bee-line on him. I just said, "I'm going to break him in half." He stepped out of bounds and it just blew my mind. He's 240 pounds and I'm 205 pounds and he had apparently hurt his shoulders throughout the year and his shoulders were real banged up. He didn't have the punch that I really anticipated. And we banged him around a lot. I remember at the end of the game sitting at my locker and everyone was trying to interview me and I was so tired, I didn't want to talk to anybody, I had just given it my all. I'd left it all on the field.

211

Penn State is different. I remember I always wanted my name across the back of my jersey. But then when I understood where Coach Paterno came from, they were a team. I bought into it. I always tried to be a coachable person. I always wanted to learn more, learn to be the best that I could be.

If Coach Paterno has a fault, and I'll just say that people see it as a fault, it's that he is loyal to his players, loyal to his coaches, loyal to his commitment to the program. Sometimes, if you're making a personnel decision and you have a fifth-year senior who was a walk-on and an okay player and you have a stud freshman or sophomore on the bench, knowing they're going to play for three or four years, Joe sometimes looks at it and says, "Hey, I'm going to play that kid cause he's a fifth-year senior. I told his parents I was going to give him an opportunity. I'm going to give him his best shot. This is probably his last year of playing football." He is loyal in that regard.

But on the flip side it's college football and it's higher education. In the sports world, it's really developed over the years that you must win at all costs.

It was kind of special at Penn State that, "Yes, I'd prefer them to win, and have the education." But in the end, it's about shaping and forming lives, preparing men to go out into the community and be a positive impact. I think Coach Paterno is hitting that right on the head. He impacted my life and shaped the person who I am today.

Mark Robinson was an All-American in 1982 and then played eight years in the NFL with Kansas City and Tampa Bay. While with the Chiefs he earned an MBA, and he and his wife, Melinda, now own and operate a Montessori School in Safety Harbor, Florida. Robinson also is active in sports broadcasting in the Tampa area, including work as the color commentator for the University of South Florida football since the team's inception in 1996 and co-hosts a Buccaneers television show.

HARRY HAMILTON

HERO

1980–1983

To me, what it means to be a Nittany Lion is having the privilege and honor of playing for a coach like Joe Paterno. The biggest reason I went to Penn State, even though I heard from more than 60 schools from my freshman through senior year of high school, was Joe Paterno's expressed interest in me as a student-athlete, and not just what I was going to bring to his football team.

If I took too many hits in the head or had a career-ending injury, then what happens? Do I basically become a piece of meat and get kicked out of the university or does the scholarship remain good and I finish my education? Those questions were posed by my dad during Joe Paterno's second visit to our house.

You can't put any more substance behind saying, "Yes, if something happens, he will keep his scholarship." Joe Paterno looked us in the eye from across the table and said it. I believe that even if he had to go into his own pocket to make that happen, he would have done it.

I was actually recruited out of Nanticoke High School [outside of Wilkes-Barre] by Penn State as a running back. My class alone was loaded with tailbacks, not to mention the ones who were already there.

I took two handoffs, I think, and then found myself in a different-colored jersey, indicating defense. Mark Robinson, who had played running back in high school, also got moved to the secondary. Years later, we were

Harry Hamilton led the Nittany Lions in tackles in his senior season with 100 when he was a third-team All-American and a repeat Academic All-American. He later won a coveted NCAA post-graduate scholarship.

also teammates in the Tampa Bay Buccaneers' defensive backfield. I think Joe Paterno's philosophy is to put the best athletes on the field. That meant that if I was going to be on the field early, it was going to be on the defensive side of the ball.

I did play as a true freshman in 1980, but Joe Paterno was even more reticent about playing freshmen at that time. Even though I did play and did travel, my time on the field was actually short-lived. I was a cornerback at first before I moved inside to safety. During spring practice of my freshman year, I spent about eight of 20 days at free safety before they moved me to hero, which is where I stayed.

Being someone who wasn't often hurt in high school, I think an injury I sustained my junior year was a telling moment. It was during a game and I had come to the sideline under my own power. I remember the shock of not being able to put weight on my leg. I didn't want to believe it. When you sit there and you cannot physically perform, you realize how quickly things can end.

Luckily the knee injury turned out to be more of a scare than anything else, and I played most of the season. We had to rely quite a bit on the offense in 1982. Defenses are supposed to be able to make plays to win games, and we were not that kind of defense. We just had to believe if we could hold the opposing teams, our offense would win the game.

The defense really came together for the Sugar Bowl. We just believed we were capable, almost beyond doubt, of stopping Herschel Walker. It wasn't so much the intensity of the hitting [in practice] as it was the film study to a man. I remember knowing the front players would be able to handle the guys in front of them and, as we moved in pursuit, we felt we were going to be there.

We did realize we were going up against a great back, so the coaches' warnings of, "You better be there," sank in because you watch the film enough to know that this guy does some things on his own. Forget about the fact that you can whip the man in front of you. That alone is not going to get it done. That's what sobered us.

You've got to remember that by the time we got to New Orleans, this team had played against some great backs. We had played Marcus Allen tough in the 1982 Fiesta Bowl. We had played against some great Nebraska backs—Jarvis Redwine and Mike Rozier. [Hamilton had 12 tackles and Penn State held Walker to 103 yards on 28 carries in its 27–23 win.]

If you think of all the hard work that has gone into [winning the national championship], there's an incredible sensation and incredible feeling. You were thankful that such a reward could be bestowed upon you and the team. You begin to think about your parents and the people in your life who brought you to that time and place and it is truly an amazing feeling.

I'll never forget the bus ride back to State College from Harrisburg after we won the national championship. There were people all along the road, waving blue and white banners and flags, honking their horns, and turning on their car lights. They were letting us know, "Thank you," and how much they appreciated it.

Even when we got to the outskirts of Penn State, it took an inordinate amount of time just to get to the locker room. When you are coming back and your bus is going one mile an hour through a sea of people, you realize the impact the feat has had on others.

When I talk to young people, I talk about positive attitude. I believe it was that attitude, the unwavering swagger, if you will, and belief that we were Penn State, that we were the best-coached and best-equipped team on the field on any given afternoon. It wasn't arrogance. It was a belief, and I think that is what made us winners.

The next year was tough, and I cannot explain it. [Penn State opened the 1983 season with three straight losses.] We had had a lot of juniors on the national championship team, including myself. You would have thought we would have been better than that.

Joe called all of the seniors into a meeting room before the Temple game, and basically we were told that if we lost this game, nobody's job was safe. It did ram home what winning in any sport means. I think collectively we just brought it together and started playing together. I can't explain why it happened that way out of the box. Nor can I explain how we were able to turn it around, except for maybe realizing that the swagger, the confidence alone was not going to do it. You actually had to go out there and play. [Penn State went 8–1–1 in its final 10 games.]

Joe Paterno is an instructor and there were life lessons in that football program. He was a coach who was not just interested in the best football team, but interested in the best human beings who also happened to play football for him.

When people would ask me in passing if it was time for Joe to give it up, I would actually take a pause and stop them in their tracks and say, "Let me explain something to you about Joe Paterno. Joe Paterno has earned the right to leave the game when he and he alone is ready." To me, anyone who suggests something other than that is missing the major point and has almost uttered what can best be termed as fighting words.

When I went to Joe Paterno as a freshman about putting more soul food on the training table, within a week there were pig's feet and candied yams. A man like Joe Paterno could stand back and say, "No, you don't suggest how I should run a football team."

During the time of the Atlanta child murders in 1981, there were green ribbons to show support for the children. I approached Joe about wearing a green wristband. If you look at a lot of photos from back then you'll see I have a green wristband on and I wore it for most of the 1981 season. Joe Paterno donned a green wristband, and I think it was for a spring game. No matter how many years he coaches, Joe Paterno will probably tell you that he's still learning things from athletes coming through there today.

That's what makes Joe more than just a football coach to me.

Harry Hamilton led Penn State in tackles in 1983 and earned third-team All-America honors. He distinguished himself as much in the classroom as on the playing field, earning academic All-America honors three times. He graduated from law school after playing in the NFL from 1984 to 1991 and establishing himself as a fan favorite with the Tampa Bay Buccaneers. Brothers Lance and Darren also played at Penn State. Hamilton is an attorney for the United States, is active in a number of charitable causes, and aided in the relief effort following Hurricane Katrina. He lives with one of his two sons in Glen Lyon, Pennsylvania.

KENNY JACKSON
WIDE RECEIVER
1980–1983

My brother Roger was a defensive back, so we competed against each other every day in practice. That was actually an extension of our childhood. We used to fight constantly growing up, playing basketball. The game would never end when we played one-on-one.

One time at Penn State we argued over who had to go into a team meeting first. It's actually a funny story. We were living in West Halls, and the football facilities were on the east side of campus. We were late for a meeting by, like, three minutes and we were scared to go into the building. I remember it like it was yesterday. Joe killed us, "You're wasting everybody's time!" I was never late after that. At Penn State, and this is the weirdest thing, if Joe calls a meeting at 4:30, everybody is there at 4:00. If you show up at 4:30, you're late.

Joe is the reason I went to Penn State, and he was the first coach to come to my house in South River, New Jersey, during my recruitment. At the time, Penn State was doing very well, and local television would have all of the Penn State highlights. I used to watch those every week, so I kind of got to know Penn State that way.

Todd Blackledge and Curt Warner were my hosts for my official visit, and I slept on a cot in their dorm room. That was a far cry from when I visited UCLA and I was in mansions and saw the Rose Bowl. Penn State was just real, everything about it.

Kenny Jackson was the Nittany Lions' first All-American wide receiver in 1982 and 1983. As the leading receiver on the 1982 national championship team, Jackson set several team records before he graduated. He is still fifth in career receptions with 109.

I also visited USC, but I didn't want to go that far away from my family and Pitt was also involved. Dan Marino was my host when I visited Pitt, and they threw the ball a lot while at the time Penn State didn't.

Joe promised me two things: that he was going to make sure Penn State threw the ball and that I was going to go to class. That was important because I was a pretty good student in high school and in the National Honor Society. When my mom and dad visited Penn State, they felt very comfortable. They never said it or told me where to go, but they just felt very comfortable there.

What I always thought should happen at all colleges, if they really cared about the kids, is freshmen should practice with the team but not play that first year. Get into school and understand what it's about. Everybody would be under the same system so it wouldn't hurt anybody.

Playing as a freshman was challenging, but Joe didn't throw me in the starting lineup, and I got a chance to understand college. Of course, it was a different time. There was no ESPN. There was no Internet. There wasn't *firethiscoach.com*. People don't realize how fast things change.

When I was at Penn State, I could go home for the summer and work out. Players can't do that anymore. Their life is consumed [with football], and there's so much pressure placed on these kids. Part of the reason for that is there's so much money generated by big-time college football. When I played, if ABC televised your games twice a season you were happy. Now every darn game is on television! I can't compare myself with kids today. I was never under a tremendous amount of pressure.

When I got to school, I didn't understand the hatred between Pitt and Penn State, I'm a Jersey kid. I wondered why Penn State fans hated Pitt so much. I learned how much that game meant by Joe picking on me all week. If I ran a bad route in practice, he'd get so mad. I'd think, "Man, you need to get off my butt." I'd get mad at him and say, "I'm going to show him this game." If that wasn't enough motivation, my best friend in high school, Troy Hill, went to Pitt and played defensive back.

I was in a zone that '81 game. [Jackson caught five passes for 158 yards and two touchdowns in Penn State's 48–14 win over No. 1 Pitt.] Sometimes it's like shooting basketball, everything you throw up goes in.

The next year, we were down 7–3 in the third quarter, and Troy was covering me. We caught them in man-to-man coverage and the backs flared out of the backfield. He kind of got picked, so he really couldn't catch up to me. I ran a drag route underneath, caught the pass from Todd Blackledge, and got into the end zone. [Penn State went on to win 19–10.]

One of the most memorable games for me came earlier that season against Nebraska.

It was the first night game at Beaver Stadium. Nebraska had Irving Fryar, Mike Rozier, all of those great players and Jersey boys, too. All of that stuff meant something to me, too, because we had played on all-star teams together.

[Nebraska scored a late touchdown to take a 24–21 lead.] We were good at the two-minute drill. We'd hit teams with a screen early. The one play I really remember is we had a fourth down and 11 yards to go. We went to the sideline and I told Joe, "Throw me the ball. I'll get it." I caught the pass and a Nebraska guy hit me, but my forward progress gave us a first down.

I just felt on that play, based on the coverages and what was happening, I could get it. [Penn State, aided by a controversial completion to tight end Mike McCloskey, scored a touchdown with only seconds remaining to win 27–24.] That was a special game, especially to come back and win it because it helped us win the national championship.

Nebraska got us back later when I was an assistant coach. In '94 we should have at least tied Nebraska for the national championship. We had a helluva team, so it evened out.

At the 2006 Orange Bowl I finally got a chance to sit in the stands with my wife and watch a game. I was always either coaching or playing, so I never really knew what the fans thought in the stands as the game is going on. I just laughed at how mad people got.

The best thing about Joe, if you're a player or a coach—and I've been fortunate to be both—is he's fair. If you've got a problem, he will work his ass off to help you figure that problem out. He's a special guy. I don't think Joe Paterno could coach a football team unless he had true student-athletes. Joe's done it the right way. He's not perfect, nobody is, but to me Penn State embodies the true student-athlete.

Kenny Jackson, whose brother Roger was a standout defensive back at Penn State, became the first wideout in school history to win All-America honors, and he did it twice (1982 and 1983) while racking up 109 career catches and 2,006 receiving yards. The fourth overall pick of the 1984 NFL draft, Jackson played for a handful of teams before retiring in 1991. He spent nearly a decade as the wide receivers coach at Penn State, tutoring the likes of Bobby Engram, Freddie Scott, and Joe Jurevicius. Jackson and wife, Ruthanne, also a Penn State graduate, live in State College with their daughter.

MICHAEL ZORDICH
STRONG SAFETY
1982–1985

WHEN I THINK OF PENN STATE and my time spent there as a player, I immediately think of the people that came into my life—solid relationships with solid people. There are some that are a core part of my life today, teammates like Shane Conlan and Dan Delligatti, who know me and know my kids, too. There are others whom I don't see as often, players like Chris Collins, Jimmy Coates, Donnie Graham, and Don Ginnetti, my roommate and friend who just buried his father last fall, as well as Todd Moules, Tim Manoa, Johnny Greene, and others who, when you do see them, you can still feel that connection. It's real. There are also coaches like "Scrap" [Tom Bradley], whom I keep in touch with; Jerry Sandusky, who's mentoring my son, Alex, at his summer football camps; and Coach Paterno. I respected them all as a player and I still do today.

And of course I met my wife, Cindy, at Penn State when I was just a sophomore. We have three kids—Michael, 16, Alex, 14, and Aidan, 12. She was a cheerleader there, and we had a beautiful group of friends. Plus, because of the games, our families got to know each other early on. Just recently Cindy pointed out that our parents were our age now when we were at school. That's how young they were. So you can imagine how much fun we had together.

When I talk to my sons about Penn State, I talk about the great tradition that we established there, particularly in the early and mid-1980s. I played in

Michael Zordich, one of the most intense and hardest tacklers of the Paterno era, will always be remembered for this run back on an interception for a touchdown in the opening minute of the 1985 season at Maryland. The crucial play launched the Nittany Lions toward the national championship game at the 1986 Orange Bowl.

two national championship games in four years, and most of the guys who were recruited with me played in three. That's something we all take pride in, especially my senior year in 1985. We weren't expected to do much and there we were, playing in the Orange Bowl for the national championship. To lose that game hurt like no other loss I have ever experienced, not even in the pros. Oklahoma was good, but we could have won that game.

That was my second national championship game. My first was in 1983 when Penn State beat Georgia in the Sugar Bowl. During the season I had started three or four games when Harry Hamilton got injured. After that, they would find ways to keep me in the game. In the Sugar Bowl I played in all of the special teams, but not a down on defense. What's pretty crazy is that after the game Joe came up to me and apologized for that. Here he was, just carried off the field, in the middle of a great personal triumph, and he took the time not only to think of me, but to approach me, a freshman. That's Joe.

Seasons 1983 and 1984 were atypical of Penn State. [In 1983 the Nittany Lions lost their first three games, then came back to finish 8–4–1. The next season, they had a 6–5 record, losing their last two games by at least three touchdowns.] By 1985 we decided as a group that we were tired of losing and the losing attitude. Now seniors, we were ready to turn things around.

Some say I set the tone for the entire season with my interception at Maryland in the first game. We weren't supposed to win. Maryland was a consensus preseason top three team and picked No. 1 by *Sport Magazine*. It was the second play. Stan Gelbaugh was the [Maryland] quarterback, and we played together later in Phoenix. The only thing I remember is that when I planted my right foot, my shoe came off and I knew the receiver [Azizuddin Abdur-Ra'oof] was fast and right behind me. My wife made me a highlight tape when I was in college, and I see myself make the play and return it [32 yards] for a touchdown. But what I see that excites me more than my making the play is that you could see the guys on the sideline and my teammates who were on the field just going crazy. The pure excitement. That's what I see, all of us in the end zone celebrating. If you ask me, more than that play, it was their reaction to it that set a precedent for our season. We were a close team that had a lot of fun winning football games.

Growing up in Youngstown, Ohio, we played sports for that very reason. The fun. We were all involved in sports. We didn't play for recognition and we didn't think much about scholarships. My parents didn't talk about all of that. I was recruited by most of the schools in the East. Pitt, Penn State, West Virginia, Syracuse, Ohio State, and Michigan were interested. My high school coach was Ed Matey. His brother, Bobby Matey, was an assistant at Pitt. The Pelusi brothers and the Cavanaughs [all Chaney grads] had gone to Pitt. My visit to Pitt was like a visit home. It was all so familiar. I told my father on the way back to Y-town, "You know, Dad, I'm probably going to end up going to Pitt." He said, "Fine. That's your decision. That's your choice."

The day Joe Paterno came to my house for the first time, my mother cooked spaghetti. My whole family was there, grandparents, too. At one point my father told Joe about his good friend, Al Perl. He was a fireman who had just had his leg amputated. My father said something like, "Al has two idols, you and Bear Bryant. If you could ever come back and visit him— that would be a real thrill for him." Joe said, "Let's go." And that's all Al Perl ever talked about after that.

My parents could tell you more about what was said during that visit and others with Tom Bradley and Jerry Sandusky. But what I could tell you is how they felt. They felt right. My decision to go to Penn State came from my gut. There is no doubt that Joe's coaching makes him a living legend. But what's more, he is genuine. Even today when I go back, he still knows my mother's name, he asks about my brother and sister. We were not just football players but people who Joe knew and cared about.

I learned a lot from Joe, certainly, for being in business now. Joe would always say, "Keep your poise and understand with hard work and time, things will work out." I think the biggest thing for me is, I've worked pretty hard. I worked *extremely* hard to stay in the NFL for 12 years. I understand what it takes. I realize that if you don't sweat, you'll get nothing out of it. You have to work for everything. Things don't always go as you plan or not as smooth as you'd like them to be. You just gotta hang in there. I understand that and just keeping my cool in bad times. These lessons are the same ones I try to drum into my own kids' heads.

That's what it means to be a Nittany Lion to me—and my family.

225

Michael Zordich, a consensus All-American in his senior season, finished his career as Penn State's 12th all-time leading tackler with 201 career stops. In 1985 he was selected as a team captain and helped lead the Nittany Lions to an 11–1 mark and the No. 3 ranking in the nation. Zordich played 12 years in the NFL with the New York Jets (1987–1988), the Arizona Cardinals (1989–1993), and the Philadelphia Eagles (1994–1998). In 1994 and 1995 Zordich was selected to the All-Madden Team, and in 1996 and 1997 he was voted by his teammates as the Eagles Unsung Hero. Zordich is the owner of a utility contracting business in Pittsburgh, Pennsylvania.

SHANE CONLAN

LINEBACKER

1982–1986

WHEN I WAS A FRESHMAN, JOE PATERNO kicked me out of practice. I was covering [wide receiver] Kevin Baugh, and when the ball was snapped, he went lame like he had pulled his hamstring. So I stopped and said, "Are you all right?" Boom, he goes and catches a touchdown pass.

Joe was on the other field and he comes running, yelling, "You stink, Conlan! You'll never play here! Get off the field! You quit!" I've never been so nervous. I thought I was going to have my locker cleaned out. Welcome to big-time college football.

Of course, I ended up playing at Penn State and we won the national championship my senior year in 1986. If it was a surprise ending to my career, that is because I arrived at Penn State as anything but a blue-chip recruit.

At the end of my junior year of high school in upstate New York I got some letters, but then I got letters back from a lot of people saying, "Thanks for the interest, but no thanks." I played at a really small school and I was the biggest kid on my team at 180 pounds. I actually played tailback. My high school coach kind of begged Tom Bradley to check me out because I had gotten turned down by everyone else.

He had never seen me play football, so he came to a basketball game. I was going to play baseball, but then Penn State came into the picture. My high school football coach had also played baseball and he told me my best chance was in football. I kind of took his guidance along with my father's and I went to Penn State.

Joe never saw me play, only on film, so I was very surprised when Penn State offered me a scholarship. Never in my wildest dreams did I think I would play for Penn State. My biggest concern was, would I be strong enough? I knew I could run with players at that level, but I had never played against a kid bigger than 200 pounds.

I redshirted my first season. We went against the [1982] national championship team every day in practice. That probably had more to do than anything with my development, especially playing against Curt Warner and trying to cover him. He was the quickest guy ever.

I probably started half the games my redshirt freshman year, and after that season I started every game. Those second and third years were kind of tough. [Penn State went a combined 14–9–1.]

My class, we knew were going to be good, so I think that had a lot to do with the turnaround. We went undefeated in 1985, but lost to Oklahoma [25–10] in the Orange Bowl. There were questions about whether I would go to the NFL after that season, but I knew I would come back. We lost strong safety Mike Zordich, who was also a co-captain, from that team, but I knew we were loaded on defense.

Joe called me into his office shortly after the bowl game and said, "I've checked around and I think you should stay another year. What are you thinking?" I said, "I'm thinking what you're thinking." I probably could have been a late first-round pick, but there's big difference between a late first-round pick and a top-10 pick, which I was the following year.

In 1986 we had some tight games, but that was a prototypical Joe Paterno football team. We won with defense and the running game. We had some great running backs. Two first-rounders [D. J. Dozier and Blair Thomas] and our fullbacks [Tim Manoa and Steve Smith] were the first fullbacks taken in the 1987 NFL draft.

We went undefeated again and played No. 1 Miami in the Fiesta Bowl. Some of the stuff Miami did before the game, I know that would never happen on a Joe Paterno–coached team. I think [defensive coordinator] Jerry Sandusky put the game plan in halfway through practice.

They told me to go tackle the guy with the ball. A lot of the times I was out on receivers. But this game, at the beginning anyway, they stacked me

Shane Conlan was
another outstanding
graduate of
"Linebacker U."
He was a consensus
All-American in 1986
when he was the heart
of the Penn State
defense that helped
give Penn State its
second national
championship, leading
the team in tackles
with 79.

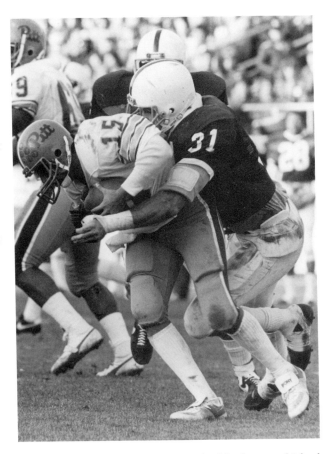

behind the two inside linebackers. They would clog up the blockers and I had
a chance to run and make plays. I loved that defense.

I hurt my knee during the game. I hit Alonzo Highsmith in the first quarter and then I got hit by one of our own guys. I heard my knee pop, but I
wasn't coming out, there was no way. I ended up intercepting two passes in
that game. The first one was my most embarrassing moment of that game.
Vinny Testaverde hit me in the face, and I took 10 steps and fell down. I was
so surprised that he threw it, and so excited, that I just tripped and fell on
my face.

When I intercepted him in the fourth quarter, I remember it was a pretty
good catch. I should have stayed on my feet and got into the end zone. We
ended up scoring and taking a 14–10 lead. You look back on Miami and how
many weapons they had, we knew they were going to come at us.

I was scared on that final drive. Obviously, I hoped for the best but I wouldn't say I knew we were going to stop them. When we won, that's the best feeling I ever had in football. I played in three Super Bowls, and obviously, it would have been different if we had won some of them, but we didn't, so that by far was the biggest game I've ever been in.

The next morning we were on the *Today* show, and in my five years at Penn State I talked to Joe more during that limo ride there than I did probably all throughout college. To be honest, I really didn't know Joe when I played. He was an offensive guy. He let Jerry run the defense.

But back then you've got to understand that we had 120 scholarship kids on the team. That's what he had to do. He's your coach first of all. Since I've finished playing, he's done so much for me. Any time I had any problems or I needed him to call someone, he would do it in a heartbeat.

I played for the Buffalo Bills and the Los Angeles Rams in the NFL, but if somebody asks me my favorite team, I say, "Penn State." Every year I get to be a bigger Penn State fan. I've never been so crushed in my life than after Penn State lost that Michigan game. [Penn State's only regular-season loss in 2005 came on the last play at Michigan.]

I was inducted [in 2005] into the Buffalo Hall of Fame, and those people know me as a Buffalo Bill. My kids and people around Pittsburgh, which is big Penn State country and where I now live, know me as a Nittany Lion. I'll take that any day.

229

Shane Conlan was a two-time first-team All-American and the eighth overall pick of the Buffalo Bills in the 1987 NFL draft. He lives in Sewickley, Pennsylvania, with his wife (and fellow Penn State graduate), Caroline, and their four children. He is involved in several businesses, including selling life insurance, and coaches his kids in various sports.

BOB WHITE

DEFENSIVE END

1982–1986

ATTENDING PENN STATE HAS GIVEN ME most of my opportunities in life, and I will always be grateful. I was a kid from humble beginnings. We lived in central Florida and at a very young age I did physical labor in the citrus groves and tobacco fields to help out around the house financially. Who knows what might have happened to me without football and Penn State? But I got here in an unusual way.

I grew up in Haines City and went to Bethune Middle School. I was a captain of the basketball team and ran track. My coach was Bob Eisenberg, who was from Freeport [Pennsylvania] and had played basketball and baseball at IUP [Indiana University of Pennsylvania]. I now refer to him as a foster brother. He was a very good coach, someone you warm up to pretty easily, and he took to me right away. He always had a lot of respect for me because I seemed to be focused and I had goals and things like that.

Ike came to the conclusion that, given my drive, given my focus, I would probably have better opportunities if I was removed from that environment. That's where this idea came for me to move to his hometown in Freeport, and eventually that's what we did. I was 15 at the time. My family in Florida consisted of my mother, my grandmother, four older sisters, two younger brothers, and my oldest brother in Atlanta. I never knew my father. My mom was not for it, but she realized it was a good opportunity for me. She went along with it, reluctantly, and allowed me to follow my goals and wishes. It

Some of Bob White's teammates on Penn State's national championship defense of 1986 grabbed more headlines, but he was one of the hardest-working, clutch players on the team. His 18 career sacks is tied with teammate Don Graham for ninth all-time.

was the beginning of my sophomore year in high school. I had never been to Freeport, but prior to making the final move I took one quick trip up during the early part of the summer.

Ike moved back a year before I actually moved up, and by WPIAL rules, we knew that I could not formally live with him. The first year, I lived with an African American retired social worker by the name of Ruth Moody and her two adopted children, Brian and Maria. After a year I moved in with Donna and Bill Zemer for my last two years of high school. Bill was the high school librarian and his wife ran a travel agency.

Ike didn't steer me to any particular college. I spent my time cracking the books and working hard as an athlete. When the recruiting started, I was contacted by about 100 schools. Penn State was my first official visit, and I was pretty sure that was where I wanted to go. But I had strong encouragement from other schools, and I took the other five visits to Pitt, Ohio State, Georgia, Florida State, and South Carolina.

Bob Phillips recruited me. Coach Phillips was a gentleman. He was very laid back. He wasn't your high-pressure-sales kind of person, but he would do a good job of being honest with you and sharing the information that you needed to know. After I graduated and came back to live and work here, I became very close to him.

Penn State stuck out for a lot of reasons. Having grown up in a big cattle-ranching town, I liked the wide-open spaces. That was very attractive to me. I also liked that when I was here on my visits, everybody I talked to seemed to talk about things that really mattered. So I walked away with a very comfortable feeling about Penn State. No one was making outlandish promises about starting right away and making me an All-American and a first-round draft pick. I was getting that from other schools. People here just said if you come here and apply yourself and work hard, good things will happen.

I wanted to be a good student but I struggled in my freshman year. I didn't grow up where around the dinner table you talked about your experiences in college because no one in my family had gone to college. I was very eager to go to college and believed I could achieve. But I had to be comfortable that the school I chose would support me and make me feel comfortable in an academic environment I was not familiar with. Penn State did that. When I came here for my visit, I was convinced that if I applied myself at Penn State, I would have the support that I needed.

Part of that was because of Joe and Sue. There were some things they wanted to do just to make sure I was committed, and they lived up to their word. Sue tutored me in English. She would work with me on papers I would write for classes. We would read books and discuss them and compare notes, whether it would be *A Tale of Two Cities*, *Moby Dick*, or *Huck Finn*. I never heard about them when I was a kid. We'd read and talk about possibly what this and that meant. I owe a lot to Sue and to Joe. I graduated with a degree in administration of justice and later on got my master's degree in counselor education in the College of Education.

There were 10 players in our recruiting class who redshirted in our freshman year and returned for a fifth year to win Penn State's second national championship. We played on two national championship teams, although we didn't play a game in '82. We almost won another in '85. We're pretty proud of being the only Penn State players to do that. [Kicker Massimo Manca, who was also in that recruiting class, played in the '82 and '86 seasons and redshirted in '83.] By the time we were juniors and seniors, we were a pretty close group and that was a big reason why we won. We started out as a bunch of guys coming in from so many different areas, like Shane Conlan from Frewsburg, New York, and me from Florida, and we all came together and truly took a liking to each other. That really was the catalyst for everything that happened after that.

233

I really don't think people realize what a strong ingredient this is—the closeness, the care for one another, the truly looking out for each other. It's taken for granted when things go well. When things don't go well, people don't realize what a huge part of that whole scenario that it is. That group had it. We truly cared for each other. The winning of football games and pulling out football games in the clutch really was a by-product of that.

The feeling was very unpleasant when we lost the championship to Oklahoma in '85. We wanted to be champions and the fact that we fell short was unpleasant, but out of that loss came the realization that we had what it took to do it. We grew from that whole experience, and it made it more certain a year and a day later that we would win, even though we were against a really great team in Miami.

We showed up with a coherent unit, a team of guys who really played well together. That clicked and that was the one thing that got us over that hump against a bunch of guys who later proved to be All-Pros: Michael Irvin,

Vinny Testaverde, Alonzo Highsmith. Some of those guys were great players, but they forgot that football is a team sport.

The most unusual thing that I remember about that whole game was the fact that we were partly into the third quarter before those guys from Miami truly realized what they were in for. They were accustomed to being flamboyant, to running their mouths, to bullying people, to talking people out of ballgames. There were clearly points in that game where you could see that it finally dawned on them that what they had been doing the whole week leading up to this game and what they had done the first half wasn't affecting those Penn State guys because we were still there going after them. By the time it sunk in, it was way too late.

They had a chance to win at the end, but the same thing happened at the end that had happened to us multiple times over the past two years and, in particular, that season. We had a group of guys who found themselves in a critical situation, and there was always that feeling, always that belief that somehow, some way, somebody in that huddle was going to make the big play. It happened multiple times. It happened at home against Maryland in '86. It happened the year before down at Maryland in '85 when we played in all that heat and they were ranked No. 1. We had to come from behind at home against Cincinnati and against Notre Dame in South Bend. Everyone was knocking himself out in every game trying to be the person who makes the play that we needed. It was no different in the championship game against Miami. So it held true even right down to the very last game of all our careers together.

What's it mean to be a Nittany Lion? It's about teamwork. No frills. Nothing fancy. All business, plain and simple. A let's-get-the-job-done attitude and the willingness and the desire to want to be a part of something special, part of something that's greater than any one individual. I'm a Nittany Lion forever.

Bob White was a three-year starter and part of the "Sack Gang" that terrorized opposing quarterbacks in the most successful era of Penn State football. Disillusioned with the politics of pro football, White returned to work for his alma mater in different capacities. Since 2001 he has been an associate director of athletic development.

RAY ISOM
Safety
1983–1986

I HAD TWO OLDER BROTHERS WHO PLAYED college football. They told me, "Make sure Mom and Dad take you early. Pick the bed you want, and when your roommate comes in just tell him this is the way it's going to be."

My roommate, Stephen Davis, came later and he was 6′8″ and 240 or 250 pounds. I had never seen anybody that big in my life and so the first thing I said was, "What side of the room do you want?" We didn't speak for two or three days. I was scared to talk to him. I was looking at this guy, thinking, "Oh my God, he's going to kill me," and he was the nicest guy in the world.

It's funny because he told me he was kind of scared to talk to me after seeing the way I played. The first year we roomed together people would call us "Mutt and Jeff" because he was the biggest recruit in the class and I was the smallest. We wound up becoming the best of friends and roomed together all four years.

I was recruited as a cornerback, and when I first got up there I didn't know if I'd be able to play. Everybody else they recruited was 6′ or taller. When I graduated from high school, I was 5′9″ or 5′10″ and I had wrestled at 155 pounds. When they first started going over plays on the chalkboard, I caught on pretty quick, so they wanted me to play safety with the freshman group until the veterans got there.

At Penn State the [free] safety makes all of the adjustments as far as the secondary, and he calls out the defensive sets. It was a good way for me to learn

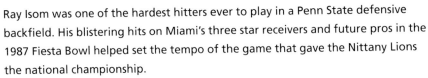

Ray Isom was one of the hardest hitters ever to play in a Penn State defensive backfield. His blistering hits on Miami's three star receivers and future pros in the 1987 Fiesta Bowl helped set the tempo of the game that gave the Nittany Lions the national championship.

the entire system, that way when the upperclassmen came, I could fit right in. When we put the equipment on, I had a couple of good hits, I guess, and that's when my roommate thought I was crazy. I didn't know any other way.

When the older group came in, Mark Robinson was the starting free safety and he was an All-American. I remember going to [secondary] coach John Bove and asking if I was going to go over to cornerback. He said, "No, I think you're doing good at safety."

When Mark would go out, the coaches would put me in. Stuff happened so fast and I was like, "This is not what's happening on the chalkboard." The offense would change and make adjustments. Everybody would turn around and look at me, and I'd be like, "Hold on, hold on!" One time [defensive coordinator] Jerry Sandusky told me in a scrimmage, "If you ever get confused and you don't know what to call, call 'Black King.'" That was our base defense. Well, he should have never told me that. The next couple of times I was in there and the offense made adjustments, I just called, "Black King."

Mark Robinson, Chris Sydnor, and Mark Fruehan would teach me the ins and outs. Without those guys, I would have been lost. When Mark Robinson got hurt, Darrell Giles and I split time at free safety. My sophomore year Darrell was number one on the depth chart and I was number one-A. I was upset because I thought I deserved to start.

Throughout spring and fall practice and even the first game of the 1984 season, I felt I played better than Darrell and that I was getting the runaround by the coaches when I asked why he was ahead of me. My frustration came to a head in the second game of the season at Iowa.

The very first series Darrell missed a tackle and Joe started yelling, "Isom, get in there! Isom, get in there!" I had a tackle and broke up a pass, and Iowa had to settle for a field goal. So the offense scored and the defense was getting ready to run back onto the field. I was putting my stuff on, and Darrell came up to me and said, "Ray, I'm back in." I said, "What do you mean?" He said, "They just wanted to talk to me. I'm back in."

I threw my helmet off, unbuckled my pants, and said, "That's it. I quit." Joe walked up the sideline, saw me, and said, "What are you doing out here?" I said, "Darrell told me I'm out." He said, "I decide who's in and out."

I grabbed my helmet and I ran out to the field. Bove was trying to stop me because they were about to run a play. I was so anxious to get out there that I ran into the game and called a timeout. I never came back out. I started for the rest of my career at Penn State.

237

Darrell and I were cool as far as friends. We hung out. Darrell knew that he was a cover safety and not a big hitter. The next year Darrell moved back to offense where he was a good wide receiver. I look back on it as an experience that I needed because in high school I always played. That made me fight for what I wanted. It's funny, I hear myself saying some of the things the coaches at Penn State said to me about not giving up. Now I'm trying to pass some of those same things on to my kids.

We went 6–5 my sophomore year, and I knew we would be better the next year. One of the biggest problems we had on that team was a lot of us weren't friends and I'm not sure we were as dedicated as we needed to be as a team.

My junior year, we got a new defensive backs coach, Ron Dickerson. He really stressed that we not only had to play together but that we had to like each other too. We hung out together and we could talk to each other. My senior year, a game at Alabama showed how valuable that proved to be.

Duffy Cobbs, one of our starting cornerbacks, had three or four sacks or tackles for losses because they kept putting the tight end on his side. We didn't have any corner blitzes in the secondary calls. Sometimes Duffy would say, "Ray, I'm going." I'd tell [linebacker] Donnie Graham, who lined up over the tight end, "Look, Duffy's going to go a lot of times when it's tight end only. Try to hold [the tight end] up a little more, that way I can help out over top of you." That was just between the players. Because we liked each other, we could do that. We had all played defense long enough to know what we were trying to accomplish.

That started my junior year, and my senior year we returned almost the exact same defense with the notable exception being Mike Zordich. By the time I left Penn State, we felt as a defense we could dominate anybody.

It was funny. In the huddle we all did our thing. Timmy Johnson, an awesome pass rusher, would be going crazy. Mike Russo would be cussing to himself, and Bobby White would say, "There's no need to be cussing." And then Shane [Conlan] would say, "We don't need to be talking about that. We need to be talking about stopping this guy!" Every game in the huddle it would be like that. It was fun, but we always knew that teams weren't going to score when we needed to stop them.

I think one of the reasons we lost to Oklahoma in the [1986] Orange Bowl is we were happy to be there. We were on vacation, we were in Florida for Christmas, and we got our butts beat. Oklahoma had lost the national championship the year before and they came to play football.

We went to the Fiesta Bowl the next year to play and win. Miami was happy to be there, talking all of this stuff, thinking they would blow us out, their wide receivers saying our defensive backs were too short.

Watching some of Miami's games, their wide receivers would catch a touchdown pass and then jump up into the stands. I remember telling coach Dickerson, "I might not make it to the end of the game because if one of them goes up into the stands, I'm going up after him. If they beat us, they beat us, but they're not going to embarrass us."

There were three or four hits early that kind of set the tone. On one play Gifto [linebacker Pete Giftopoulos] hit one of their players, and we're like, "Hold him up! Hold him up!" We were determined that they were going to pay for everything they got.

Brian Blades had a brother, Bennie, who was a safety. He was a hard hitter and a talker. When we were on the field, Miami's defense was on the sideline talking. Brian ran the same post pattern that Michael Irvin had run earlier and fumbled after I hit him. The ball was thrown a little high and I didn't go for the ball.

I remember looking to the sideline and telling his brother, "You better come get him, he ain't gettin' up!" Brian rolled over and ran straight to the sideline. I said, "Now you put a Pamper on him and send him back out here." That was the hardest hit I had in that game.

I got so mad at [cornerback] Eddie Johnson near the end of the game. Miami had a fourth down deep in its own territory late in the game. They ran a little 5- or 10-yard out, and Eddie went for the interception. The next thing you know, we're chasing Brian Blades down the sideline. At that time I wasn't worried about them scoring. I was more mad at Eddie and said, "What the heck were you going for the interception for?" That's when Shane said, "Ray, stop yelling, you've got to call a play!"

Next thing you know they're deep in our territory and it's like, "Hey guys, this is it." Gifto got the interception in the end zone and the thing is, Duffy was behind him and I was behind Duffy. Gifto is running down the field, and the game's over, and we're screaming, "Fall down! Fall down!"

After the season I got chosen to play in the Japan Bowl. They flew us into San Francisco after the game and we went to our hotel room. I got a phone call, and it was [Miami running back] Alonzo Highsmith, and I'm thinking, "Oh no, here we go." He said he wanted me to go for a drink with him, Jerome Brown, and Winston Moss. I said, "I don't know you guys. You might get me down there and jump me or something. I'll see you on the plane."

239

We get on the plane, and Jerome Brown comes up to me and says, "You're that little Isom guy, ain't you?" I said, "Yeah." I went back and had a drink with those guys and we actually started hanging out together. They said, "Man, we thought we were good. You guys are *good* defensively. I can't believe you shut our offense down like that."

Looking back, I wouldn't change a thing. I loved my career and my experience at Penn State. If I could do anything different it would probably be keeping in better contact with the guys.

One of the leaders of Penn State's celebrated "Smurfs" secondary, Isom was a second-team All-American in 1986 and still ranks among the school's leaders with 10 career interceptions. He played for Tampa Bay for two years before retiring due to injuries. Isom lives and works as an insurance claims adjuster in the Harrisburg area. He and his wife, Tracey, have four children, three of whom they adopted, and Isom helps coach or cheer for them in various sports.

JOHN SHAFFER

QUARTERBACK
1983–1986

M Y FRESHMAN SEASON IN 1983 WE PLAYED in the first Kickoff Classic. Penn State was coming off of a national championship and matched against a tough Nebraska team. It was my first trip to New York City and Giants Stadium. We were beaten badly, 44–6.

A memory from that game was when I was almost called in to play. Quarterbacks coach Bob Phillips was on the sideline talking to Coach Paterno, and I remember Joe asking Coach Bob if "we should put Shaffer in to play?" I was standing pretty close to them, and I thought, "Oh no, don't put me in. We're getting killed, I'm a freshman, and just not ready." Fortunately for me, they chose not to put me in.

Joe wasn't pleased with the performance of either junior quarterback. The following Monday we were preparing to play Cincinnati and I got to the quarterbacks meeting room early. Coach Bob was already there. He said, "We're going to get you ready to play, we want you to play against Cincinnati and possibly start against Iowa." I was shocked and nervous. Ultimately, I did play against Cincinnati. Against Iowa, Doug Strang, a junior quarterback, started, had a great game, and began what ultimately became a great career. Doug and I split time the following year.

In 1984, my sophomore year, we finished 6–5. Needless to say, Joe wasn't pleased. He made winter conditioning and winter workouts very tough. We were yelled at a lot and we spent extra time honing our skills. This disciplined

John Shaffer may have been the most maligned winning quarterback in Penn State history by fans and the media. The only defeat in his career came to Oklahoma for the national championship in the 1986 Orange Bowl, but he came back the next season to lead the Nittany Lions to their second national championship.

approach carried into an even tougher spring practice. After that winter and spring, we knew we didn't want to repeat 1984.

My junior season was the beginning of a great run for Penn State football. We had a lot of young talent and we won many games by only a few points, but we won. We became known as the team that "won ugly." Winning close games and never giving up no matter what the score served our team well in the pursuit of a national title. We learned to never walk onto the field expecting to lose. We always expected to win.

The 1986 Orange Bowl game was a highly publicized fight for a national championship. A lot was made of my performance and my comments after that game. I certainly didn't play very well, and Oklahoma had a great team. They beat us handily [25–10]. We spent a lot of time the week prior to that game talking to the media. We did interviews at all hours of the day and night. We did "live shots" back to cities in Pennsylvania for the 11:00 PM news. This really affected me and many other players. I've seen this overexposure affect many teams playing big games. It really took our minds off of the real reason we were there. In the end, hype or no hype, Oklahoma was a better team. Oklahoma's defensive backfield was the best that I've ever played against.

242

One event never really mentioned in the media was what happened after we got back to the hotel after the game. The previous year my mom had a serious brain tumor removed. Following the operation, she took medication that helped her but sometimes caused seizures. As you would expect, there was a lot of pressure, emotion, and disappointment that night for all of us. When I got back to my hotel room, my phone was ringing. It was my grandmother, and she said I needed to come to the hotel lobby immediately because my mom was having a seizure. In the end, my mom was fine, but the entire Shaffer family spent the rest of the night and into the next morning in the emergency room of a Miami hospital.

Fallout from the Orange Bowl loss began a very tough stretch for me. My confidence was hurt, and many Penn State fans vented and let me know how they felt about the game and my performance. In hindsight, it was a tough process to go through. I wouldn't wish it on anyone, but it was typical of athletics. In all sports, you always need to prove yourself. Nothing is ever given to you, and you have to earn your position every day.

When I got back to State College, I sat down with Coach Paterno and Coach Bob. After that meeting it was clear to me that I didn't have the starting quarterback job. The pressure continued to build. I went into every single workout following that January meeting never knowing what small thing would tip the scales in my favor. Matt Knizner, the other quarterback, and I were friends, but it was as fierce a competition as I've ever been in, in my life. The starting quarterback job was something I had worked for my entire life, and to have seemingly lost it was awful. I can't tell you how many times when the lights weren't on and no one was watching, I was practicing, working out, throwing. I'm sure Matt was doing the same thing.

Joe decided he would name the starting quarterback 10 days before the first game against Temple. He ultimately announced that I would be the starting quarterback. In hindsight, that competition was very tough to go through but it was a valuable learning experience. It helps me now deal with the controversy and competition I see in my current role.

The first game against Temple went extremely well for Penn State. [Penn State opened its 100th football season with a 45–15 win.] We all had a great game. That year we had a new quarterbacks/receivers coach, Jim Caldwell. He was a great coach and a great person and role model. His new philosophy served us well in that first game and the rest of that championship season. Coach Caldwell really allowed us to play to the offense's strengths. We concentrated on throwing to the tight end more with a more controlled pass offense. We had many more audibles, and many more decisions were made at the line of scrimmage. This really opened up the offense. After the Temple game, I certainly believed in myself again.

243

The Fiesta Bowl was the icing on the cake of a great season. [Penn State capped a 12–0 season by upsetting Miami 14–10 in the Fiesta Bowl to win the school's second national championship.] It was extremely important that we had already dealt with the hype of a national championship game. We were very prepared for the media circus, and much credit goes to our sports information director at the time, Budd Thalman. Budd was a secret weapon for us that week. Miami's players spent much of the time trying to win the game in the papers. They were greatly affected by the hype. Miami had a bunch of very vocal, confident players who thought they'd won the game before it started.

It is still easy to remember that game, the plays called, the players, and the emotion. It was a great moment in Penn State history, and it was the ultimate validation of what Coach Paterno preaches and the type of teams he puts on the field. That victory speaks to the players he recruits and the kind of people he makes successful. We were a great team. We had some very, very talented individuals but were nowhere near as talented as Miami. We just had the better team that night.

Years later I took my oldest son, John, to Penn State to watch a preseason practice. That day the team was practicing in Beaver Stadium. Johnny and I walked onto the field and stood in the end zone. Coach Paterno came over to say hello. After some small talk, he asked Johnny if he knew where he was standing. Johnny, of course, said, "Yes, we're in Beaver Stadium." Joe responded, "No, no, no. You're standing in the end zone. Your dad didn't make it here very often." It was very funny for both of us.

John Shaffer has been at Merrill Lynch in New York City since earning an MBA at Penn State. A managing director at Merrill Lynch, he distinguished himself as a director of football teams, going 66–1 as a starter in games he started since seventh grade. Shaffer won 25 of 26 starts at Penn State and ranks among the school's top 10 in career passing. He and his wife, Marta, also a Penn State graduate, have four children and live in Summit, New Jersey.

TREY BAUER

LINEBACKER

1984–1987

I LIKED PENN STATE GROWING UP, but I was really an Ohio State fan. I loved Woody Hayes, and Art Schlichter was my favorite player. I went to football camp after my junior year in high school, and that's when I really got exposed to Penn State. I really liked the coaches, I really liked Jerry [Sandusky], and my parents thought the world of Joe.

One of the reasons I went to the football camp was because of my dad. He was my high school coach and he thought it would be a great way to get evaluated. He said, "We'll have a better idea what kind of player you are and see if you are able to compete at that level. It would be great to see what the Penn State staff thinks of you."

I was there for a week, and after the third day, Franny Ganter came up to me and said they were going to offer me a grant. I told him I didn't know what that meant. He said, "Well, we're going to give you a scholarship. We'd love to have you." I told my father that and, of course, he didn't believe me. He was like, "Okay, you're there for three days, and they offered you a scholarship?"

I did not get a scholarship offer from Ohio State. It's a long story: I had kind of gotten into an argument with the recruiting coordinator at the time and we kind of had it out on the phone. I basically hung up on him and I knew I wasn't going there.

It's tough to say whether I would have gone to Ohio State if I had received a scholarship offer. I never took an official visit there. When I went to State College and saw it, it looked like everything I imagined a college would be: the old buildings, small town, and atmosphere.

My freshman year, I got hurt in camp and it was tough. I was a kid from north Jersey, a tough guy, that whole thing. I thought I should have been playing, but I missed two weeks of training camp, so I was done, basically, for the year. I was having a tough time coping with being away from my parents. It was a real tough adjustment for me.

One story I'll never forget happened during my freshman year. I got into trouble in study hall—it really wasn't my fault—but I got thrown out anyway, and Joe was not happy. I then showed up late for a team meeting, and Joe became even more upset with me. We had a team meeting every Sunday, and my sister was in town. We were out late the night before and, needless to say, I didn't look my best, walking in 10 minutes late. Do you know Joe Paterno time? You've got to be 10 minutes early and to this day I set my watch 10 minutes ahead. Anyway, here I came in with a hat on and I had long hair, which he hated, and I was 10 minutes late.

There was a collective gasp from the team as I came in, and Joe started screaming at me. I saw him after the meeting, and he told me, "Here's the deal: I've had it with you. You'll never play at Penn State. I will give you your unconditional release, I'll call any coach you want in the country and try to get you into another school. You might as well transfer because you'll never play here." Needless to say, I was hurt and very scared by what he was telling me.

I called my father and told him what had happened. He said, "I'd throw you off the team, too. You're a pain in the ass. You don't listen to him, you've got long hair, and you're a punk." I was very upset with him telling me this, but I knew I had to change or I would not be at Penn State very long.

I tried calling Joe to set up a meeting and explain my situation. I finally got a chance to see him and said, "Listen, I'm not transferring. I'm going to stay here and play." He was like, "Well, you're never going to play here." Obviously, it worked out for me. I have all the respect in the world for Joe. I just really believed I had the talent and the will to do it and wanted to prove it. I got my chance, cut my hair, and was never late to another meeting. I also never got thrown out of a study hall again.

Although overshadowed by his All-American linebacker teammate, Shane Conlan, Trey Bauer was known for his mean and nasty style of play on the field and his fiery temperament, which sometimes landed him in Joe Paterno's dog house.

During the '84 season, we were in pretty much every game but lost the games Penn State would usually win. After we lost our last game to Pitt to finish 6–5, Joe called us out in the press and basically said we were a bunch of crybabies. There was a lot of soul-searching there, believe me. Winter conditioning was not to be believed, and in the spring every practice was as intense as any game I played during the '84 season. It was really difficult, but that set us up for a really good training camp.

We weren't even ranked going into the '85 season. We were coming off the worst season Penn State had had in 20 years and were opening against Maryland, the No. 1–ranked team in the country. The preparation going back from winter conditioning to training camp, that really set the tone for the whole year. Preseason practices were so hard that guys were literally limping back to their dorm rooms to take naps between practices. Games were a joke compared to the practices. We upset Maryland [20–18] and went on to win the rest of our regular-season games.

We thought we were going to kick Oklahoma's ass in the Orange Bowl. Todd Moules was pancaking Brian Bosworth all night long. We just turned the ball over too many times and lost 25–10. It was really disappointing because we knew we were better than they were and the score didn't indicate that.

We had a lot of guys who could have left but came back, and anything short of winning the national championship would have been a disappointment. If you look at the '86 season, every game someone came up big. As Joe used to say, you kind of have to have a swagger about you, you have to really believe you can do it. By putting all the time and effort we did into preparing for it, I don't think there was a question that somebody was going to come up with a big play.

[Top-ranked Miami and No. 2 Penn State each finished the regular season undefeated and were selected to play for the national championship in the Fiesta Bowl.] We watched films of Miami for six weeks and we didn't have any doubt that we could beat them. I was really ticked that we were seven-point underdogs. We really didn't get the respect of the media because Miami was so great and everything else.

They were just talking crap from the beginning of the game. Just running through our warm-ups, that's how it started. It's like hitting a hornet's nest with a stick: at some point you're going to have to pay the piper, and they did.

All the smack Michael Irvin was talking was crazy. What did he have, five dropped balls in that game? You want to talk the talk, you've got to walk the walk. And to a large extent, they didn't. I think the thing that stands out in my mind is that every single play was so intense. Not that we ever took breaks in other games, but it seemed like every single down we were playing for keeps.

They played exactly the way we thought they would play. If Jimmy Johnson had half a brain, he would have run Alonzo Highsmith 50 times that game, but he didn't. You're not going to win any game turning the ball over seven times. I remember there was a still shot taken of Gifto intercepting the

248

ball, and it was intended for Brett Perriman but there were six of us around the guy. [Pete Giftopoulos preserved Penn State's 14–10 win by intercepting Vinny Testaverde in the end zone.]

If you could describe what the game was like in one picture, that would be it. That's kind of what we wanted, we wanted him throwing the ball where he didn't want to throw the ball. No one really believed that we could do it and we did it. I said in the press conference after the game, "I think we would have beaten them nine out of 10 times." Regardless of the fact that they had so many great pro players, I just really think we kind of had their number.

You could tell how happy Joe was. He believed in us, and we believed in him. As a group we didn't always agree with everything he did, and he didn't agree with everything we did, but we were all pulling in the same direction.

Classic Joe: we were playing in the Citrus Bowl after the '87 season, and I was a captain. A bunch of guys wanted to go see Def Leppard in concert. I went to Joe and said, "Listen, guys want to go to the concert, but curfew is 10:00. Can we make it 11:00?" And he said he'd think about it. So he said the next day at our team meeting, "Bauer came up to me and said you guys want to go to a concert to see a bunch of dead leopards. I'll extend the curfew, but just don't get in any trouble." We just started laughing, and he said, "What the hell is so funny?"

You always knew where you stood with Joe. Everyone knew he was the chief, but he tried to reach out to everyone and get on their level. I think he truly believed it when he told me I'd never play there. He's like your dad, he gets smarter as you get older. My kids are getting a little older and getting into sports. I go to their games and I go to their practices, and people know that I played at Penn State and want to ask me about it. It comes up a lot, and it's 20 years later.

Just like the opposing players who went against the three-year starter at linebacker, Trey Bauer has his hands full these days. He and his wife, Maureen, have twins and triplets—can you hear Joe Paterno laughing at that one?—and live in Garden City, New York. Bauer, who is the president of a financial services firm, ranks among Penn State's top 10 in career tackles and was a third-team All-American selection in 1987.

STEVE WISNIEWSKI

GUARD

1985–1988

I PLAYED JUNIOR HIGH AND HIGH SCHOOL BALL in Houston, Texas. My brother, Leo, who played at Penn State, is seven years older than I am, so I grew up rooting for Penn State. I remember when Leo was getting recruited and at that time I guess I was about an 11-year-old kid. Coach Paterno showed us around the locker room and the coaches' rooms. He took a ball cap out of his locker and put it on my head and said, "One of these days we're going to be recruiting you."

I think from that time forward I was hooked. I knew if I ever got to that level, Penn State was going to be the place for me. Large schools across the country ended up recruiting me, and I was blessed to basically go wherever I wanted to go. I really believed the education was more important than the football experience. I wanted to go somewhere where I felt confident I could get a good education and also play for a competitive football program.

I never envisioned myself as a great NFL star, so football was kind of my way to steal a college education. Through my brother's experience, I knew Joe Paterno was serious about education, that it wasn't just lip service. I was most serious about Penn State and the University of Virginia. Virginia had a really good business school, and I didn't know how serious Penn State was about recruiting me, so I thought maybe my chances of playing were better at a smaller school like Virginia.

Rather than follow his brother on defense, Steve Wisniewski became one of the toughest and meanest guards who ever played at Penn State. Even though he played on teams that stumbled in 1987 and 1988, Wisniewski became Penn State's third offensive lineman to become a two-time All-American.

I ultimately signed with Penn State, and in my freshman year [1985] I backed up Todd Moules, a team captain. My first two years, I was incredibly spoiled. I was part of teams that ended up going 23–1. The national championship experience in 1986 stands out to me.

I had double pneumonia in the week-and-a-half leading up to the Fiesta Bowl. I was so sick that, other than practice, I would just stay in my room. I had the shakes, I was sweating, and I had a fever. I had lost so much weight that, going into that game, the biggest one of my life and arguably for the school, I jumped on the scale and I weighed 238 pounds.

That was less than most of the linebackers I'd be facing. Up front I was going up against All-Americans like Jerome Brown and Dan Sileo. The feeling of victory was great because that team epitomized the heart and soul of a team. It wasn't like we had all the All-Americans like the University of Miami, but we just played with so much heart and believed in each other.

That national championship didn't go to the team with the most stars. It went to the team in college football that played most like a team. I played 13 years professionally, I was named to eight Pro Bowls, and I won a number of awards and honors, but that remains the greatest moment in my sports career. The feeling of elation wasn't so much, "Look what I did." I was just so happy for my teammates and John Shaffer, our starting quarterback and a classic example of a guy that gave everything he had, every single game. I was just so happy for Coach Paterno. To this day I've never experienced anything like that. My last two years were very frustrating because we felt like we were letting the university down.

To be undefeated, undisputed national champion and then to struggle so dramatically was very difficult. Coach Paterno has said this well: you learn more about yourself in defeat than in victory. You see if anyone is going to point fingers and give up and want to quit. That didn't happen with us.

I give Coach Paterno credit; he never changed. The head coach who went 23–1 was no different from the head coach who went 13–10 my final two seasons. He stayed steady, he encouraged us, we prepared hard every week.

Here's a funny Coach Paterno story: I was at Penn State helping my brother film a football clinic. This was approximately 10 years after I graduated, and I was playing for the Oakland Raiders at the time. We stopped by the coaches' office to say hello to some of the coaches. It was early in the morning and I had a baseball hat on because I hadn't showered that morning.

I heard Coach Paterno down the hall, and it was obvious he was coming to the meeting room. Coach Paterno walks through the door and looks up at me. He hadn't seen me for 10 years, but in a fraction of a second he said, "Steve Wisniewski, didn't I teach you better than that? Get your hat off in the meeting room. A gentleman doesn't wear his hat indoors."

After I got my hat off, he greeted me warmly and wanted to know how I was doing, how my family was doing, and everything else. He's never changed who he is as a person, he's never changed his core values. Some people are wishy-washy and go with the times. He stays constant. He's such an incredibly sharp guy that he'll remember your father's name and your mother's name. He remembers things about virtually anybody who ever played for him.

One of the greatest things I learned from my Penn State experience was the concept that no one is bigger than the team. I'm looking here in my study at my old Penn State helmet and it's plain white, and I've got a few jerseys around and my name's not on the back of the jerseys. The concepts and the values instilled in us—the team comes first, believe in each other, never speak poorly about a teammate—have stuck with me for life.

One of the greatest things Coach Paterno has said, when asked about his greatest team, is, "I don't know. I'll tell you in 20 years." He really believes his greatest team isn't which one had the fewest losses. His greatest team is what becomes of the men he coached. That's a rarity in collegiate and professional sports, but that just epitomizes the class and values of Coach Paterno.

Steve Wisniewski earned first-team All-America honors in 1987–1988. The first pick of the second round in the 1989 NFL draft, he got traded from the Cowboys to the Raiders and spent his entire career (1989–2001) with the Raiders. Wisniewski made the Pro Bowl eight times and will get serious consideration for the Pro Football Hall of Fame. He hasn't slowed down in retirement as he works in software sales and as a licensed Christian minister while also doing sideline reporting for radio broadcasts of Raiders games. He and his wife, Jeanne, and three children live in Danville, California.

ANDRE COLLINS
LINEBACKER
1986–89

IWAS ONE OF 19 CHILDREN, AND NOW that I have kids of my own I just really appreciate what my mother and father were able to do for us. My mother is probably the biggest reason I went to Penn State out of Cinnaminson High School in southern New Jersey. I kind of had my bags packed for Illinois. They wooed me with all of their different uniforms and all of their fancy colors and my name was on the back of the jersey. Dick Butkus, Red Grange, they really play up that tradition there.

I missed the national signing day because I was so undecided. Finally my mother pulled a little chair into my room and said, "It's time to sign those papers to go to Penn State." So I signed the papers and miraculously [assistant coach] Franny Ganter showed up at the front door ready to collect them. Looking back, I guess Mom always does know best.

Going to Penn State for me was the absolute best decision. I probably could never have had the same college experience anywhere else and certainly not the same opportunity that Joe Paterno, [defensive coordinator] Jerry Sandusky, and [linebackers coach] Joe Sarra provided for me. The football education I got at Penn State is what fueled my opportunity to play in the NFL.

I actually started my career as a cornerback at Penn State. Then I kind of ate my way to safety, and then I ate my way to strong safety. One spring day after my sophomore season, Paterno called Brian Chizmar and me into his

Andre Collins was the best of the Collins brothers to play for Penn State and led the team in tackles in 1988 (110) and 1989 (130). He also is tied with Jack Ham for the most blocked punts in a career (4) and most in a season (3 in 1989).

office. He said, "I need a linebacker and it's going to be one of you guys. When you come back on Monday, I want to know who it's going to be." Chizmar said, "Hey, I'm the starting safety and you're the back-up." I agreed. I saw the opportunity to go to linebacker and basically it was going to be my job to lose.

I left school that year at 200 pounds and returned in the fall at 220 pounds. I was tired of food. I didn't want to see food. And all summer Joe was saying stuff like, "We're not going to be a very good defense with Collins at linebacker," and he was right. I knew nothing about playing that position. I had spent all of spring practice at safety.

I went straight from safety to weak inside linebacker. A lot of the credit for my development goes to Joe Sarra, who made me tough in a linebacking sort of way. He just gave me the skills and got my footwork together. He taught me how to read things. In the greater scheme of things, Jerry Sandusky put together a game plan that was going to allow me to do what I did best: run and make tackles and be creative with what we did. Moving to linebacker was actually something that saved my career at Penn State.

We didn't have a winning season that year [Penn State went 5–6 in 1988], but the following year we had one of the best defenses in the country. It was hard being a part of the first losing season in 50 years with all of that great tradition and all of the players really do buy into the Penn State tradition. Contrary to popular belief, we loved the uniforms, especially loved the road ones with the white pants, the white jerseys, the black shoes, and white hat. We take a lot of pride in that.

To put it bluntly, Joe beat the crap out of us that winter. We had to get up at 5:30 in the morning, which is something we had never done. We had to trudge through the snow to Holuba Hall for team aerobics. Men just aren't built for aerobics, and that woman, she crushed us.

Then after that we would have to wear a collared shirt to the dining hall. Joe just laid down his law. It was collared shirts. You had to wear socks. There were no walkmans allowed in the football facilities. I just remember that being an awful, awful winter. By 3:30 in the afternoon, you're sleepy and starting to fear that next morning of aerobics. It was just a long, tough winter, but he whipped us into shape.

Training at Penn State was one of the hardest, toughest things I had ever done. Our practices were the same way. We beat on each other as if it were a championship game. When you got into the real game, you were just battle-ready. You were tough, there was nothing you hadn't seen. The games were almost like a walk in the park after practicing against our first-team offense full-speed almost every day.

I used to like to fight a little bit on the practice field like so many other players. One particular time, it was the coaches' clinics scrimmage when high school coaches from Pennsylvania, New Jersey, the New York area, and Ohio all come to Penn State for the weekend. So we were in Holuba Hall, and coaches were around the field four and five deep.

[Tight end] Al Golden came off the ball and, for whatever reason, it was pick-on-me day. He gave me a little extra after the play, and we got into a fight. Joe said, "Aww nuts, Collins! Get outta here!" So he threw me out of practice in front of all these coaches. This is before my senior year, and I was a preseason All-American and excited about practicing.

There was a dead silence, and I screamed, "C'mon, Joe! For crying out loud, it wasn't me!"

He said, "It's never you!" He was making a point to all of them that you don't take anything from anybody. You're the coach and you're the boss. I hit the showers.

In 1989 we had a chance to be really special, but we lost our homecoming game [17–16] to Alabama. It was a heartbreaker. Even though we lost, that was college football at its best. Penn State–Alabama. The stadium was packed. It was the most beautiful October day. The quiet that permeated campus that night just really hit home about how much Penn State means to the students and to the alumni and how much winning those ballgames means.

I used to race over to the locker room every afternoon just to hear what Coach Paterno was going to say next. It was always so exciting to listen to him talk about what was going to happen that day, throwing in his words of wisdom. For me, it was a thrill. Listening to my brothers talk about him, it was the same thing for them, and I have so much respect for him even now.

There's always a little bit of that underdog thing with Penn State, being ripped off of three or four national championships, including 1994. Penn State never really got the respect that it truly deserved.

For me, being a Nittany Lion is about working hard, being blue-collar, no-nonsense Penn State. Here we are in our all-white uniforms, but we know and you know that we're hitting harder than you, that we've prepared better than you, and that we practiced harder than you all week, so come get your licking. That's how it was for us, and I think that still exists today.

My wife went to the University of North Carolina at Greensboro, and whenever she sees a Penn State person, they're always decked out in Penn State or they've got a flag and stickers all over their car. She says, "What is going on up there? It must be some kind of cult." I say, "Well, you just have to experience it to understand why the fans and the student body and the alumni are like that. It's just a special place."

In my mind, we're the greatest college football tradition that exists.

The Collins name is one of several that is synonymous with Penn State football and it is easy to see why. Andre, a first-team All-American in 1989 and a finalist for the Butkus Trophy, led Penn State in tackles in 1988–1989 and is one of five brothers who played for Penn State. The others were Gerry, Phil, Jason, and Aaron. Collins played in the NFL from 1990 to 1999 and is now the retired players' director for the NFL Players Association. He and his wife, Ericka, have three children and live in Arlington, Virginia.

The
NINETIES

DARREN PERRY
HERO
1987–1991

I HAD DREAMS OF BEING AN NBA PLAYER instead of an NFL one. Had I been a little bit taller I think I would have tried to take that path. Growing up in Virginia, Alonzo Mourning went to a rival school. I remember Georgetown coaches coming down to watch him play a high school game, and that night I happened to score 30-some points.

After the game my basketball coach said one of Georgetown's coaches asked about me. But he told them I was already going to Penn State on a football scholarship. I said, "Oh man," because Georgetown had smaller guards and I thought maybe with my quickness I could fit into its system. That may have been wishful thinking, and I had already committed to Penn State.

Throughout the recruiting process I had been torn because I really liked North Carolina. It had a beautiful campus and was a lot closer to home. It's funny, I didn't have a fantastic visit to Penn State as far as those guys rolling out the red carpet. They pretty much put you in a dormitory and tried to show you the true college experience and what it would be like as a freshman. North Carolina was different. They put you up in a big, fancy hotel and had you meet the governor.

I had become friends with Keith Goganious, and we had talked about going to an in-state school like Virginia. Keith decided to go to Penn State, and I was going to North Carolina at the time. I hadn't told my mom that I was going to North Carolina. Then I thought about it and ended up going

Darren Perry was arguably Penn State's best defensive back in the 1990s and is tied with Pete Harris for second in career interceptions with 15. He also is tied with Dennis Onkotz with three career touchdowns on interceptions.

to Penn State. Penn State was coming off a national championship, and if you went to North Carolina you were going to a basketball school where football was maybe an afterthought.

It was tough that first year [1987] because you're trying to feel your way through it. You're not playing—Willie Thomas, Leroy Thompson, and Gary Brown were the only freshmen in my class who actually played, and it was only sporadically—because the speed of the game is so much different than in high school.

After my redshirt freshman year I wanted to transfer. I was playing a little corner and a little safety and kind of going back and forth. I thought I should be playing more and, when I wasn't, I said, "You know what? I'm leaving this place. We're 5–6, we're struggling, and things aren't going well. I'm not happy here." I wanted to get home more often. It was a seven-hour trip by car, and I didn't even have a car.

I stayed except one time after my redshirt sophomore year I walked off the field during spring practice. I was having a tough day and I was still being shuffled back and forth between various positions. We were practicing at Beaver Stadium, and Ron Dickerson, our secondary coach at the time, yelled at me for something. I said, "Enough of this crap," and I just started heading out of the end zone.

I had played hero during the '89 season and alternated with Gary Brown, who had been moved from tailback. I became frustrated with that. I thought I was doing a good enough job that it didn't warrant someone taking snaps with me—that had a lot to do with me walking out of practice. That was probably my toughest time there because you go into your sophomore, junior year and you want to start establishing yourself as a player. I felt they were trying to take that away from me.

Ron and I kind of had a heart-to-heart the next day. I came back and just kept working, and things started falling into place for me after that. I kept getting better and better, and they eventually moved Gary back to offense.

Starting out in 1990 we lost to Texas and then to USC, and those were two games we felt we could have won. We followed the losses with seven-straight wins and were a confident group going into a late November game at No. 1 Notre Dame. We felt we had nothing to lose. For the big, big games, Joe never got uptight. Then the games that you didn't think were that important, that's when he really put the hammer down.

We got down early [21–7], but nobody hung their heads. I remember being on the sidelines talking to Mark D'Onofrio and Keith Goganious, saying, "Hey, that's it. No more drives." They got a couple of big plays on us but they weren't doing anything we couldn't stop.

After we scored to tie the game in the fourth quarter [21–21], we figured if they gave us the ball back, the way our offense was going, we were probably going to score again. So we got to a third down and we were playing a cover two, but it was man-to-man coverage underneath. Reggie Givens was playing one of their wide receivers with help over the top from myself along with Willie Thomas. I just remember Rick Mirer dropping back and staring at the guy. Reggie had good coverage underneath, and the ball just sailed on Mirer. I was right there to make the interception.

I had had a couple of touchdown runbacks that year, but I had also had a guy come up behind me in the West Virginia game on about the 2-yard line and poke the ball out. So when I made the interception, I was thinking about that because I was kind of showboating a little in that West Virginia game. I was running but I wasn't running because I had to be as careful as possible and just get the ball in the middle of the field.

I think the way things were going, we felt, "Hey, we're supposed to win this ballgame." I think that's the belief that everybody had on the sidelines. I was confident Craig Fayak would make the field goal, and he did.

263

When we got back to State College that night, you'd have thought we'd won the national championship. It was so crazy that we didn't even go out that night. We just sat around our apartment and kind of reminisced and talked about what a great feeling it was to beat them because everybody contributed. Everybody felt like they had a part in the victory.

Going into the next season, we felt everything was in place for us to win a national championship. We had so many starters coming back on defense and we were experienced at all the key offensive positions. We started out with Georgia Tech in the Kickoff Classic and it had just come off a co-national championship. We knew winning the game would be a great way to set the tone for the season.

We went out there and really handed it to them. [Penn State beat Georgia Tech 34–22.] Then we came back home and blew out Cincinnati 81–0. I think I played a quarter in that game.

USC didn't have anything that year, but in a nationally televised game they upset us [21–10]. We probably had the mindset that all we had to do was show up and things would fall into place for us, but they didn't. They jumped on us early and we never really responded.

We kind of got caught up at looking down the line because we had Miami on the schedule. We kept thinking, "This is going to be great. It's the first time Penn State's played Miami since that national championship game. We're going to be undefeated and they're going to be undefeated." Had we beaten Miami [Penn State lost 26–20 in the Orange Bowl], I still think we would have had a good chance of playing for a national championship. We finished No. 3 after beating Tennessee in the Fiesta Bowl. That's when you sit back and say, "We should have a playoff system," because we were playing our best football at the end of the season.

Looking back, I'm glad I stayed at Penn State. It was the best four years I had in my life. If I had to do it all over again, I wouldn't change one thing about it. It made me grow as a person and as a football player. To me, what it means to be a Nittany Lion is representing a great tradition, a program that stands for not only a lot athletically but academically, as well. There's a pride there that may be unlike any other school.

Darren Perry's 15 career interceptions are tied for second on Penn State's all-time list. A first-team All-American in '91, Perry's three interception returns for touchdowns are tied for the most in school history. An eighth-round pick by the Pittsburgh Steelers in the 1992 NFL draft, Perry started the first 110 games of his career and played in the NFL from 1992 to 2000. Perry, who intercepted 32 passes for Pittsburgh, joined the Steelers' coaching staff in 2003. He, his wife, Errika, and four daughters live in the Pittsburgh suburb of Wexford.

TERRY SMITH
WIDE RECEIVER
1987–1991

O NE OF THE THINGS JOE ALWAYS TOLD ME during my recruitment was, every four years, one of his classes played for the national championship. I definitely wanted to be a part of that and play at the highest level, and it didn't get any better than Penn State. It also helped that my dad is a Penn State graduate, though my older brother, Harvey, played for West Virginia.

My cousin Marques Henderson was a senior at Penn State my freshman year, so he helped make my transition a lot smoother. I still remember my very first practice—this was when freshmen reported before the upperclassmen. We had a quarterback named Doug Sieg in my class, and he had one of the strongest arms I've ever seen. I was running a 10-yard slant and he threw the ball so hard it split the web between my pinky finger and my ring finger. I'm thinking that I just got 10 stitches put into my hand, I'm probably going to be out for a little bit.

Well, I was right back out there for the second practice, and that was kind of my initiation into big-time college football. I had another one not long after that. It was a few weeks later and the veterans were in camp. Brian Chizmar initiated me as well after I went across the middle. He hit me pretty good. I was seeing stars, I was a little dazed. He said, "Welcome to big-time football." I didn't miss any time though.

I redshirted my first year and then was our number four receiver in 1988. We really didn't know how to take a losing season [5–6]. We were all

265

Terry Smith was known as a "big play" receiver and was an exceptional downfield blocker. His 55 receptions in 1991, including 10 at Southern Cal, is second only to Bobby Engram and O. J. McDuffie in the Penn State record book for catches in one season.

disappointed that we were the first team to have a losing record under Joe. We vowed that it would never happen again and we worked extremely hard during the off-season and re-committed ourselves.

I started in 1989, and we never got blown out of a game. We just didn't know how to win that year. [Penn State went 8–3–1.] We knew the next year we could get those one or two plays that make a difference in ballgames.

We started off a little shaky with close losses to Texas and Southern Cal. I think part of it was we had worked so hard during the off-season and our preseason training camp was probably the hardest of my five years there. For the Texas game [a 17–13 loss], I don't think we were fresh enough. I think we were a little worn out from camp and just couldn't get our legs back.

Then we went out to USC and got caught up in the travel and playing out in the Coliseum. We played a good game but we just couldn't make the plays at the end to get the victory. We had a team meeting and pulled together and vowed it wasn't going to be like the previous years. We got hot and won quite a few games in a row.

The Notre Dame game, we knew we had a chance. All week we were watching film and we knew we had to contain Rocket Ismail. The first half of the game he did get loose, and towards the end of the second quarter Willie Thomas put a hit on him. I think he got a deep thigh bruise, and it took him out of the game. From that point on, it was our ballgame. We had faith Craig [Fayak] would make the field goal and we had momentum, too, so we knew it was right. That's pressure for you. You're in South Bend with all of that history and tradition and Notre Dame was No. 1. That [24–21] win was a big-time thrill.

Most of our guys returned for that following year. We had an experienced quarterback, the offensive line was strong, and our defense was pretty much intact. We felt it was our year but we started out with an early-season loss [21–10] to USC. That loss woke us up again and we won a few games in a row.

We ran into Miami, which had a 50- or 52-game winning streak at home in the Orange Bowl. We beat them in every facet of the game except the scoreboard. [Smith caught a pair of touchdown passes in Penn State's 26–20 loss.] We beat them up and down the football field, but two long plays just broke our backs. Miami was a great team that year and it ended up sharing the national championship with Washington.

We played a great game and just didn't finish it. We re-dedicated ourselves, refocused, and got ourselves back on the winning track. We ran the table from there, went to the Fiesta Bowl, beat a tough Tennessee team [42–17], and finished No. 3. By the end of the season, we were the best team out there.

I got into coaching in 1996. My first year at Hempfield High School in Greensburg, Pennsylvania, we made the playoffs for the first time in forever. We lost to North Hills in Pittsburgh, which had LaVar Arrington. We were leading 14–0, and then LaVar did a LaVar-like thing and just took over the game.

In 2002 I took over as head coach of my alma mater, Gateway High School. It wasn't long before Tom Bradley, the coach who had recruited me at Penn State, started coming around. My stepson, Justin King, was on the team and by his senior year he was widely considered the top defensive back prospect in the country.

It was really, really crazy because he could pretty much go anywhere. You name them— USC, Oklahoma, Texas—and they were coming to Gateway. I told Justin he had to pick a school that fit his personality and that was best for him—not for me, not for his mother, not for his friends, or anyone else.

Through the whole recruitment he really liked Michigan, he really liked Florida, and he really liked Penn State. His first pick was actually Florida. He was going to commit there and then the school went through a coaching change.

We had gone on an official visit down there, and he met with the president. The president told him, "Ron Zook will be our coach the next four or five years." Justin took that as a bald-faced lie, and it caused him to re-evaluate the whole recruitment process. If a guy could sit there and tell him that and then a week and a half later fire the guy, who's telling the truth?

With Penn State and my experiences, I knew what Paterno was saying was true. Michigan, we didn't know if they were telling the truth. Tom Bradley also did an excellent job of recruiting him as well. Every area, he turned out to be the best recruiter for Justin.

When Florida kind of fell out of the picture, Michigan pretty much took everything for granted. They didn't think a kid like him could go to Penn State. They had a certain arrogance that they had him in the bag. Justin felt like if he went to school there then that's probably how they would treat him. He just didn't like it.

People ask me why Penn State people are so loyal. Unless you go to Penn State and play football there, outsiders will never understand it. It's a pride. It's a loyalty. It's a trust. We can get a sideline pass to any football game. My brother, Harvey, played for West Virginia and he can't get a ticket. It's a family. We're all in it together.

You see players from all different generations and there's just that mutual respect. It's an awesome feeling, and I was proud that Justin chose to be a Nittany Lion.

Terry Smith ranks sixth on Penn State's all-time receptions list (108) and seventh in receiving yards (1,825). His cousin, Marques Henderson, started at hero on Penn State's 1986 national championship team. In addition to being the head football coach at Gateway High School, Smith is the athletics director. He and his wife, Alison, also have a daughter and live in Pittsburgh.

O. J. McDUFFIE
WIDE RECEIVER
1988–1992

I REMEMBER CRYING THREE TIMES AT PENN STATE: after we lost games we very easily could have won against Miami in 1991 and '92 and right before the start of classes my freshman year.

Oh man, is Joe tough, especially on the freshmen. He's really trying to mold that Penn State-type of football player. One time I called home crying, saying, "Mom, I don't like it here. The coaches are jerks. The players are jerks." I didn't know if I was going to be able make it.

That I ended up at Penn State was a bit of a surprise and not just because I grew up in Ohio. I wasn't really into Penn State because, as a kid, it's all about the flashiness and you look at Penn State's uniforms and go, "Oh my gosh, are you serious?"

[Secondary coach] Ron Dickerson recruited me and he was just a great person, my mother loved him. It actually came down to Penn State and Notre Dame, even though Ohio State was my hometown school.

They had fired Earle Bruce when I was in high school, and John Cooper came in. He came to my high school to visit me and he didn't even know what position I played or anything about me. That kind of turned me off.

The Monday after I got back from a visit to UCLA, I got a package and it had a six-page letter that Joe Paterno had handwritten. A lot of other schools tried to use different things against Penn State, saying, "Young guys don't play and you'll never get to play baseball there." Joe always emphasized the positives, saying I was going to get an education and get a chance to play for the national title. The fact that he sat down and wrote that letter really impressed me and really impressed my mom.

I went to a small high school, and people were already wondering if I could compete at the highest level of college football. It's a heck of an experience and certainly a humbling one because you were always the man at every other level of football; even as a freshman in high school I started on varsity.

But when you get to Penn State or places like that, everybody's little peons at first. A lot of kids fold because they're so used to getting things handed to them. I was motivated by my competitiveness. I didn't want to lose at anything, and there was no way I was going to sit back and let three or four guys be ahead of me at wide receiver.

The first year in general was a long one, even though I got to play a little bit. We weren't very good, and it turned out to be Joe's first losing season ever. It's a whole different thing for a kid to go in and try to play major college football and balance that with school and social life and everything else. After that first year I couldn't wait to get back to Cleveland, go home, and get back to my friends in high school. When I returned in the fall, I never left Penn State.

I thought I was well on my way after my sophomore year, but I got hurt in the 1990 season opener when [wide receiver] Dave Daniels came down on my leg. I didn't need surgery after tearing the medial collateral ligament in one of my knees, but I had to rehab it for six or seven weeks, so the coaches decided to redshirt me.

That's how I think I got to be the best receiver I could be because I got a chance to work against our first-team defense every day in practice. I was out there getting pounded, but I liked bringing out the best in them because they were bringing out the best in me.

The one thing I did miss was when we beat No. 1 Notre Dame on the road. The funny thing about that is I was in Philadelphia with one of my teammates. We hung out with his family and watched the game.

We were supposed to stay until Sunday, but once Penn State won the game we drove back to campus. We had to get back just to enjoy the victory. I just wished I could have been a part of it, especially since Notre Dame had been my No. 2 choice coming out of high school. Finally getting a chance to play

O. J. McDuffie was not only an outstanding receiver who still holds the Nittany Lions' record for most receiving yards in a game, with 212 against Boston College in 1992, but also a fine punt returner, leading the team in returns in 1991 and 1992.

against those guys next year was great. I killed them, and that was a fun game because I scored three touchdowns.

We were really close to winning the national championship in 1991. The Miami game really messed it up for the rest of the season, and that basically happened to us two seasons in a row. That's the way it is in college football, you lose one game and you think that's it.

I thought we were the best team in the country by the end of the '91 season, and no one gave us a chance in the Fiesta Bowl against Tennessee. They had so many stars—Carl Pickens and Dale Carter—and Tennessee showed us so little respect at some of the banquets. They didn't think we should have been there.

It seemed like some of the media were not giving us much of a chance to win that game either because of Tennessee's talent level, speed, size, and strength. We just went out there and played Penn State football and hit them in the mouth, offensively and defensively. They got up on us early and then we just went on a tear where they didn't know what hit them. [Penn State rallied from a 17–7 deficit to win 42–17.]

I told coach Paterno right after the game, "I want to come back." He said, "Wait a minute O.J., let me see where you're going to go in the draft and we'll go from there. If you're going to be a first-rounder that means you've done all you can do for Penn State. You're about to get your degree and you can always come back and get that."

After he did his research he said, "Well, it looks like you're going be a late first- or early second-round pick." I said, "I definitely want to come back." That made it so much easier. I took classes in the spring and then I only needed one class in the fall to graduate.

That was a tough season because every other Penn State sports program was playing in the Big Ten except for us. Actually, some of us seniors had to go to Big Ten Media Day in Chicago. All of the other teams were excited and we're sitting there thinking, "Why are we here? This is such a waste."

We put so much into the Miami game and played our butts off. A couple of plays went the other way, and we came up short again [17–14]. It was all downhill from there and a lot of people kind of quit. [Penn State lost five of its last seven games after starting the '92 season 5–0.] I remember the Boston College game. I was so upset because they were just killing us with their tight end, Pete Mitchell. I had over 200 yards receiving in that game, but I couldn't get anybody to come along with me, no matter what I said on the sidelines. [McDuffie's 212 receiving yards are still a single-game Penn State record.]

Even though the season didn't go the way we wanted, I definitely think I made the right decision to return for my senior season, and not just because it almost gave me a guarantee of being a first-round NFL draft pick. I didn't think I needed it then, but in hindsight I really did need to polish my skills and have some more big games against big schools, so a lot of scouts recognized what I could do.

The college experience, there is nothing like it. A couple of guys from high school I'm still cool with, but everyone who went through the growing pains with me at Penn State and the crying and the hugging and the partying and the fun, those are my best friends now and that's what it's all about. I understand what [USC quarterback] Matt Leinart was doing [in 2005] when he returned for his senior season even though he may have been the first overall pick of the NFL draft.

You always hear the term, "Lion's pride," and for me that really surfaced when the team struggled prior to 2005. No matter what, I always wear my Penn State stuff proudly. I used go to meetings with the [Miami] Dolphins with my Penn State stuff on because I know what it means to be a Penn Stater. It's not about wins and losses. It's about what kind of man you develop into and how you go into the community and represent yourself and your family and the university.

If a coach from another school was getting heat, a lot of his former players wouldn't care. We genuinely cared and told people to leave Joe alone because we're proud to have played for a man like that. We're grateful for what he's done for us and the way he treated us.

I'm blessed to have made that decision to go to Penn State because I've talked to other [players] and they have very little or zero love for their university. At Penn State, we're very proud people and we'll continue to be because of Joe and our experiences there.

The second Penn State wide receiver in school history to earn first-team All-American honors (1992), McDuffie is still prominent in the Penn State record books, and his 63 receptions in '92 are a single-season record (tied with Bobby Engram). He also played baseball for one season at Penn State before long bus rides and games in cold weather convinced him to concentrate on football. He played for the Miami Dolphins for nine seasons and became one of Dan Marino's favorite targets. McDuffie, who led the NFL with 90 receptions in 1998, is still a fixture on the South Florida sports scene as he is a talk show host for 790 The Ticket in Miami. He lives in Fort Lauderdale and his next-door neighbor is another former Lions great, Ki-Jana Carter.

LOU BENFATTI
DEFENSIVE TACKLE
1989–1993

I WANTED TO STAY NEAR MY HOME in northern New Jersey, four or five hours away. I visited Nebraska and was also recruited by Notre Dame, Rutgers, and Syracuse. Once I went up to Penn State my senior year, I just fell in love with it. Penn State was clearly the place I needed to be. It was just a gut feeling.

My freshman year I redshirted as a defensive tackle, and it was overwhelming. I went against Dave Szott and Roger Duffy, two guys who went on to the NFL, every day in practice. They beat me up pretty good. I started my redshirt freshman year. I had worked hard that summer and my goal was to start. At first it was tough but I got really comfortable. That's where I wanted to be.

I started 49 straight games and I didn't even realize it until the second to last game of my career. My redshirt freshman year I think we were 17th or 18th in the polls when we went into Notre Dame. I can remember starting the game, and we weren't doing so well. We just weren't playing together and we were down 14 points going into halftime.

At halftime I remember [linebacker] Mark D'Onofrio getting up on a table and screaming, trying to help us identify what we needed to do. He said, "Listen, this is one of those moments when you can get out or join in." In the second half we came back and tied it, Darren Perry had that late

Lou Benfatti is one of the few players who started every game he played for Joe Paterno. Benfatti started from his redshirt freshman season on, and in 1993 he won the Hall Award as the team's outstanding senior.

interception, and Craig Fayak kicked the field goal [for a 24–21 win]. You don't really forget those types of games.

We had some bumps in the road in 1991. It was just one of those things where we outplayed ourselves. We still only lost two games and went out to Arizona and played Tennessee in the Fiesta Bowl. I remember Reggie Givens making some big plays in the second half, and it's fun when you're able, in the most important time, to make the plays that you practice over and over [Penn State won the game 42–17.]

We had built up to that Miami game the following year and started 5–0. The fans were so loud, and there were just two or three plays that turned the game. I remember Darren Krein making the interception and scoring, things like that just kind of swung their way and took the wind out of our sails. We ended up losing a 17–14 heartbreaker.

It's one of those things where you get a little depressed and I think the following game, when a couple of things didn't go our way against Boston College [Penn State lost 35–32], we just didn't follow through with some of our assignments and finished the season 7–5.

Going into the Big Ten my senior year was really interesting. Joe had asked fullback Brian O'Neal and myself to attend the Big Ten media conference, and it was an honor being a captain and representing one of the top universities in the country. Everybody was gunning for us that year. Hey, they're pretty comfortable with who they have there. What are we trying to do coming into their territory?

It was a fun to see the big-time tradition of Michigan and Ohio State. The one thing Joe did my senior year was develop a breakfast club. He felt he had gotten out of the loop of the players. Players from all the different classes had breakfast with him every Tuesday, and we just shot the breeze and talked about current situations that were going on. It helped him see where we were coming from as players and student-athletes.

We were close to playing in the Rose Bowl that year. We had a couple of letdowns at key points in key games. After the 24–6 loss at Ohio State, we won our last five regular-season games and then beat Tennessee [31–13] in the Citrus Bowl. It was a good ending to my football career at Penn State.

Joe just does not let you quit. He never, ever gave up. As a leader, he was constantly raising my game to another level. That's not very common these days. He helped me understand where I was and where I was going as a player and as a person.

What does it mean to be a Nittany Lion? You never give up. You battle. There's a pride that you have. There's a certain way that you carry yourself, especially upholding the tradition of the men who have fought to get the name of Penn State where it is.

276

Lou Benfatti earned second-team All-American honors in 1992 and was a first-team All-American in 1993. He played three seasons with the New York Jets before a serious neck injury cut short his playing career. A school administrator, he and his wife, Jodi, have four children and live in Jefferson Township, New Jersey.

CRAIG FAYAK

KICKER

1990–1993

First and foremost, being a Nittany Lion means winning but also winning with dignity and winning with integrity, and that's something I've carried over with me in the business world and everything that I really do. It's certainly important to win and we all want to—that desire to win is critically important—but you can't win at all costs. There has to be a certain amount of dignity and integrity that goes along with it.

The second thing is learning how you can get through any situation, regardless of how a situation may look at the present moment, if you're around people who you trust and love and work together as a team. At the end of the day, it's going to work out and it's going to work out well for you. It's also having calmness under pressure. That's especially true for a kicker. I had many situations in games where maybe we didn't play so well early on and it looked bleak, but toward the end we always seemed to pull it out.

The Notre Dame game late in the season of my freshman year is the best example. We were down 21–7 [at halftime] at their place, and they were No. 1 in the nation. They were beating us up pretty good, and I can remember Jerry Sandusky and Coach Paterno saying, "Hang in there," and "We're going to pull this out." It didn't feel like that at halftime.

But we came back to tie it in the fourth quarter and, with less than two minutes left, Darren Perry intercepted a pass [by Rick Mirer at midfield] and

Despite being hampered by injuries in the latter part of his career, Craig Fayak was one of Penn State's "clutch" kickers and an outstanding scholar-athlete who won a prestigious NCAA post-graduate scholarship in 1994.

ran it back to about the 20. My knees sort of buckled. The gravity of the situation lands on your shoulders and you start to think about, "This is really going to come down to us kicking a field goal."

Franny Ganter was the kicking coach. Neither he nor Coach Paterno said a thing to me. Absolutely nothing. They did that on purpose because one thing the coaches at Penn State know how to do well is how to motivate every player, and every player is different. Some need a kick in the pants. Some need to be left alone. They knew right away that I was the kind of person that if you just let me be alone, I would gather my thoughts and I would do my job. That's how they always treated me in my entire career at Penn State.

So I was very nervous at first, but once I stepped on the field, that all went away. That's why the routine is so important. When you get out there in a game, you put it on autopilot and you just go. Everything looked the same, everything felt the same. The snapper, the holder, the goal posts, the dimensions for the kick, it was all the same as practice. It was by far the most focused I think I've ever been in my life. I was very confident. Bob Ceh was the center and Bill Spoor was my holder. Those two were so instrumental, not only in that kick but certainly in my first two years at Penn State. Bill had such a calming presence and he didn't flinch at all during that kick. Bob put that ball back there all the time, very consistently. So I never had to worry about a bad snap or a bad hold. It never even entered my mind. It allowed me to focus on just kicking the football.

Right before Bill put his knee down on the ground for the spot, I said, "Hey, it's just like kicking in my backyard. I've made this kick a million times." I wasn't being cocky. I was just confident. And that's exactly what happened. I knew it was good as soon as I hit it. I saw the trajectory and I knew it was right down the gut. I don't get overly excited in any situation, really, so I just threw my hands up and looked at Bill as if to say, "What do we do now?" and he just grabbed me and everyone jumped all over me. It was a pretty exciting feeling. I remember distinctly in the locker room [quarterbacks] coach Jim Caldwell, whom I was close to, just giving me this look in his eye as if to say, "You really have no idea what you just did and what this is going to mean for your life."

I had just kicked the field goal to beat the No. 1 team in the nation and I guess they just assumed I knew to go into the media room. I was just exhausted. I showered and I was so excited to get home I walked out into the bus. I'm sitting on the bus eating my lunch when someone came and told me they wanted me in the media room. They had been looking all over for me. Here I was an 18-year-old freshman and I just guessed they didn't need me.

I wasn't very highly recruited, although I received a lot of letters. West Virginia wanted me to walk on, Oklahoma recruited me to play baseball and football, and William & Mary had a scholarship offer, but that was it outside of Penn State. Jerry Sandusky recruited me and Jerry was a big reason why I went to Penn State because of his integrity and just who he is. They recruited me as an athlete. They knew I could kick, and when I got there they needed me right away as a kicker. But they always kept me around as an emergency quarterback, too. I finally got to play quarterback late in my senior year when I took four snaps against Northwestern.

I kicked for four years, and Notre Dame was the high. The low was the Miami game my junior year. It was just devastating. I missed a couple field goals and one chip shot that we should have had, and we lost [17–14]. But that's when I had my back trouble and it was just an emotional and painful time for me. Before my junior year I started to lift heavier weights, especially with my legs, and really started to get stronger. Those first few games of my junior year were some of the best games I ever played. But the way I was lifting weights and my kicking technique caused my vertebrae to start to crack, and I rehabbed for almost a year. I didn't play for the last half of that season. I was really never the same kicker after that, but I really learned a lot about myself going through that. It helped shaped who I am today.

I do remember the field goal I kicked in my senior year [1993] at Ohio State that made me the all-time leading scorer. At that point in your career, you really don't think about it because records aren't really that important at Penn State. It's really about the team. But in hindsight it was one of those kicks that was really important because it was a validation of all the ups and downs I had gone through in my career. It was a muddy, muddy game. It was snowing. It was cold. The wind was blowing in my face, and for some reason Coach Paterno sent me out there for a 49-yard field goal. We had a lot of trouble in pregame, just snapping the ball, holding it, and I was almost shocked when he sent me out there. I guess I got a bit lucky. I hit the ball perfectly. It floated and went through.

I signed with the Cowboys as a free agent. I was there for a few months, got cut, and went back to Penn State. I had a couple of classes to finish my degree and I coached the kickers and defensive foreign team for the '94 team. That was my recruiting class, Kerry Collins and Kyle Brady and those guys, but they had been redshirted. So I was with them every step of the way to the undefeated season, Big Ten championship, and Rose Bowl, and it was really fun to be around them.

Of course, Joe Paterno is the symbol of Penn State. He sets the tone for all of it. While certainly Joe can't control every action of every player every time, he's just so consistent with setting a tone for what it means to be a Nittany Lion. The program is all about consistency, whether you're going to class, whether you're in the locker room, whether it's game time, whether it's after a game, whether it's the off-season, or whether it's during the season. There is stability and consistency with how they approach not just football but life in general.

Those plain uniforms and black shoes say it all. Once you put them on, you know it's something special. I would never in a million years change it at Penn State. It's our brand. It's who we are. It's just so simple and yet so emblematic of who we are and what we stand for. I think it's great and I love it.

Craig Fayak's 282 points is still Penn State's career-scoring record, and he also holds three other career records: in field goals (50), attempts (80), and consecutive field goals (13 in 1992). Since 1999 he has worked for a pharmaceutical marketing and sales company, and is currently in charge of domestic sales operations. He lives in the heart of New York City.

KYLE BRADY

TIGHT END

1990–1994

AFTER PLAYING IN THE 1994 CITRUS BOWL, we were getting cleaned up in the locker room. Some of my teammates were joking, saying, "Hey, it was good playing with you." I said, "Hey, what do you mean? I'm coming back next year." They were like, "Yeah, right."

They really thought I was going to skip my fifth year and enter the NFL draft. I'm glad I didn't now because I would have missed the '94 season [Penn State went 12–0], and I wouldn't have been drafted as high as I was [ninth overall in 1995].

The '94 season fulfilled a promise Joe Paterno had made to me, one that helped steer me to Penn State. He said, "Kyle, if you come to Penn State, I'll guarantee you that you'll either play on an undefeated or a national championship team. Every player I've ever recruited has had an opportunity to do that if they've stayed here and played out their years."

Another big factor in my going there was Jerry Sandusky. He was the defensive coordinator but he was the one who recruited me. Some of these coaches would tell you anything you wanted to hear. Jerry was just very honest. He said, "Hey, I can't make you any guarantees. You come here, work hard, do your best, and see what happens."

Even the recruiting visit was a real experience. Penn State puts you up in a dorm room with one of the freshmen or sophomores. You see and experience exactly what you are going to see and experience your first couple of years at Penn State.

The last day I was there happened to be my 18th birthday. My mom and I were getting ready to drive back to Harrisburg, and they told me to stop by the football office to pick something up before I left.

We got there and Joe and Jerry were there. Joe went into his office and came out with a cake with burning candles on it and sang, "Happy Birthday." I wish I would have had a camera because that would have been a classic moment to capture on film and to show my grandchildren.

I visited Miami, Michigan, and Virginia. I liked Miami a lot and I was also thinking of going to West Virginia since one of my best buddies from high school was going to Morgantown and my girlfriend at the time was there also. Deep down I felt Penn State was the best place for me.

My freshman season in camp, I was actually playing a good bit with the second team and catching some balls and blocking pretty well. One day I was blocking somebody, and the pile kind of came down on my ankle. I thought it was broken because I heard a lot of popping and cracking. It was real painful and turned out to be a pretty severe high-ankle sprain.

It was around the third or fourth game that the coaches were starting to prepare me to play, and I was probably only going to go in on two tight end, goal-line situations. I asked Jerry Sandusky if I could redshirt. He told Joe, and Joe let me do it. I'm glad I did it because I wouldn't have been there for that fifth year, the undefeated season. Not that I coasted by any means that first season.

We called Tuesday practices "Bloody Tuesdays" because we really got after each other. I would walk off the practice field feeling like I had just played in a game, having the equivalent of soreness and fatigue as I had after high school games. The exhaustion level you feel is just tremendous and then you've got to go to study hall for two hours.

For me that discipline was as close as I experienced to being in the military. The whole thing was such a wake-up call for me because I didn't have much discipline before that. We had mandatory breakfast between 7:00 and 8:30 and classes after that. Meetings started at around 2:30 and we had practice until 5:30 or 6:00. Then we had mandatory dinner and study hall from 7:00 to 9:00.

I remember going home one weekend when Penn State was traveling to see my high school team play. The game seemed so slow. I wished I could put the pads on and do it at that level one more time, having improved already so much just because of the demands that were placed on you.

My redshirt freshman year [1991], I didn't know what kind of season it would be because Al Golden was back. He was one of the captains of the team, and I respected him a lot. He ended up getting hurt early so I started several games.

We beat Cincinnati real bad [81–0], and I scored a couple of touchdowns and ran a few people over on the way to the end zone. I think that game may have had people saying, "Oh wow, maybe he is going to live up to the hype." As the year went on, Al got healthy, but I still played a lot and scored four or five touchdowns that year.

Nothing seemed to go right for me the following year. I got a real bad virus during preseason practice so I missed the majority of it. When I did get back I had a few neck problems; it was just one thing after another.

Troy Drayton started doing really well, and the coaching staff started using him a lot of different ways. He had been a big wide receiver who moved to tight end, and everything worked out well for him. He ended up being a second-round pick by the Los Angeles Rams in 1993.

284

Any time you have those nagging injuries, it's hard to get on track, and Joe was on me because he knew I had a lot of potential. I thought I was working hard in practice, but he mentioned one time in the newspapers that he thought I was having a little slump.

Sometimes your confidence can fluctuate a bit when you don't see yourself doing the things you want to do. You have the tendency to start pressing and trying too hard in those situations, which makes it worse sometimes. Joe was frustrated with what was going on with me, and I was frustrated, too. Sometimes he'd get on me at practice and I didn't want to hear it. One time in the paper I think I said I wanted more opportunities or I wasn't happy with my role, something like that.

I went to practice one day and there was a green jersey in my locker, which was a demotion. I was so angry about that. I knew what he was doing, that it was just a head game, that he was trying to get me to respond the way he wanted me to. I just didn't want to deal with it at all.

I walked off the practice field and Craig Fayak, who was my roommate, thought I was just going to the bathroom. He said, "You had enough, huh? You heading out?" I said, "Yep, you got it." I walked into the locker room, took my stuff off, put my street clothes on, and just got in the car and left.

Kyle Brady is considered one of the best tight ends ever at Penn State and gained special recognition for his blocking, which was an integral part of the offensive line schemes that helped lead the undefeated 1994 Nittany Lions to the Big Ten title.

I was driving down the road, not sure if I was really leaving for good or just doing it for a little while. I thought about transferring to a Division I-AA school and playing out my years there. Deep down I think I didn't want to quit. I just needed some time to settle down a little bit and, obviously, I returned to Penn State.

With Troy gone after that season, Penn State went back to the more traditional use of the tight end and utilizing what abilities I had. The first season in the Big Ten was almost a feeling-out year. We did pretty well, going 9–2 in the regular season. We lost to Ohio State, and Michigan had a big goal-line stand against us. We could have easily been 10–1 and gone to the

Rose Bowl that year. The next year we understood what it was all about, winning the conference and getting to the Rose Bowl.

Things went pretty well in 1993 for me, and I thought real hard about going pro. As a player, you start to hear rumblings of "Oh, there's some teams out there that would like to have you" and sometimes you would have agents call you.

I wrote a letter of inquiry to the NFL. The league has a service where it interviews a few general managers and sees where you might go. It came back saying I might go anywhere from the fourth to sixth round. There were other people telling me there were teams that were real high on me. I later found out that if I had come out, the Cleveland Browns were going to draft me in the second round. That's when Bill Belichick was there and he was all set to draft me in the first round at the 10th spot when I came out the following year.

Going into the '94 season, we felt confident that we were significantly more talented than we had been the previous years. We didn't feel like we would lose any games that year because of the rhythm the offense was in and just the feel we had for one another. We had a good understanding of what it was going to take to succeed. We had put in all the time during the summer that was necessary to succeed, did everything Joe asked of us, and proved it on the field. There was a general feeling in the locker room that it was our time.

The Illinois game seemed like it was almost a conspiracy, that somebody was trying to sabotage us. The hotel lost electricity and couldn't make our pregame meal, so they had to order in pizzas. There was a lot of noise and a lot of parties going on near the hotel, and guys had trouble sleeping the night before the game.

Not only did all of that go haywire, but the first half went haywire. We were losing 21–0 at one point and then 28–14. But on that final drive, there was that certainty that we were going to get it done. [Penn State drove 96 yards for a touchdown late in the fourth quarter to beat Illinois 35–31.]

We went undefeated that season but didn't get a chance to play Nebraska for the national championship because of bowl tie-ins. Every other level in college football has a playoff, and you ask yourself, "Why?" Right now, it can be honestly said that there has never been such a thing as a national champion in Division I-A college football. They've all been mythical. It's a shame the system is what it is.

If I had to do it over again, I'd pick Penn State. Although there were some tough times and some ups and downs, overall it was a good experience. I'm glad I got to play for a coach like Joe Paterno, who was also serious about academics. I'd be glad to send my own kid to Penn State one day if he wanted to play there.

I play with guys now from all different schools, and you can see with some of them that there isn't the discipline and the understanding of what it takes to succeed on a consistent basis, and not just in football. Joe really teaches you about what it means to be a responsible citizen and a contributor in society.

A first-team All-American in 1994, Kyle Brady's 76 career receptions rank second to Ted Kwalick in school history for career catches by a tight end. After starting his NFL career with the New York Jets, Brady blossomed in Jacksonville, and the 228 receptions he had for Jacksonville from 1999 to 2004 were the fifth-best of any tight end during that time span. He and his wife, Kristi, have a son and live in Jacksonville, where they are involved with multiple charitable causes.

KI-JANA CARTER
RUNNING BACK
1991–1994

AGE 18 TO 22 IS PROBABLY ONE OF THE MOST important times of your life. That's when you learn responsibility and discipline, and Joe Paterno really stresses that and instills that into us. My days at Penn State were some of the best times of my life.

Not that I ever would have guessed I'd end up at Penn State since I grew up 10 minutes from Ohio Stadium as an Ohio State fan. The one thing I knew about Penn State was I hated their uniforms because they were so bland. The summer before my senior year of high school my coaches wanted to talk to Penn State defensive coordinator Jerry Sandusky about some things for that season. They made plans to drive to Penn State and they asked me if I wanted to go and look at the school.

I didn't really have anything else to do in the summer other than working out, so I went with them and met David Daniels. We hit it off and I later met O. J. McDuffie and Leonard Humphries. We just talked about school and being from Ohio and stuff they had to go through being a top athlete from the state and going to an out-of-state school. I was impressed that they took the time to talk to me and spend time with me, and I thought, "This might be something I might like."

Eventually, I told the [Penn State] coaches I'd take an official visit there and, lo and behold, O.J. was my host. He always called me to check on how I was doing and didn't pressure me into going to Penn State. He said, "If you

Ki-Jana Carter's spectacular running for the vaunted 1994 Lions' offense made him a consensus All-American and the runner-up for the Heisman and Maxwell Trophies. His exciting 83-yard touchdown run on Penn State's first play from scrimmage in the 1995 Rose Bowl was one of the most dramatic in school history.

ever need to talk to me, here's my number," and I really appreciated that. I visited other schools, and some of the players would say, "You need to sell yourself to us. Why do we need to sell ourselves to you?" Penn State was the other way around.

I decided in the end that Penn State was the place for me. I wanted to go to a college that not only focused on football but grades, too. I was one of the first people from my family ever to graduate from college, so that was a big thing for me. Joe Paterno had a great track record for graduating players and for how the players conducted themselves off the field.

Even after I verbally committed to Penn State there was still enormous pressure on me to go to Ohio State. Ohio State gave me tickets to a basketball game one time, and I wanted to go watch Jimmy Jackson. I knew him and met with him a lot when I was getting recruited. When I got there, I had people telling me, "Change to Ohio State, you still have time. You need to stay home and support your Buckeyes." After that I didn't go back to another game because it was just too much.

I didn't waver on my decision, and my mom really stayed firm on Penn State, saying, "That was your first choice." She loved Joe, and I think that's a big thing for Penn State. Parents respect what Joe does because you see a lot of places where, once the four or five years are up, the program doesn't care about the player anymore unless he's one of the best in its history.

We had the number one recruiting class that year in the country and the unique thing was that everybody got along from day one. We didn't have a bunch of egos. I think it really hit me that the coaches were going to redshirt me when we played Cincinnati [in 1991]. We beat them 81–0, and it seemed like everybody besides me got to play.

Joe took me aside after the game because he knew I was mad. He said, "We're probably going to redshirt you. I know you're disappointed, but keep working hard like you've been doing and good things will happen to you before you leave this program." After that my game days came during practice. You had some of the upperclassmen getting mad because I was running so hard and I said, "I want to get better because I want to get out there and play, too."

When Richie [Anderson] decided not to come back [after the '92 season], Stephen Pitts, Mike Archie, and I talked. We said, "Everybody's going to try to make a controversy out of everything and who should be playing. Let's go out there and work hard and push each other to be the best." It was a friendly competition. There was never any animosity or jealousy.

Before our third game of the season at Iowa Coach Paterno and [offensive coordinator] Fran Ganter came to me and said, "You're going to start this week." I had a good game against Iowa and just kind of settled in as the starter. I knew I had to carry the torch from our past running backs and help this team get to its ultimate goal of winning the Big Ten.

We came close that first year in the conference, and the Michigan loss is tough to take to this day. Physically we beat them, but they made more plays than we did and stopped us on their 1-yard line four times. Coach Paterno's so adamant about mano-a-mano, wanting to run the football up the gut. After I got stopped on a run up the middle on third down, I was like, "Coach, I run a 4.3 [in the 40-yard dash]. Pitch me the ball and I'll outrun everybody to the pylon." For one yard, ain't nobody going to catch me to the corner, that's how I felt. Basically Michigan had 10 guys over our center and stopped us on fourth down when we went up the middle.

Two weeks later the conditions were bad at Ohio State, but they just beat us. I cried because I played my heart out and I was devastated, being from that area. After that Ohio State game I didn't lose again at Penn State.

During the off-season it was, "Look, it's Pasadena or bust." Our first meeting I stood up and tried to be a leader. I said, "Publications are talking about Ohio State this and Michigan that. We're going to take this thing one step at a time like a ladder. But we're going to be undefeated. We're going to be in the Rose Bowl."

We started 6–0 with a tough win at Michigan, and the Ohio State game two weeks later was just sweet redemption for me. They were in our house and we were going to make them our houseguests, go out and, from the first play on, hit them in the mouth. I didn't get a chance to really reflect on everything until near the end of the game when I was on the sidelines and we were killing them. The whole off-season the year before I kept hearing from people in Columbus and players even, "See, we told you you should have gone to Ohio State." I said, "We'll see next year," and I got the last laugh on that one. The score [63–14] could have been a lot worse, but Joe didn't want to run it up.

I feel better when people reflect back on what might have happened had I played in all of the games. I only remember playing two full games, against

Michigan and Illinois. Rashaan Salaam [of Colorado] won the Heisman and he deserved it because he had 2,000 yards. I only had 190 carries. Salaam had 100 more than I did, and he only had one more touchdown and 400 more yards than I did. Had I played every game to the end, I think I would have had around 2,200 yards.

The runner-up finish in the Heisman voting wasn't even close to being the most disappointing one I had to endure that season. We finished second to Nebraska in both polls, even though both teams were undefeated. The best analogy with that is getting 100 percent on a test and getting a B. I get a little gratification now because the reason they're doing the BCS is our team. ESPN [in 2005] did something on the top teams of the last 50 years, and I want to know why our team was number three or four and Nebraska's '94 team was not even on there? If they were so much better than us, then why weren't the '94 and '95 Nebraska teams on that list?

We watched Nebraska and Miami play in the Orange Bowl while we had our midnight snack the night before the Rose Bowl, and [NBC announcer] Bob Costas called it the national championship game. After Nebraska won, I said, "Bleep what Bob Costas said. We're going to go out and win this game and show everybody we're the best team in the country. He doesn't have a say in who the true champion is."

We got the ball at the 17-yard line on our first possession of the game, and the first 15 plays were already scripted. I said, "Let's take this to the house," and center Bucky Greeley said, "I'll meet you there." [Carter broke free for an 83-yard touchdown run and finished with 156 rushing yards and three touchdowns in Penn State's 38–20 win over Oregon.]

The possibility of going to the NFL didn't really hit me until our last game of the regular season against Michigan State. That's when everything started swirling, all of the Heisman stuff and Big Ten and All-America awards. People were saying, "You might be a high draft pick next year," and I said, "Well, when that time comes, I'll think about it." I really had a tight-knit group, and none of that stuff affected what I was doing on the football field. I didn't decide anything until after the Rose Bowl.

Joe came to me after the game and said, "You did all you could for Penn State. Who am I to tell you to stay because I want you to stay? You can take care of your mom now." The big thing for me was I was going to graduate that spring. During the whole NFL process I took 18 credits. Granted, I was traveling a lot, but when I put my mind to something and focus, I'm going to get it done.

It's hard to say in one word what it means to be a Nittany Lion, but it goes beyond football. It's about respecting people and loving your neighbor and treating others how you want to be treated. It would be hard to find a player at Penn State that if someone met him he would say, "He's a real jerk." Hands down, I would go to Penn State if I had to do it all over again.

A serious knee injury sustained during the preseason of his rookie year prevented Ki-Jana Carter from fulfilling his promise in Cincinnati, although he did play in the NFL from 1995 to 2004. Carter averaged a whopping 7.8 yards per carry on the way to 1,539 yards and 23 touchdowns in 1994. A consensus All-American, he finished second in both the Heisman and Maxwell Trophy voting and was the number one overall pick of the 1995 NFL draft. Carter, who is involved with real estate, lives in Fort Lauderdale, Florida, and is the next-door neighbor of fellow Penn State All-American O. J. McDuffie.

BOBBY ENGRAM
WIDE RECEIVER
1991–1995

I GREW UP IN SOUTH CAROLINA and there was a lot of pressure on me to stay in the South coming out of high school. But I kind of fell in love with Penn State after attending summer camp there.

As soon as my father and I left campus after my official visit, he said, "I know you're coming here." I guess he saw it all over my face and in my eyes. We were extremely close, and I think he felt really good about the place as well.

He was big into academics. He just didn't want me to be the typical football player. He wanted me to get my degree and do something meaningful with my life. He threatened many times to pull me off teams if I didn't keep my grades up from middle school on.

On the first day of classes my freshman year I was in the Schwab Building and my academic advisor, Don Ferrell, came and got me out of class and took me to Joe's office. I walked in, and there's this eerie, somber silence. Joe and [starting wide receivers] Terry Smith and O. J. McDuffie were in there. Joe said, "I've got some horrible news," and he told me that my father had been killed in a car accident.

I kind of laughed. I thought it was a joke—I didn't think there was any way that that could happen. I glanced at everyone in the room again and saw how serious that it was and I was speechless. From that moment on my whole life changed.

Bobby Engram is considered the greatest clutch receiver in Nittany Lions' history. He still holds nearly all of Penn State's receiving records, including career receptions (167), yardage (3,026), touchdowns (31), most games over 100 yards (16), and most touchdowns in one game (four against Minnesota in 1993).

The thing that really hurt was my father never got a chance to see me play one college football game. That kind of sticks with me to this day, but you move on and realize things happen for a reason.

I had played as a true freshman, so going into 1992 I was touted as, "Okay, we're really waiting for this guy to break out." I was battling for a starting job and I had a pretty good training camp.

I ended up going out one night and doing some stupid things. [Engram was charged with felony theft and got suspended from the university for a semester. After a groundswell of support that included a letter from South Carolina's Speaker of the House of Representatives, he received probation.] Again, my whole life changed. It happened almost one day to the year my father died. I don't say that to use it as an excuse. I say it because I was a young kid going through a lot of issues. I was angry, I was hurt, I was confused, but I tried to act like I had it all together.

I kept a lot of things bottled up inside and didn't talk to a lot of people. In terms of what I did, I take full responsibility for it, but anybody who knows me knows that was out of character.

That turned out to be a reality check. I got hate mail, a lot of people dogging me, saying I didn't belong at Penn State. My name was all over ESPN and every newspaper saying I had been kicked out of school. I wanted to leave Penn State, I'm not going to lie, and my mom said, "Nope. You are going to stay up there and you are going to face the music."

I ended up getting a job and staying with Pat Daugherty, who owns The Tavern and to whom I still talk today. I rented a room at his house for a while, and it was perfect because he lived off-campus and he and his wife gave me a place with solitude where I could get back on my feet.

It was a killer every Saturday to have to watch those games, especially when Penn State was at home. I'm supposed to be on the football field making plays and here I am at home watching it on TV, not knowing if I'm going to get that chance again.

I did get reinstated to school and the team, and on our first play [from scrimmage] of the 1993 season, I took a screen pass to the house. I remember getting a couple of tremendous blocks from my linemen and I was just so determined to get that ball into the end zone every time I touched it. [Engram caught eight passes for 165 yards and four touchdowns.] Never in my wildest imagination did I dream I would do that in my first game back.

We came close to winning the Big Ten in our first season in the conference. We had a tough loss to Michigan in which we had a first down on the 1-yard line. They stopped us four times and then ended up going down and getting a score. Then we lost a tough one at Ohio State in the snow and the rain.

Honestly those two losses planted the seeds for the 1994 season. Michigan and Ohio State, those were the big dogs in the Big Ten. They're saying, "You can come in here and beat everybody else but you can't beat us," so to speak. We took that personally and once we started playing the '94 season we realized pretty quickly that we had something special.

The Michigan game in Ann Arbor was a back-and-forth battle, and we had to put together a drive near the end of the game. On the touchdown, the coaches called a post route for me, and I remember seeing a seam where their guys weren't sure what was going to happen. [Quarterback] Kerry [Collins] fired the ball on a direct line right on time. I remember snagging it and saying, "Just hold on to this ball." I remember how silent it was after I made that catch. You could hear a pin drop. That was a beautiful thing.

297

It's hard to explain to this day the catch I had two weeks later against Ohio State. If I'm not mistaken, Kerry scrambled, and when he did I broke across the field and he gave me an opportunity to make a play. The pass was behind me, but I was able to get my right hand out and I just stopped the ball dead in the air, like it stuck to my hand, and I pulled it in. [That play symbolized Penn State's dominance in a 63–14 win.]

Ohio State had a good team, but I think we were just hell-bent on paying them back from the year before. They had big offensive linemen, and we had small defensive linemen. I think their plan was to flood the field and pound the ball since the wet field had taken away a lot of our quickness.

I would go back to catch a punt and let the ball hit the ground. It would just splat and stop right in its tracks, that's how much water was on the field. We wanted to pay them back and we just exploded and never looked back.

The Illinois game later that season was a unique situation. We lost all of the electricity in our hotel the morning of the game. We had pizza and subs for breakfast. We got to the stadium so late that we only had about 10 minutes to warm up.

They were up 21–0 before we knew what had happened. I never thought once that our perfect season would come to an end. Call it naïve, confident, cocky, or whatever, but we just had a belief in ourselves that after four quarters of football we were going to come out on top.

I'll never forget that last drive. They had [linebackers] Simeon Rice, Kevin Hardy, and Dana Howard and a couple of good cornerbacks who went on to play in the NFL. It started snowing, we were on our own 4-yard line, and we were on the road against the number-one defense in the country.

I got hit so hard one play I got my helmet knocked off, but we didn't care. We just made plays [Penn State drove for a touchdown and held on for a 35–31 win].

It pisses me off to this day that we finished the season with a perfect record and finished second in the polls to Nebraska because it wasn't right. It should have been a split.

All we could do was win every game, and Joe wasn't in the business of running up the score. I just wish we would have had some way of settling it on the field like we saw USC and Texas do in the 2006 Rose Bowl. Then there would be no dispute.

I was extremely close to leaving for the NFL after the '94 season. I had a serious girlfriend at the time—she is now my wife—and she was really in my ear about finishing school. She had talked to my mom, and I knew my mom wanted me to get my degree and my father would have wanted me to get it.

I also felt I needed to be loyal to Joe even though he never said, "I need you to come back for me." [Quarterback] Wally Richardson and I had played against one another in high school, so I wanted to come back and be a playmaker for Wally as well. Finally I felt it couldn't hurt to come back and spend another year under [wide receivers coach] Kenny Jackson's tutelage. I look back and I think I did the right thing.

We lost a couple of tough games in '95 and were down late in the regular-season finale at Michigan State. We had about three different wide receiver screens that we ran that year. On one of them I would come straight down the line of scrimmage, and we would release the linemen. It was essentially like a punt return: get the ball in my hands and let me read blockers and try to make people miss.

We actually called that play two times in a row at the end of the Michigan State game when we were on their 5-yard line. The first time we called it, I was wide open and I would have walked into the end zone but I didn't get the ball. I told Joe, "Call it again," and he said, "Get the ball to Bobby." Then he said, "You better score."

Michigan State played it so well the second time that, after I caught the ball, all I saw was one white jersey and a bunch of green. If you ask for the ball, you've got to make the play. I was able to split two defenders, duck underneath them, and keep my balance. Once I saw I had a shot at the goal line I just went for it with everything I had. [On what would have been Penn State's final play from scrimmage, Engram scored a touchdown to give the Nittany Lions a 24–20 win.]

Penn State was a place where I really grew up and had a chance to become a man. You have good times, you have some bad times, you face adversity, but through it all you've got a support system and know you're around good people.

A first-team All-American in 1994, Bobby Engram also won the inaugural Biletnikoff Award that year given to the best wideout in college football. He is the only player in school history to post 1,000 receiving yards in a season and he did it twice (1994–1995). Engram, Penn State's all-time leading receiver, has been playing in the NFL since the Chicago Bears selected him in the second round of the 1995 NFL draft. He started at wide receiver for the Seattle Seahawks in 2005 and played in Super Bowl XL. He and his wife, Deanna, also a Penn State grad, live with their three children in the Seattle area. Their youngest son's middle name is Simon, the first name of Engram's father.

JEFF HARTINGS
GUARD
1991–1995

Back in the early 1990s, schools were still allowed to give 105 scholarships. If not for that, I don't think I would have been offered a scholarship by Penn State. There were four other offensive linemen in my class: Marco Rivera, a guy by the name of Scott Stratton, who I think was maybe the top offensive line prospect in the country, Andre Johnson, and Keith Conlin. I was the fifth guy with no fanfare really, no all-state, and from a small-school division in Ohio.

People always ask me why I went to Penn State, and there are two reasons: the chance to be coached by Joe Paterno and the chance to win a national title. Also, I figured if I could play at Penn State, then I'd have a chance to play in the NFL, and that was my ultimate goal.

What really helped me out, strange as it may seem, is I tore some meniscus in my knee during my first preseason camp. I needed surgery and missed the whole season. All I did was eat and lift and rehab my knee—I went from 245 pounds to 265 pounds before spring practice the next year. That gave me enough strength and enough weight to be able to compete. Getting up to 265, that's where Paterno loved guys. That was the perfect weight. He never allowed me as long as I was there to get over 280.

In 1992 I was sometimes playing as much as half a game as a redshirt freshman. I was like, "Oh my goodness. Are you kidding me? I'm a redshirt freshman and I'm out here in the fourth quarter against the Miami

Jeff Hartings, one of the leaders of the powerful 1994 offensive line, was a two-time first-team All-American and Academic All-American. In 1995 he won a National Football Foundation and College Football Hall of Fame graduate fellowship.

Hurricanes?" We started 5–0 but lost to Miami 17–14, and the season kind of unraveled. [Penn State finished 7–5.]

What the young guys learned more than anything from that season was to have the right attitude, and that's something I felt like that team definitely lost. Instead of the focus being on football after the Miami loss, guys started thinking about other things and just playing the season out. I started the following season along with two of my classmates: Marco Rivera and Andre Johnson, as well as junior center Bucky Greeley. Keith Conlin, another classmate, joined us on the starting offensive line for the '94 season.

I think it was the bowl game where the '94 offense really came together. I remember Tennessee was practicing with no pads and just having fun, and we were doing two-a-day practices. We never complained. We wanted to win, and we believed that Joe was going to do what it took for us to win the Citrus Bowl. Tennessee went up on us in the first quarter 10–0. At the end of that first half we ran a draw play that totally surprised Tennessee, and Ki-Jana Carter ran it in for a touchdown. In the second half we pretty much dominated Tennessee. [Penn State won the game 31–13.]

That game made us realize, "Man, we're pretty good. We just beat the No. 3 team in the country." I remember walking away from that game feeling like, "Next year is our year. We are loaded with talent."

For me one of the defining moments of that season happened in training camp. The defense pretty much put it to our offense one day, and Ki-Jana said of Joe, "He's been telling the defense exactly where we're running the ball. We're going to be alright." I remember thinking, "If he's that certain of it, then I'm going to believe him." We went up to Minnesota and beat them 56–3.

Going into the Michigan game, I don't remember being nervous at all. We were beating teams real bad. We went into halftime leading 16–3, and we had a touchdown taken away by a really bad holding call. I remember thinking the first half was almost too easy. Maybe we felt like we'd come out in the second half and score 25 points and beat this team pretty easily. Michigan came back. fought hard, and tied us up. We had to make a play at the end of the game to win.

The Ohio State game was probably one of the most dominating football games Penn State has ever played. We felt like there was no way Michigan should have had that game close. We let up in the second half, but I think we rode the momentum from that 31–24 Michigan win into the Ohio State game and took the attitude that we're not letting up anymore on anybody.

Everything worked. Kerry Collins had a great game, Ki-Jana had huge holes to run through, and we were just too good for them that day. [Penn State beat Ohio State 63–14 at Beaver Stadium.]

After the Michigan and Ohio State games, we went to Indiana and felt like we were going to win pretty easily. We gave up three late touchdowns, and it definitely had an effect on the polls because we lost a lot of votes. Personally, I always felt all we had to do was go undefeated to win the national championship. In recent years before that there were teams losing one game and still winning the national title. If we had finished the season beating every team 45–10, there's no way a voter could have justified taking us out of the No. 1 spot, no matter what Nebraska did.

I remember before the Illinois game, the locker room was as quiet as it ever had been. I don't know if it was because we had lost the No. 1 spot in the polls, but we did kind of come out sleepwalking. [Illinois scored three early touchdowns to take a 21–0 lead.] We scored a key touchdown to make it 28–14 at the half. Our team was always at its best when we got challenged.

Before that last drive I remember looking up in the stands feeling, "Man, this is going to be awesome when we make it to the other end." [Hartings's block helped Brian Milne score from the 2-yard line, capping a 96-yard drive that provided the decisive points in Penn State's 35–31 win.]

It was very exciting playing in the Rose Bowl. The night before the game everybody was watching the Nebraska game obviously hoping they would lose. After Nebraska came back and beat Miami, we felt like we were going to have to beat Oregon really good. Oregon was better than a lot of people thought, and it was tied 14–14 in the third quarter before we finally pulled away 38–20. How could you not at least give us a share of the national title? I just don't respect the fact that you can vote a team the national champion without two undefeated teams playing each other.

Could you really say Nebraska was better than we were? I don't think they were better at all. I always felt if we had played them we would have won because their strength, if I remember, was their defense, and our offense was pretty much unstoppable. I'd have much rather played Nebraska and lost than to be able to claim an undefeated season.

I didn't really consider coming out for the NFL draft that year. I felt like I needed to get bigger and stronger. One of my goals was to be a first-round draft pick, and I didn't feel like I'd be one after that year. I still weighed only 275 pounds, and most guys coming out weighed over 300 pounds. Plus, we had a really good team coming back, and the thought of going after that national title definitely factored into my decision to return to Penn State.

I think our defense was about the same from '94, not dominant but pretty good. Our offense wasn't as experienced as it had been in 1994 and not quite as explosive. Bottom line is, we didn't score as quick and didn't score as often as we had the previous season.

We had Ohio State beat, and they came back in the last minute and beat us. Wisconsin was a real close game, and Northwestern was close. When you lose three guys that go in the top 10 of the draft [Carter, Collins, and tight end Kyle Brady], that makes a big difference. I think we all felt very good about the way we finished that year, although we wanted to win the national title or at least the Big Ten. With our recruiting class, we definitely felt like we had a chance to win three Big Ten titles in a row, but that shows how good the Big Ten is.

I take great pride in the fact that Penn State was willing to take a chance on me and give me a scholarship. We had some great years there, and I'll always admire Coach Paterno for what he has done. I take a lot of pride in the fact that I played for Coach Paterno and played for Penn State University.

Showing he was as much student as he was athlete at Penn State, Jeff Hartings was a two-time Academic All-American as well as a two-time All-American (1994–1995). He was named a National Football Foundation and College Football Hall of Fame Scholar Athlete. A first-round pick by the Detroit Lion in the 1996 NFL draft, Hartings helped the Pittsburgh Steelers win Super Bowl XL and he played in the 2005–2006 Pro Bowls. He and his wife, Rebecca, live with their five children in the Pittsburgh suburb of Baden.

COURTNEY BROWN
DEFENSIVE END
1996–1999

I WAS FORTUNATE TO GO TO PENN STATE's football camps during the summer and get familiar with the school and the coaches. When the recruitment process started, one of the big things for me was familiarity with the people there. Penn State felt comfortable.

There was a lot of pressure on me to stay in South Carolina, even to the point where some people—at different football activities and banquets— were aggressive in making their feelings known about how I should play for a team in the state. I visited Notre Dame, Penn State, Virginia Tech, Georgia Tech, and the University of South Carolina. When the time came to make a decision, I just really felt most comfortable at Penn State.

I knew if I was going to play my freshman year [1996], I was going to have to get up there early, and I left for Penn State a few weeks after my high school graduation. I was recruited as a defensive end, and a lot of the guys up there were so much bigger than I was, so I had a lot of catching up to do if I was going to compete for playing time that first year.

I guess the coaches liked what they saw in training camp and decided to play me my first year. The first game, I got to play towards the end and I got a sack. It was fun because my whole family had come up for the game [Kickoff Classic in East Rutherford, New Jersey].

After my freshman year I knew I had a chance to win a starting job but I also knew I had a lot of work to do. In 1997 we played Michigan late in the

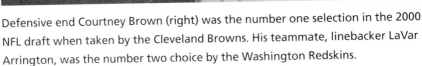

Defensive end Courtney Brown (right) was the number one selection in the 2000 NFL draft when taken by the Cleveland Browns. His teammate, linebacker LaVar Arrington, was the number two choice by the Washington Redskins.

season and both teams were undefeated. It was tough because they jumped on us early. [Michigan beat Penn State 34–8.] In that situation, you've just got to keep fighting and keep grinding. That's how it is in the Big Ten. It's a tough, grinding conference.

Going into '98, I just wanted to take it up another step. My defensive line coach Larry Johnson encouraged me and told me we could do some very good things. I wanted to become a more complete player and be prepared to have success. [Brown earned MVP honors in the '99 Outback Bowl after recording two sacks and four tackles for losses in Penn State's 26–14 win over

Kentucky.] You want to finish on a good note, and I think the game was a springboard for next season. I wasn't really thinking about going to the NFL. I wanted to finish school, and I didn't really hear a lot of what would happen if I did come out early, so I decided to stay.

Unfortunately things didn't pan out the way we had hoped in 1999, and we struggled at the end of the season. [Penn State lost its final three regular-season games.] The Minnesota game, any time you lose you don't feel good about it, especially a situation like that. You always remember people bringing it up and it's tough, but that's football. Sometimes you have games like that and you just have to deal with that and move on. That's life. That's football. You have ups and downs. There's a lot that can be said about that season and that Minnesota game. We all gave our best effort and did what we could. We all wanted to do more and knew we had the ability to do more, but it just didn't work out.

Getting drafted first overall that following April was a unique situation. I had never experienced anything like that before and it was truly a blessing. You think about all of the guys you played with and all of the guys that play football, to be picked first in the draft and come into the league that way is just a mind-boggling thing. It's almost indescribable.

Joe Paterno always talked about pushing through obstacles and never giving up. Those are some of the things I remember about Joe and being at Penn State. It's hard to find another like him. He demanded a lot from his players, not just on the field but off the field, too. He had a standard about what a Penn State student-athlete is all about and it goes for everybody.

If I had to do it over again, I would definitely choose Penn State. I really appreciate that I had a chance to earn a degree there, play football for Joe Paterno, and be a part of Penn State's history. To me, what it means to be a Nittany Lion is doing things the right way to try and succeed in life.

Courtney Brown can make a strong case for being the greatest defensive end in school history. He owns school records for career sacks (33) and tackles for losses (70). A first-team All-American in 1999, he was also named Big Ten Defensive Player of the Year for that season. The first overall pick of the 2000 NFL draft, Brown has played for the Cleveland Browns and Denver Broncos. He and his wife, Candace, also a Penn State graduate, have a daughter and live in Parker, Colorado.

The
NEW
MILLENNIUM

MICHAEL HAYNES
DEFENSIVE END
1998–2002

BOTH OF MY PARENTS WERE IN THE MILITARY, and in July before my senior year of high school, we moved to New Jersey. A lot of my teammates were going up to Penn State for football camp and, wanting to get to know them, I decided to tag along. I already had scholarship offers from Boston College and East Carolina—I got them the previous year when I attended their camps. Because I had only played overseas, they literally based my scholarship offers on what I did at football camp.

I had never played football in the States, and I was really focused on the upcoming season—more than I was on where I was going to go to college. As my senior year progressed, we had a couple of injuries, and the next thing I knew, the coach was putting me in on defense—up until then, I had primarily played fullback. That's when I really started to excel, getting sacks and tackles.

Penn State offered me a scholarship early during my senior season. Nebraska wanted me as a fullback; so did Wisconsin. Kenny Jackson did a great job recruiting me. He said, "Look, if any school can beat us academically, then by all means go there, because football is football. If you go to any of these schools, you'll be fine. Go back and talk to the coaches. See if they'll let you pursue the degree you want."

At the time, I didn't exactly understand what he meant. Then I started talking to the coaches and told them I really wanted to study animal science

In 2002 Michael Haynes had a breakout season as he set a new Penn State record by causing seven fumbles. He tied Larry Kubin's 23-year mark for most quarterback sacks in a season.

and maybe one day become a veterinarian. You really saw the true colors come out, because some of the schools were trying to convince me to change majors. Joe Paterno said, "If that's what you want to do, as long as you have the grades to do it, then knock yourself out." In the end, it wasn't that close between Penn State and my other finalist, Nebraska.

I left for Penn State the day after I graduated from high school. I went to my first summer workout, and I was horrible. The other guys in my group were [LaVar] Arrington, Brandon Short, and [Brad] Scioli. I was so far behind everybody. We were running 300-yard sprints for times, and I think I only made three out of 14. I was so far behind, and everybody was laughing at me. It was embarrassing, being in the back and throwing up in front of everybody. The workouts between high school and college are so different; it really is night and day.

That first year [1998] I redshirted, but I got to see the leaders on that team. I followed Brandon Short around a lot. I talked to LaVar a lot and Courtney Brown. Those three were the ones whose brains I constantly picked on why they did what they did, and how they handled the team on and off the field. Brandon Short told me, "Look, to be a leader, they don't always have to like you."

That's something we were missing the two years we were 5–7 and 5–6 [2000 and 2001, respectively]. I think we really struggled because we didn't have leadership. It was more "every man for himself." My senior class had a dinner one night, and we talked about what we wanted to do. Obviously, we wanted to get back to a bowl game, so we decided to take it upon ourselves to get things right again. That winter and summer we were very, very hard on everybody, making sure everybody showed up for workouts, making sure everybody was fine academically. I'm not going to lie, a lot of the young guys really didn't like me. I told them, "Look, either you get it done or you ain't going to play."

312

When that case with R. J. Luke and T. C. Cosby came up, I could have kept my mouth shut and let the courts handle it. But I felt that, if they're wrong, they're wrong. [Luke and Cosby were charged with felony assault stemming from a fight at a fraternity house in July 2002, and Haynes testified for the prosecution. Both were acquitted.] This was the first time I actually had to deal with someone who got seriously hurt. This guy had to go to the hospital. He had to get major surgery, and that was something I could not deal with.

The morning after the incident, police were knocking at my door because they knew I knew what had happened. So, in my mind, I really didn't have a choice. But I got branded for a little while because, at the time, nobody else was willing to stick his neck out. Coach [Larry] Johnson did a real good job of supporting me through that. I was real nervous about it, but he said, "If you do it, make sure you're doing it for the right reasons, and as long as you can live with yourself, forget about everybody else."

One guy cannot bring down an entire program, which was kind of what was happening. I felt that my testifying was helping the program, because we were admitting, "Hey this guy messed up," and we weren't trying to hide it. A lot of the guys who got mad at me? They were the troublemakers, anyway.

We had great individual players that 2002 season, but we had holes that other teams were able to exploit. The atmosphere for the Nebraska game was absolutely crazy. It was a very emotional experience, because we knew we had a good team. We all felt we could go out and play with anybody. A lot of the media were acting like we couldn't stop the option.

Defensively, one of our proudest games was against Ohio State, even though we lost [13–7]. It was a very hostile environment—a lot of people were doubting that we could control Ohio State's offense because they always have a big offensive line. But we held them without an offensive touchdown.

That season, I was able to trust my ability, and it all started to click. Jimmy Kennedy helped a lot in watching film and figuring out what I could and couldn't do and in just boosting my confidence.

Anyone who goes through that program understands the work ethic it takes, because Penn State does not cut corners. Nothing was given to us. If you got a degree from Penn State, you earned it. If you were a starter for Penn State, you earned it.

I don't care if we win, lose, or draw, I'm Penn State proud. After those two losing seasons, it was very obvious the respect we lost. I take a lot of pride because I honestly feel that, at least in my senior year, I did a better job than the seniors in the past as far as laying down the law and making sure people understood what it took to win.

313

Michael Haynes tied Larry Kubin's record for sacks in a season (15) in 2002 and earned first-team All-America honors while also winning the Big Ten Defensive Player of the Year award. Haynes, whose 25-1/2 career sacks ranks third on Penn State's all-time list, got taken with the 14th overall pick of the 2003 NFL draft by the Chicago Bears. He graduated from Penn State with a degree in animal science and hopes to attend veterinarian school after his playing days are over.

LARRY JOHNSON

TAILBACK

1998–2002

MY DAD (AND NAMESAKE) IS THE DEFENSIVE LINE COACH at Penn State, and I graduated from State College High School. However, I was not a lock to go to Penn State, even though a lot of coaches assumed I was going to choose Penn State because of my father.

I really wanted to go to North Carolina, but at that time, it was in the middle of a coaching change. Mack Brown had left for Texas, so I decided to go with a more stable place and chose Penn State.

There were a lot of tailbacks when I got to Penn State, and I redshirted my freshman year. That same season, Eric McCoo led the team in rushing as a true freshman.

It was always tough sharing time the next three years, especially for a running back like me. A lot of guys who are scatbacks can get eight or nine carries a game and be fine with that. I was a guy who needed 20 carries or more to get going. The fourth quarter is when I got most of my big yards, if I didn't get going early. I did the best I could with that time and ended up being the team's leading rusher my junior year.

Going into my senior year in 2002, I knew I'd finally have the position to myself. Any time the seniors got a chance to speak, we tried to convey that we were trying to bring Penn State back [after back-to-back losing seasons in 2000 and 2001], that we were trying to show an example for the younger kids.

We ended up having a great season [9–4] compared to the couple of seasons we had had in previous years. It's devastating to know that we could have been in the national championship game. I felt we had enough talent to beat that Ohio State team. [Penn State held Ohio State without an offensive touchdown, but lost 13–7.] At Michigan, we got hosed on a call where my brother [Tony] was called out of bounds even though he got both feet down after making a catch. If we kicked a field goal there, we would have won [Penn State lost 27–24 in overtime]. Our only loss in which I felt we truly got beat was against Iowa.

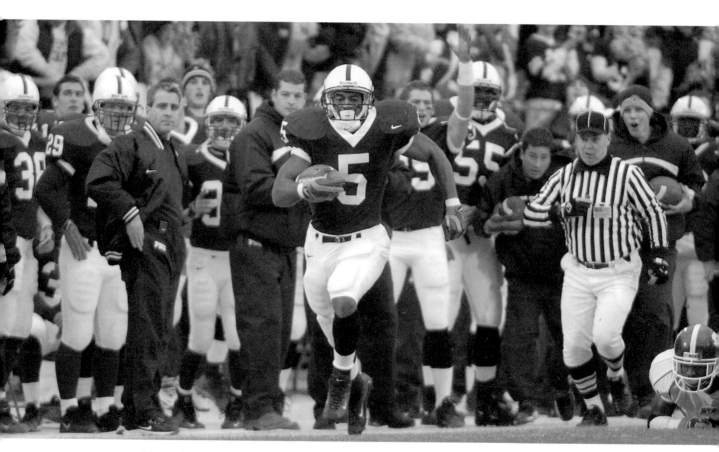

This touchdown run by Larry Johnson against Michigan State in 2002 put him over 2,000 rushing yards for the season. Johnson led the nation in rushing yards (2,015 yards, bowl games are excluded) and all-purpose yards (2,575), and finished third in the Heisman Trophy balloting.

Going into the regular-season finale [against Michigan State], I knew I had a chance to go over 2,000 yards rushing. I thought it would come down to the last series in the fourth quarter for me to reach that milestone, but I ended up gaining 279 yards in the first half.

If I had kept playing, who knows? I might have broken the NCAA single-game rushing record that LaDainian Tomlinson set. But Coach Paterno kept it classy, and I didn't play in the second half.

The run in which I broke 2,000 came on a basic toss play. They stacked the box with eight guys, but they ended up overpursuing. I cut back and squirted through this little, narrow crease. After that, there was nobody there. Michigan State had overplayed the run because it didn't want me to get the record.

I just ran as fast as I could. I knew I'd broken the record when all of these flash bulbs started going off as I hit about the 2-yard line. It was just a great day for me. My dad hugged me and said, "I'm proud of you. You deserve it." It kind of hit me what I had accomplished when I got on the sideline and looked up at the scoreboard. It kept showing my rushing yardage.

Just seeing that screen and looking at everybody else and how happy they were for me is something I'll never forget. That is when I realized I was in the upper echelon of running backs who came through Penn State.

I was one of five finalists for the Heisman Trophy, but I knew I wasn't going to win. In the big games we lost, some [critics] claimed that I didn't have enough rushing yardage. The voters apparently wanted to see someone like me take over a game, but it can be tough for a running back. A quarterback is touching the ball every single play, so it's a little bit different.

I also knew I wasn't going to win because we had so much talent on the East Coast, and Carson Palmer was the only one from the West Coast who was really getting recognition. [Johnson finished third in Heisman balloting, behind Palmer and Brad Banks.]

Joe and I had some differences when I was at Penn State, but our relationship is cool now. I come back and talk to him every so often.

Graduating from Penn State and being an athlete means you're in the ultimate fraternity. When I'm on the field, I have people who work for NFL Films come up to me, and they're so proud to say, "Hey, I'm Penn State class of 1970…" Everybody is so proud to be a part of that university, it makes you feel even more important because you are somebody who has been through the program and made a difference.

A consensus first-team All-American in 2002, Johnson posted an impressive triple crown, winning the Maxwell Award and Walter Camp Award—which are given to the top player in the country—as well as the Doak Walker Award. His brother Tony played at Penn State from 2000 to 2003 and is seventh on Penn State's all-time receptions list with 106. An emerging star for the Kansas City Chiefs, Johnson set team records in 2005 with 211 rushing yards in a game and eight consecutive 100-yard rushing games. Johnson, who made the Pro Bowl for the 2005 season, also owns 527, a clothing store in downtown State College.

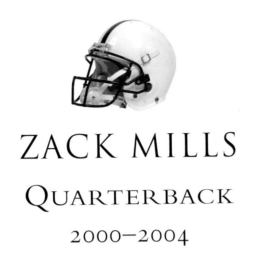

ZACK MILLS

QUARTERBACK

2000–2004

ICOMMITTED TO PENN STATE IN APRIL of my junior year in high school. They offered three quarterbacks scholarships, but what had been discussed and agreed upon was that they were only taking two quarterbacks. I committed even after Zac Wasserman did because, as I looked at it, I would rather be competing against someone my age. He was more highly recruited, but that stuff doesn't always hold up. At the same time, I believed in my abilities. And he would have to come in and learn the offense and fit in just as much as I would.

I redshirted my freshman year. In my second year, I got into the season opener against Miami when Matt Senneca got hurt. When Matt came off the field, I was running around, scrambling, trying to find my helmet. I had put it underneath the table where the phone was to talk to [quarterbacks coach] Jay Paterno, so we had to burn a timeout. I went in there and got hit pretty good right away, so that was kind of my welcome to big-time college football. I remember throwing a little pass out to the flat to the fullback, but it didn't even get to his feet, just from my being nervous.

Once I settled down, got into kind of a rhythm with some shorter passes, and made some first downs, things got a little easier. If you look at the guys who were on their defense—Jonathan Vilma, D. J. Williams, [Ed Reed], Mike Rumph, Vince Wilfork—all of those guys are in the NFL. Looking

Injuries and an erratic receiving corps hindered Zack Mills throughout his career, but he still was able to become Penn State's top career total offense leader with 7,796 yards. He also holds the record for passing yardage in one game, with 399 against Iowa in 2002.

back, I'm proud of the way I came in there and handled myself. I didn't get too rattled and made some plays.

The Northwestern game later that season was a funny situation. There was less than two minutes left, and we were trailing 35–31. All of a sudden, Matt went down. As one of the team doctors went out onto the field, I grabbed him and said, "Keep him down as long as you can so I can get warmed up." The thing I remember was just trying to let the guys know I wasn't nervous being in that situation even though I was only a freshman. There were fifth-year seniors who desperately wanted this win [Penn State was 0–4 at the time], and I just wanted to let them know that I was relaxed and focused. I said something like, "What's up, fellas? You guys ready to go score?" It kind of loosened up the huddle and let them know I didn't come in all wide-eyed and shaking.

The winning touchdown came on a play that we used a lot that season. It was designed for Eric McCoo to go out in the flat and turn it upfield. We ran it the next week against Ohio State when we scored on a 20-yard pass. We were on about the 5-yard line there, and I think Joe Paterno called it. I was thinking, "There's not enough room for this. This isn't going to work." So when I called the play, I said, "McCoo, look early if you're open." As soon as I came off my fake, I put it right to McCoo, and he was able to get in for the winning touchdown.

The next week against Ohio State, I threw a couple of picks, one of which was returned for a touchdown. We were getting killed on the scoreboard, but we were moving the ball on offense. Honestly, I wasn't worried about being down by so much [Ohio State led 27–9 in the third quarter], but I knew we needed to do something quickly.

Earlier in that game, I'd had a couple of runs, and on third down it just opened up for me. I believe [Chris] McKelvy made a block, putting a guy on the ground and going down himself. I jumped over McKelvy, and as I was coming down, [OSU safety] Mike Doss bumped into me. I guess he got blocked into me, but he didn't make an attempt to wrap me up or anything. I bounced off of him and was right near the sideline. He propelled me forward, and from there I just ran as fast as I could. Right after that touchdown, we got a turnover, and two plays later we scored. We actually took the lead on the first play of the fourth quarter and ended up winning 29–27. [The victory was Joe Paterno's 324th, moving him into first place on the Division I-A list for all-time wins.] It's something I look back on now; and no one can take that away from me. It's a memory I'll always have.

In our last regular-season game at Virginia, we were winning and were driving for another score when I fumbled, and the ball was picked up and returned for a touchdown by Virginia. The tapes we looked at later showed my knee was down before I fumbled, but that was a tough call to make. Joe would always refer to that when he pushed for a replay system the next year. Then he would add that I should have held on to the ball, anyway.

The next season we had a big game early against Nebraska. Nebraska ended up not being as good as people thought that year, but we may have started their spiral down. It was a statement game for us. We had some success at the end of the previous year, but we ended on a down note at Virginia.

The crowd was ridiculously loud, the loudest I've ever heard there. We couldn't convert in the first half, and then in the second half we had a couple of big plays and scored. It kind of opened up from there, especially that big interception by Rich Gardner. It was a great night, a great atmosphere, and again, one of those memories I'll always keep with me. [In front of a crowd of 110,753, a Beaver Stadium record, Mills led Penn State to a 40–7 victory.]

Looking back, we were only a couple of plays from going undefeated instead of losing three games during the regular season. Look at Michigan. [Tony] Johnson was in bounds after making a catch late in the game but was called out. We would have been in field-goal range if they'd given him that catch. And then against Iowa, we came back from a huge deficit but lost in overtime. The Ohio State game came down to one bad throw. Chris Gamble picked it off and ran it back. If he hadn't done that, we would have kept our 7–6 lead and probably would have won, as they didn't score the rest of the game.

In the bowl game against Auburn, I had trouble getting zip on the ball, and most people probably assumed it was because of my shoulder. But to be honest, I never really had any problems with my shoulder, it was more the tendinitis in my elbow. I do remember that being a huge problem throughout that year. By Wednesdays my elbow would be killing me from practice, so I'd have to cut down on my throws, monitor my arm, and ice it. Then we went into the bowl game against Auburn, and it didn't help that I was throwing into a 25-miles-per-hour wind. I got an MRI after the season, and it showed pretty extensive tendinitis.

The next two seasons were very frustrating, as frustrated as I've ever been. I could deal with losing and not playing well, but it was frustrating taking a lot of the heat and not being able to tell people that it's not all my fault. The ones who followed the game understood that, but there were thousands of other people who didn't. That's where you get your boos, the emails, and the prank calls from. I was a year too late with Joe getting all of the freshmen receivers for the [2005] season, so that's frustrating. But what are you going to do? My high school basketball coach always said, "If life were fair, there wouldn't be seeing-eye dogs."

The end for me was bittersweet. I wouldn't call the 37–13 win over Michigan State redemption. It always leaves a good taste in your mouth when you end up with a win, but it didn't take away the sour taste from what had happened the previous two seasons. We still finished 3–9 and 4–7. One win doesn't count as six or seven.

Don't get me wrong, it was very nice to go out and have a decent game and find the end zone—the coaches even pulled me in the middle of a series so I could get an ovation. For every negative email I got, I'd get about 10 positive ones. Walking off the field that last time at Beaver Stadium, I just felt that I wasn't in the moment. For five years I was such a part of that program, and the next day there was a squad meeting that I was not a part of.

If I had to do it over again, I'd go to Penn State in a heartbeat. I have made so many connections and friends, and when I run into somebody now, it's, "Zack, you're one of the players I respected as much as anyone just because of what you went through." I think people understand what was going on, and hearing that makes me feel a little bit better. It was a great opportunity and a great ride.

Things didn't work out as I had hoped football-wise, but everything else did. I got a degree, and if football doesn't work out for me, I've got plenty of people who would be more than willing to help me out with a job opportunity. I don't regret going to Penn State at all. The only thing I regret is the number of wins I had, but there's only so much you can do about that.

A four-year starter, Mills holds the school record for passing yards in a game (399). The two-time Academic All–Big Ten selection is also Penn State's leader in career total offense (7,796 yards). Mills is in his first year as a graduate assistant coach with Temple, whose head coach is former Nittany Lions tight end and coach Al Golden.

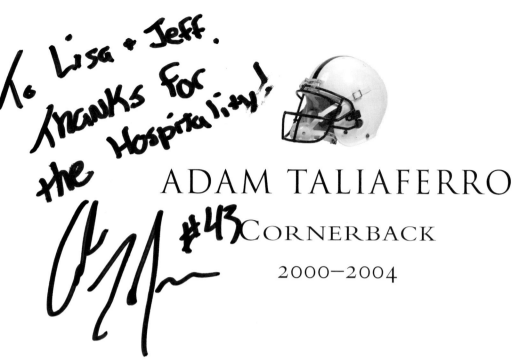

ADAM TALIAFERRO

#43 CORNERBACK

2000–2004

I WENT TO PENN STATE'S SUMMER CAMP before my junior year of high school, and I had fun. I do remember when I got home, I told my mom, "I could never go there." It seemed like it was in the middle of nowhere, and I had grown up just outside of Philadelphia in southern New Jersey. I could never see myself being there for four years of my life.

But during my junior year, I went to a few games and saw the atmosphere there. It was like nothing I had ever experienced. Afterward, I had the opportunity to talk to Coach Paterno and saw how genuine he is. During my recruitment, I talked to a lot of coaches, and I could tell which ones were fake and were just telling you what you wanted to hear.

Throughout the whole process, Coach Paterno was really honest. He wasn't promising me anything, wasn't telling me I was going to be an All-American or was going to start right when I got there. He told me he thought I had a good opportunity, not only football-wise but in terms of what Penn State could do for me academically. I thought that was really cool, and I really took a liking to him more than any other coach I talked to throughout the recruiting process.

It's good that I wanted to play cornerback instead of tailback, because when I looked at the guys who were playing corner and the ones who were at running back, the cornerbacks looked a lot more like I did. The running

Nearly 110,000 people stood on their feet and cheered as Adam Taliaferro walked and then jogged onto the Beaver Stadium field on September 1, 2001, before the season opener with Miami. Almost a year earlier he had been paralyzed after fracturing a vertebra while making a tackle against Ohio State in Columbus.

backs were huge at all of the colleges I visited. I said, "I'm not going to be the guy getting hit. I don't want to get hurt."

I couldn't have been happier during my first preseason because I really didn't have many expectations going in as a freshman. For me, any amount of playing time was a bonus. I remember our first preseason scrimmage—I was playing second-team cornerback, and I dislocated my thumb. I didn't think I was going to be able to play for the rest of the year, but Dr. [Wayne] Sebastianelli put pins in my thumb, and I got back out there with a cast.

As a freshman, I was amazed at how much they actually wanted me to get back on the field. I remember the first practice in which I had my cast on. I was kind of feeling down and had a long pass caught on me. Coach Paterno was the first person there to let me know about it. He told me he'd send me back to New Jersey if I didn't start playing better. You hear that from Coach Paterno and it kind of lights a fire underneath you.

When I got hurt, Penn State was right there. [Taliaferro fractured the C-5 vertebrae in his neck while making a tackle at Ohio State in 2000 and was initially given a 3-in-100 chance of walking again.]

Coach would fly in to Philadelphia to see me during the season. I don't know how many head coaches would have done that. I mean, they would have done it once or twice, but he did it consistently. I remember he came to the Christmas party at Magee Rehabilitation Center and was signing autographs for everybody there. Just as special was Mrs. Paterno, because she would drive down from Penn State and bring me cookies.

Penn State and my teammates, they were there for the long run. They could have stopped coming once they knew I was going to walk again, but they didn't. Along with my teammates, the fans of Penn State were second to none. Every day, I was getting cards from people who were Penn State alumni. I had never met them in my life, but they said, "Hey, we're here if you need anything, just let us know." That made me realize that Penn State's kind of like a big family.

325

When I got back to Penn State [summer session of 2001], Coach [Tom] Bradley and Coach Paterno made sure I stayed involved with the football team. I helped out with the defensive backs, and during practice I would help out with the signals, just to get the guys ready for game day when Coach Bradley was going to be doing the signals. I would also help out by watching tape with some of the younger guys.

They weren't real big tasks, but it was great being back out there on the practice field with the guys and feeling like I had a purpose with the team. I did everything I did before I got hurt, except play.

I remember the day of the Miami game [Penn State's season opener in 2001] from the time I woke up, wondering what it was going to be like, wondering what I was going to do coming out of the tunnel. I was fortunate to have everyone who helped me along the way there. It was right before we left the football building to take the bus over to the stadium. I was sitting in our training room, and Dr. [Wayne] Sebastianelli could tell I was a little bit nervous. He said, "What's wrong?"

I said, "I don't know what I'm going to do. I don't know if I'm going to be able to run out."

He just sat there and told me, "Hey, you made it this far. Whatever you do, people are going to appreciate."

Riding the bus over to the stadium just brought back so many memories from the times I had played. Going into the tunnel and seeing all of the fans there for the first time, it just felt surreal, like I wasn't there. It made me recall what I had been though over the last year, from not being able to move to standing there at that moment.

Then, hearing them call my name, I think adrenaline just took over, and I was able to jog and skip a little bit. It was one of the most amazing things, because when I was in the tunnel I really didn't think I was going to be able to do it. Then you hear all the fans up and cheering—it brought it out of me. It was definitely a moment I'll always remember. I had tried to run up until that day, and even my therapist said, "Hey, maybe you shouldn't try [to run], and just walk." But when you hear [109,313] people cheering just for you…I don't know if I could do it again.

To me, just from what I have been through, I feel Penn State is like a big family. I didn't understand what they meant when they chanted "We Are…Penn State!" at the games when I first started going to them. It really hit home for me after being hurt that when they say "We Are…Penn State!" it's really a family thing.

Everybody supports everybody 100 percent. Being a Nittany Lion means you have a family of maybe 80 on the team and another million behind you, from Penn State fans and alumni around the country. Penn State for me is second to none. I couldn't have picked a better school. Although I got hurt, I couldn't have been at a better place.

Adam Taliaferro's remarkable recovery was chronicled in *Miracle in the Making: The Adam Taliaferro Story*, which was also published by Triumph Books. He is in his second year of law school at Rutgers University.

MICHAEL ROBINSON
QUARTERBACK/WIDE RECEIVER/RUNNING BACK
2001–2005

I'M PROUD TO BE A MEMBER OF THE TEAM that brought Penn State back. We had a couple of bad years, and everyone was bad-mouthing us, telling us we were no good and didn't have any talent. That's why winning the Orange Bowl and finishing third in the country means more to me than anything— and doing it for Joe Paterno, because he always had faith in us.

We were really upset after Alan [Zemaitis], Poz [Paul Posluszny], and I came back from the Big Ten meetings before the season. The media didn't give us much respect. When we first got there, they had this big press conference where the players sit at their team table and the media from different cities go around and interview you. A lot of media didn't stop and ask us questions.

Some people just looked at us and asked us dumb questions. I got a question about how we and Illinois were close to the bottom of our conference last year and, "What could we expect from a game like that?" It was insulting. When Coach Paterno got up to talk the next day, some of the fans in the crowd and some of the other players were laughing at him, like he was washed up and needed to let it go. We felt insulted as a team and as a program. I'm just glad we could turn some people's heads.

Michael Robinson not only was successful at quarterback but also as a wide receiver, running back, and punt returner. Coach Joe Paterno praised him as "one of the best football players we have had at Penn State in the years I have been here. He is a great athlete and an outstanding leader and he made a big difference in our [2005] season."

We felt pretty strong going into the season. Some people would say, "Oh, Mike, why did you guys have so much confidence after the last couple of years?" We had confidence because, as seniors, we knew we were only a play or two away from having a totally different record these last couple of years. We felt that we had the players in the right positions and the right leadership to go out there and just make things happen this year.

We felt that half our problems in the last couple of years were that, mentally, we weren't prepared to win games. We had to just come out with a little bit of Penn State swagger. Joe always talks about a Penn State swagger, and when we came out and played South Florida in our first game, we had that swagger, and it carried us on to the Orange Bowl.

We knew our first Big Ten game at Northwestern would be our first test, and I still can't believe I would throw three interceptions and fumble away a touchdown at the 4-yard line. But even when we were behind by 16 points at halftime, I had confidence that we would win.

I understood that turnovers do happen. I just kept plugging away. At halftime, Joe just kept on saying, "Mike, just keep playing. Don't become hesitant. Just keep going in there, and things are going to finally happen." Like Joe always says, "You take care of the little things, then the big things take care of themselves."

I know a lot of fans had given up when we had a fourth down and 15 back on our own 15-yard line with only about a minute and a half left and no timeouts [Northwestern led 29–27]. I looked in the huddle, and I asked everybody if they were ready. Guys were ready. It just seemed like practice for some odd reason. It didn't seem like it was the present situation. It didn't seem like we had to make it happen. [Isaac] Smolko made an excellent catch, probably the catch of the year. He got open [for a 20-yard gain and a first down], and we went from there.

When I threw that touchdown pass to Derrick Williams near the end of the game, they sent their front eight on the blitz. I felt it, and I changed the protection to give myself about an extra second. I just knew that Derrick was going to be one-on-one with someone, and I knew when he's one-on-one with anybody in this country, we'll win that match-up. I got hit pretty hard and didn't see the catch, but I knew it was a touchdown. Like I said, I just kept plugging away, and we won.

That gave us the confidence that we could do what we thought we could do. From the start of preseason practice, we believed we could go to the Rose

Bowl and play for the national championship. We almost did it, and if we hadn't lost that Michigan game on the last play, after they got some breaks from the officials, who knows how things might have turned out?

The Orange Bowl was a BCS bowl. We beat a great Florida State team with a tradition of winning. At the same time, we felt we were one second away from playing USC or Texas, and we knew we could play with those guys. We understand everybody wanted to see that game, Texas-USC, but we still feel that, on any given day, we could beat any one of those guys.

A lot of people didn't think I could be a quarterback here, and I heard the criticism. [In his first three seasons, Robinson had more playing time as a wide receiver, running back, and punt returner than he had as the back-up quarterback. He led the team in pass receiving in 2004, and before the 2005 season, many sportswriters and fans believed he should play there instead of quarterback.] When I would hear that, it just made me stronger. It made me want to go out and practice more. It made me want to take more drops, work on my footwork, and try to become the best quarterback I could be so that, at the end of the season, I could just say, "I told you so."

330

I wasn't thrilled about not being the starting quarterback, especially when I felt I was giving my all to compete for the job. At the same time, I understand from the coaches' standpoint why they did what they had to do. If I was the quarterback, what receiver did we have that was going to be able to stretch the field vertically? Wherever I could help the team was where I wanted to play, because I'm definitely a guy [whose] team comes first as long as we're winning games. When we still weren't winning games, I'd say, "Coach, give me a chance."

He'd say, "Stay with us and be patient. Your day is going to come." And it definitely did.

One of the reasons I went to Penn State was because they told me I could compete at quarterback. Bill Kenney recruited me. He never lied to me. Neither Coach Kenney nor Joe nor Jay [Paterno] promised me I was going to come in and start. They said, "You're going to compete for the [quarterback] position, but we can't promise you a starting job." That was one thing interesting about Penn State that really attracted me to them.

In my freshman year at Varina [High School near Richmond, Virginia], I split time at tailback and played safety and cornerback from time to time. I only played tailback in four games—not complete games—and I led the team in rushing as a freshman. That's when my coach really figured he had to start getting the ball into my hands. In my sophomore year, I split time at quarterback and continued to play safety. Then in my last two years, I was all quarterback and some safety.

The recruiting process was interesting because half of the SEC was recruiting me for safety and the other half for quarterback. Most of the Big Ten recruited me for quarterback. Pretty much all of the ACC recruited me at quarterback and linebacker, and the West Coast colleges wanted me for quarterback. So I had a variety of where I could go depending on what I wanted to play.

It ended up with Penn State first, Maryland second, and Virginia Tech third. I felt at home at Penn State. Virginia Tech started a great tradition, and being in the state, I obviously thought about following behind Michael Vick, but I just didn't want to live in anybody's shadow. As for Maryland, Coach [Ralph] Friedgen and his coaching staff were at Georgia Tech, and when they made the switch to Maryland early in the recruiting process of my senior year, I got interested in Maryland.

I almost quit in my sophomore year because I was frustrated. I was ready to transfer, and Alan [Zemaitis], who was one of my roommates, said, "Mike, what are you doing?"

I said, "I gotta get out of here. I just don't know my place here. I don't see it working out for me here athletically."

He said, "Do what you're going to do, man. I'm still going to love you, and you'll still be my boy. Just keep in contact with me." He gave me five and that just meant so much to me, and I stayed.

Of course, I'm glad I did. Playing for Penn State and going through what I went through is going to help me greatly in the future. Everywhere you go, there are Penn Staters, and I know that will help me. And what I've been through here, as far as having to wait my turn, having to be patient, to keep plugging, to play where I can play just to get on the field, I think has made me a stronger person first and foremost, and a stronger athlete.

I feel honored that I could play for Joe Paterno. He epitomizes what it is to be a great person and a great leader, and I look up to him. I can't believe some of the things he's been through, especially in these last couple of years. He really bore the brunt of it on his own shoulders. Coach Paterno's a great man, a great leader.

I will never forget when I was invited to the hospitality suite after the Orange Bowl. Someone asked Joe to have his picture taken with me and Franco Harris. Here I am standing next to Coach Paterno, one of the greatest coaches on any level of any sport ever, and Franco Harris, one of the legends of the NFL and of college, and they wanted me in the picture with them. It really meant a lot to me and really made me feel a sense of Penn State pride and a sense of accomplishment in my college career.

That's what it means to be a Nittany Lion. Pride. Respect. Class. I'll always be a Nittany Lion.

Michael Robinson graduated with degrees in advertising and broadcast journalism and was a four-time Academic All–Big Ten. In his senior year, he was named the Big Ten Player of the Year by the *Chicago Tribune* and Offensive Player of the Year by the Big Ten coaches, while finishing fifth in the Heisman Trophy balloting. Robinson broke Kerry Collins's season total-offense record with 3,156 yards and became the first Penn State quarterback to rush for at least 10 touchdowns in a season. In the 2006 NFL draft, Robinson was drafted as a running back by the San Francisco 49ers.

TAMBA HALI
DEFENSIVE END
2002–2005

I LOVE PENN STATE. I don't think there is anywhere else in the country that has what we have there—the coaches, the staff, the facilities, and the faculty. It's more than just football. They want you to get an education and everybody works with you, regardless of who you are, to help you get that education.

That's one of the reasons I went to Penn State. I thought going there would be a better chance to leave with a degree than anywhere else. We had a great season [in 2005], but it was just as important to me to get the degree.

We won the Big Ten championship and the Orange Bowl, but I'm still not satisfied with the way the season ended. We accomplished as many goals as we could and can't be ashamed of that. We didn't get the national championship, but we got as close as we could get. [Penn State was third in the final BCS rankings, after beating Florida State in the Orange Bowl 26–23 in triple overtime, and finishing with an 11–1 record.]

Because we lost the Michigan game, some people claimed we would still be in the same position, behind Texas and USC. But what if we had won and somebody lost? You never know. Unfortunately, we lost that game at Michigan, but I still think we need the referees to make the right calls. [Penn State lost to Michigan 27–25 on the last play of the game, after officials put more time on the clock following a Michigan out of bounds play.]

As a team, we knew we were going to have this type of a year. No one believed us when we told them. Anytime the media interviewed me, I said, "I personally feel there is no team in the Big Ten that can beat us this year." We knew we weren't as bad as everyone said we were [even though we'd had losing seasons four out of the last five years, including the last two].

We were frustrated because for most of our games, we weren't getting blown out. Our games were always close, like that Iowa game [in 2004]. They won 6–4. We wondered, How did that happen? And then they went on and won the Big Ten.

You couldn't blame the offense, and you couldn't say we were doing enough on defense. If you don't let the teams score, it's a tie ballgame and you go from there. What was frustrating was that we knew we were always good. We had a lot of talent on the field.

We had success because of teamwork in trying to get it done the right way. Some of the guys that were here before had this thing in their minds that they were playing for themselves, trying to get theirs, not worrying about the team so long as they did well. We all got together—seniors, juniors, sopho-mores, and freshmen. We realized this was what we had to get done. If any-body stepped out of line, the upperclassmen usually came in and laid it on the line. We figured that if we did it as a group, we all would get recognized.

We came into every game like that, and it was amazing what happened. We knew we were going to come back in the Northwestern game. I didn't have any doubt about us winning. [The Nittany Lions rallied from a two-point deficit in the last two minutes, going 80 yards on the passing of Michael Robinson to win 34–29.] I just sat on the bench with [co-captain] Alan Zemaitis. We never got up. We just said, whatever happens here happens. We prayed and we watched, and it happened. I think that's where it all started.

Even though I knew the team would have a good year, I didn't think I was going to have the type of a year I had. Before the season started, [defen-sive line] coach [Larry] Johnson said to me, "Erasmus James [of Wisconsin] got the award last season as [Big Ten] Defensive Lineman of the Year, and you're going to get that award this season." We looked at how many sacks I had missed for the previous year, and I had missed about 13 sacks and only had two. It wasn't that I couldn't play the position. I was still learning it because it was my second year.

I didn't make it in my mind that I was going to get that award. I just went out and played. Being the Big Ten Defensive Lineman of the Year is credited

Tamba Hali had just three quarterback sacks before the 2005 season, but by the time the year was over, he had entered the Nittany Lion's record books with the fourth most sacks in one season (13), including a crucial one late in the Ohio State game that caused a fumble and virtually clinched Penn State's upset victory.

to my teammates on the defensive line—Scott Paxson, Jay Alford, and Matt Rice. If those guys didn't take on that double team, I couldn't come off the edge.

I think my best game was against Wisconsin just because it was my last game at Beaver Stadium. I had purpose in my heart. I had talked to my mom [in Liberia] on the phone before the game. It was very emotional. So I came out there to make people believe that this is Penn State football, that we were as good as we thought we were, and personally, I didn't want to leave that field with a loss. [Hali tied the school record for sacks in a game with four as Penn State beat Wisconsin in a battle for first place in the Big Ten.]

The play everyone seems to remember is my sack of Troy Smith at the end of the Ohio State game. We were always told as defensive linemen that we had to make a play. I wasn't purposely thinking in my heart, *This is the time to make the play*. I was just thinking, *Do what you have to do*. I used my hand on the tight end and I took a couple of steps at full speed. Troy was still holding the ball, and I just accelerated. He fumbled, Paxson recovered, and that sealed the deal. [Hali's sack with 1:21 left helped preserve Penn State's 17–10 victory and thrust the Nittany Lions into the top 10 rankings for the first time in three years.]

I guess I did the right thing when I didn't leave Penn State in my freshman year. I was playing behind three All-Americans at the time—Anthony Adams, Jimmy Kennedy, and Michael Haynes—and I thought I should be playing. As I look back, that was a positive thing because I was young and learning the system, and had the opportunity to play behind three guys who are professional players now.

If I have any regrets about anything that has happened to me at Penn State, it's that my mother has never seen me play. She's still in Liberia, and I've been away from her for 11 years. [During the civil war in Liberia, Hali's mother, Rachel Keita, his two brothers, and a sister fled the country. The children joined their father, Henry, who already was in the United States, but their mother and other siblings have been unable to immigrate due to governmental problems.]

My father has seen most of my games, and I'm happy about that. He's in Teaneck, New Jersey, where I played high school football. I didn't start playing football until my freshman year. I played defensive tackle, defensive end, and stunting linebacker. I was the number-one prospect in New Jersey, and I got heavily recruited. My top five schools were Southern California, the University of Miami, Maryland, Syracuse, and Penn State.

I watched one of the Penn State games, and I saw Courtney [Brown], LaVar [Arrington], and Brandon Short, and they played exactly the way I felt I could play. They were just relentless. I told my coach, Dennis Heck, that I liked Penn State, and Fran Ganter started recruiting me. Franny really didn't put me under any pressure. It was more making me feel comfortable with what he was trying to do.

To be honest with you, Penn State was my worst visit. I was pretty much bored. But I liked it here because I wasn't coming here to party. I was really coming to go to school and play football. Coach Paterno came to my high school, and he was a very up-front guy. He had a plan for every player, to put in their minds that they wanted to come here to get an education, go to classes, be a good citizen, and abide by all the rules he established. So I made my decision about three days before the signing deadline. People kept telling me, "Tamba, he's going to retire soon." I'm done, and he's not retired yet. So I came here and played under a guy who's a coach for the ages.

I love Joe Paterno. Joe and I have this relationship—he doesn't have to tell me twice. He tells me one time, and I will get the point. In one game this year, the Northwestern game, he said I stunk up the field in front of the entire squad. It didn't bother me. I took what he said and made it a point that, in the next games, I was not going to make anyone feel like I was stinking up the field.

Joe really teaches you how to be a man and how to handle situations, how to look at things differently, and how to grow up fast. He always has this knowledge about people, and he's always interested in their family. When you go through this program, you are experiencing life from an inside perspective. You're not really in the real world, but you learn things that are important and you learn to honor and respect each other. I'll always be thankful I went to Penn State.

337

Tamba Hali graduated with a bachelor's degree in communications, majoring in broadcast journalism. He was a consensus All-American defensive end in 2005 and the Big Ten's Defensive Lineman of the Year. He led the Big Ten in sacks (11) and was finalist for both the Bronko Nagurski and Ted Hendricks defensive awards. Hali was selected in the first round of the 2006 NFL draft by the Kansas City Chiefs. He was the 20th overall pick.

PAUL POSLUSZNY

LINEBACKER

2003–present

GROWING UP, I WASN'T REALLY AWARE of how special and important Penn State football was. I was a Penn State fan and did go to several games when I was younger with my dad and friends of the family.

Tom Bradley recruited me, and we got along great. He was probably one of the main reasons I decided to come to Penn State, because I felt really, really comfortable around him. Since he was the defensive coordinator, I knew I was going to be working a lot with him.

Once I came on a recruiting visit, that's when I started to learn about "Linebacker U" and all of the tradition that's involved here. It came down to Penn State and Pitt. Two or three days after one of my unofficial visits here, before my senior year of high school, I decided to commit to Penn State.

I thought I would take the normal track and redshirt my first year. When I first started practicing, I wasn't very good technique-wise, I was just running around a lot. One thing I experienced very quickly at the college level that doesn't happen in high school is that [offensive] linemen cut-block you. You're not allowed to do that in high school football in western Pennsylvania, so that was a huge adjustment for me. I would get cut all the time because I wasn't used to seeing guys that big and that fast.

I just tried to continue to work hard throughout the first two or three weeks of our season. I had been practicing with the first and second units for a week or two, and before our first Big Ten game against Minnesota,

In 2005 Paul Posluszny, seen here with ESPN's Chris Fowler at the College Football Awards Show, was the surprise winner of the Butkus Award, given to the nation's outstanding linebacker. He beat out favorite A. J. Hawk, a senior from Ohio State.

[linebackers] coach [Ron] Vanderlinden told me Friday night at the hotel, "We're going to play you tomorrow." I was obviously very excited, and as I started to play more and more, I felt comfortable as the season went on.

The first two years were very, very tough to go through, especially coming off a state championship my senior year at Hopewell High School. Coming to Penn State, I thought we would go to serious bowl games every year and win Big Ten championships, but things just didn't work out that way at first.

We all wanted to be successful and win games, and when all of the losing happened [Penn State went a combined 7–16 in 2003–2004], it just made all aspects of life a little bit tougher. It was tough to walk around campus knowing we were 3–9. When I went home, everyone asked, "What's wrong?"

In 2004 we needed a goal-line stand to beat Indiana. That was our first Big Ten win on the road in a while, and it gave us confidence against Michigan State. We ended the season with two big wins, and all of that really carried over to the following fall.

We needed a starting point for success and to put our foot down and say, "All right, let's go, let's turn things around." I really think if you look back on it, you could say that was it. Beating Indiana, in the grand scheme of things, isn't as big as beating, say, Southern Cal. But at that particular time, it was big for us because it was on the road and we were able to make plays that just gave us a lot of confidence.

When we went to Big Ten Media Day before the 2005 season, it was a huge thing for us as captains because we saw that everyone had written us off as a team. They thought we were going to be at the bottom of the Big Ten again.

We knew that everyone wanted to talk to players from Michigan, Ohio State, and Iowa—and they deserved that attention because they had been great the previous couple of years. But our team and our coaches knew we could be something special. To realize that the whole world thought we weren't going to amount to anything really put everything into perspective.

We came back home and knew we could have a great year. We had a lot of seniors, a fifth-year guy at quarterback [tri-captain Michael Robinson], and a strong defense. We really felt confidence in ourselves.

If we didn't win the Northwestern game [Penn State won 34–29 on a late touchdown], I think that could have changed the whole course of the season. That was a tough game for us and one we probably should have handled a little bit better.

We had guys who were able to make plays in the fourth quarter when the game was on the line, and I think that really showed us we were a different team. In previous years, we would have lost that game and continued down the same path we were on. By winning a game in that fashion, I think that showed us how special we could be, that we could get through difficult times.

The Minnesota game the following week was a pretty big game for us. We weren't supposed to win, and the offense did a great job controlling the clock and scoring a lot of points. And we controlled [Minnesota running back Laurence] Maroney.

On a goal-line stand, we had a good idea where the ball was going to go. Our defensive line did a great job of taking care of all the offensive linemen up front so there was a wall of guys on the ground. By the running back's body motion, it looked like [Minnesota's Gary Russell] was going to jump, so I was able to time it right and we made some good contact in the air. Thank God everything worked out, because if he would have jumped over me, that wouldn't have looked good at all. Joe would have definitely had something to say.

The whole week leading up to the Ohio State game was unbelievable. It was the start of Paternoville, and we had a pep rally Friday night before the game. We just felt like, "All right, this is our chance. This is our big shot right here to put ourselves on the national scene." [ESPN's] *College Gameday* was there, and it was really important for us to win that game. That was the loudest stadium and most excitement that I've been a part of since I've been here.

Michigan was a good, tough team. I don't think we necessarily played as well as we could have. They ran the ball a little bit on us early and were able to make some plays offensively that really shouldn't have happened.

Michael Robinson played an outstanding game, and we did our best. We just came up a little bit short. [Michigan scored a touchdown on the last play of the game to beat Penn State 27–25.] It was really tough because our undefeated season went out the window on one play with one second left.

If someone had told me, "Okay, your defense is on the field. You have one play left. If you make the play, you win." I would say, "All right, Penn State wins, no doubt in my mind." For some reason, that just wasn't our day.

I think everyone on the team not only wanted to win the Big Ten but to show the nation that the program was back and that Coach Paterno still had it, that he's able to do things the right way with the right guys and not bend or break any rules.

He had taken a lot of heat, and he didn't deserve it at all. It was the players who were going out and playing badly and losing football games. To get back in the national spotlight, I think all of the players just wanted that for Coach. [Penn State went on to win the rest of its games, capturing the Big Ten title and claiming the first BCS bowl bid in school history.]

In the Orange Bowl, when I got carted off the field and passed by the student section, I could hear fans cheering my name. That made me feel great under the circumstances. I had just done something to my knee, and coming out of the game, that was definitely uplifting to hear.

Even if I hadn't gotten hurt in the Orange Bowl, I probably would have returned for my senior season. All of the people whose opinion I really respected said it seemed like the right decision to come back. When Tom Bradley, Joe Paterno, Ron Vanderlinden, Shane Conlan, and Jack Ham all say, "You could go in [the first round of the NFL draft], but we think it would be the best decision to come back," you've got to listen to those guys. No one knows more about football than they do.

What it means to be a Nittany Lion is being a small part of something that's so big—part of a program that takes young kids from all different backgrounds and develops them into not only great football players but people who are going to be great fathers, great husbands, people who are going to have a positive impact on the world.

We know there's a great history with all the guys who came before us. They're in the NFL and the Hall of Fame, but they're also the vice president of Merrill Lynch, doctors, and lawyers. I think that's the best thing about being a Nittany Lion: I know I'm part of an elite group.

A consensus All-American in 2005, Paul Posluszny also won the Bednarik and Butkus Awards, given to the top defensive player and linebacker, respectively, in college football. He posted 100-tackle seasons in 2004 and 2005, and was the first junior to serve as a captain for Penn State since 1968.

HONORABLE MENTION

*These men did not play football
for Penn State, but through their words
and deeds, they proved that they know what it
means to be a Nittany Lion.*

FRAN FISHER

BROADCASTER

1966–2001

I WAS PENN STATE'S PLAY-BY-PLAY BROADCASTER for so long that some fans believe I was there in 1906 when "Mother" Dunn became the school's first All-American. They might actually be surprised when they learn that I saw my first Nittany Lions game in 1932. I'll give you another little tidbit: I played alto sax for the Blue Band in 1942. So I was a Penn State fan long before I joined the broadcast team in 1966.

My family lived in Pittsburgh when I was 10 years old, and I watched Waynesburg beat Penn State at Beaver Field. It was an upset, 7–6. My sister was a cheerleader for Waynesburg, and we used to go to all of Waynesburg's games. But I became a Penn State fan even though they lost. As a little guy, I thought the place was beautiful, all that green grass and stuff.

As for marching in the Blue Band, I went to college at Penn State in 1941 after transferring from Bethany College in West Virginia. I marched in the Blue Band for one football game, and then I quit to join the navy. It was a mistake. I should have stayed in school. I married my high school sweetheart in 1944, and by the time I got back to my home in Greensburg after the war, it wasn't easy to pack up your wife, move up to State College, and go back to school. So I never went back.

I started covering Penn State sports while working for radio station WKVA in Lewistown. In '66 I became the [football] analyst for the radio network, and I took over the play-by-play in 1970 around the same time I was

344

Fran Fisher (right) teamed up in the broadcast booth with George Paterno, Joe's younger brother, for seven years (1994–2000), and it was probably the most popular Penn State sportscasting duo since the Lions first started broadcasting games in 1927. *Photo Courtesy of Fran Fisher.*

hired full-time by Penn State's public broadcasting radio and television stations. I've broadcast a lot of sports on radio and TV for Penn State, and not just football—men's and women's basketball, wrestling, gymnastics, soccer. You name it, and I've probably done it.

In 1967, Joe Paterno's second season, Joe asked me to go on the [statewide] coaches' show, *TV Quarterbacks*, to narrate the game films, and I did that until the show went off the air in 1986. I stopped doing play-by-play after Penn

State won its first national championship at the 1983 Sugar Bowl. By that time, I had been working in the athletics department as the radio-television film coordinator for several years, and I became an assistant athletics director overseeing the Nittany Lion Club and the club's fund-raising effort.

The year I retired in 1988, they created a call-in show for Joe on the radio network, and I began hosting that. I was enjoying my "nursing home" days, doing the call-in show, emceeing pep rallies, traveling to the away games with my old friends, and having fun at all the tailgates. And, if you didn't already know it, tailgating outside Beaver Stadium is a great experience.

Before the 1994 season, the guy doing the play-by-play, Bill Zimpher, got a job with the [Miami] Dolphins and they asked me to go back on the broadcasts with George Paterno. I was reluctant because it had been 12 years, but George helped convince me. Of course, I couldn't have been happier with the way the '94 season turned out, with the Big Ten championship and the Rose Bowl victory. That season was one of the greatest offensive performances in the history of college football, and it's too bad those kids were denied the national championship. I guess that's the albatross for Penn State, because I was broadcasting when the same thing happened in '68, '69, and '73.

George and I had a great time in the booth over the next few years, and I miss him. [George Paterno died in 2003.] He was a character, but he was an outstanding color man and didn't hesitate to criticize his brother about football. I retired for good in 2001, not only from play-by-play but also from the call-in show and the emceeing. But I still have season tickets, and [my wife] Charlotte and I go to as many away games as we can.

Joe Paterno put Penn State on a national scale by playing a national schedule and getting to bowls, but it was a good college football team before that. Bob Higgins had good teams, especially that Cotton Bowl team in 1947. And Rip Engle, who was an innovator to a degree, had better teams in his first couple of years than most people realized. Look at who was there—Lenny Moore, Rosey Grier, and those guys.

If there is anything that defines the change in football at Penn State, it can be traced to Penn State College becoming Penn State University [in 1953]. When it was Penn State College, it was a college football team. When it became Penn State University, it became a "universal" football team, and that's when the upswing started.

One of my early memorable games is the Pitt–Penn State game at Pittsburgh in 1948. I particularly remember [fullback] Fran Rogel's performance that day. Every time he carried the ball, the whole Pitt defense knew it but couldn't stop him. And he must have carried 16 or 17 times. Pitt was ahead 7–0 with the clock winding down and Penn State had to go 80 yards just to tie. But a tie probably meant going to a bowl game. They went right down the field and were on about the 2-yard line with a couple of seconds left. This time "Punchy" couldn't get in. The guy that stopped him was Walt Cummins, who was from Greensburg and later became the assistant AD for Pitt. That's the first game I really, really felt bad that Penn State lost.

I don't think I felt that way again until we lost to Alabama in the Sugar Bowl [in 1979]. And I also felt bad after the Orange Bowl in '86 when John Shaffer, who was the quarterback, took so much criticism. That was a disheartening game because we could have won it, and it was for the national championship. I really felt sorry for John because everyone seemed to blame him. But he came back the next year and took us to another national championship. Those were the three games I remember being disappointed.

But the best games far outnumber those disappointments. I remember the first national championship game in the Sugar Bowl in '83 and the Nebraska game at Beaver Stadium that '82 season. I'll never forget the scene coming back from the '83 Sugar Bowl, coming up through Lewistown and all the people along the way. The buses had to stop on the highway outside of Lewistown because there were so many people. It was unbelievable.

The Nebraska game was the greatest game ever played at Beaver Stadium. I never saw the stadium like that after we won [27–24 in the last minute]. People wouldn't leave. They were parading around the playing surface, not misbehaving, but just in an aura of pure joy. It was an amazing sight.

I also remember the win over Miami in '67 that turned Joe's career around and the 15–14 victory in the '69 Orange Bowl against Kansas. And I think the Cotton Bowl game with Texas in '72 might have been the most significant bowl win in Penn State history. That was a wishbone team that couldn't be stopped by anyone, and they didn't even get a touchdown. It was a statement being made by Penn State.

Of course, there was the '87 Fiesta Bowl, when I was a spectator again, although I did emcee the pep rally. There were so many people there around the swimming pool at the team hotel that they were standing on the roofs of the cottages. I was afraid those roofs would collapse and people would fall into the pool. That pep rally matched the one at the Orange Bowl after the '73 season when Cappy introduced his kid brother Joey, who was dying of

347

leukemia. It was very emotional when Joe [Paterno, John Cappelletti's] mom and dad, and Joey were sitting right down in the front row, and Cappy introduced Joey.

It's amazing how this team and this heritage attract people. They want to be as close to Joe as they can get. They want to be as close to the players as they can get. It may be true elsewhere, but I've never seen anybody, in all honesty, attract people like Joe does.

Playing football for Penn State is a very special fraternity, and it's a special, special situation with a feeling and a meaningfulness that just can't be shared. No player is placed above others, even if one is an All-American and the other a walk-on.

No one player typifies a Penn State player more than Steve Smear. I have never seen anybody as a player, as a graduate, or as an ex–Nittany Lion who is more humble and more appreciative. Steve was a very good player, but when he was playing here, he had a guy on the other side of him, Mike Reid, who was all-everything. Steve could have been jealous, but he was Mike Reid's biggest supporter. Steve was so team-oriented.

348

I also remember guys who never played who were important to the team. I'm talking about the foreign team and the walk-ons. For some reason, I remember Cliff Buckwalter, who never played. I remember him because Joe had a rule for *TV Quarterbacks* that you had to interview every senior before underclassmen. People didn't care about Buckwalter because he never played, and it was a tough interview. But these kids were always very charming and understanding, and they weren't embarrassed that they weren't playing because they had bought into the team concept.

I have spent the better part of my life being fortunate enough to be associated with the combination of a University, a team, a coach, and a program that sets high standards and keeps them, and I'm better off for it.

Although he has been officially retired for years, Fran Fisher continues to be a familiar face around the Penn State football program. His sports marketing company, which includes his sons, Jeff and Jerry, serves clients that include the University athletics department as well as local businesses that advertise to reach Penn State fans. Fran and his wife, Charlotte, who are avid spectators at most Penn State athletics events, live in State College.

BRAD "SPIDER" CALDWELL
HEAD EQUIPMENT MANAGER
1987–Present

I WAS THE VARSITY MANAGER FOR THE FOOTBALL TEAM at Curwensville High School for four seasons and also did baseball and wrestling. For college, I went to DuBois branch campus my first year. I told my high school coach I really loved being a manager, and it really helped get me out of my shell. He worked the football camps in the summer at Penn State, so he made a couple of phone calls, and they said they'd accept me as a student manager.

I'll never forget the first day I walked in here. It was reporting day for the whole team, and it was total chaos—phones ringing off the hook, players coming in and out, needing this, needing that. I was changing a face mask and thinking, "How am I ever going to fit into this rat race?" I was nervous as all get out, and here I am more than 20 years later, so I guess I adapted pretty well.

I was only here one week when I got my nickname. I was born with severe scoliosis of the spine. I have half a shoulder blade on one side and a couple of ribs missing. I'm 5′2″ but I've got long arms and long legs. The players were all sitting in the locker room one day, waiting for a squad meeting. I took off across the locker room floor to get something. I was hunkered down real low, taking big, long strides, and I had my arms way out. Guys laughed, and one of our defensive linemen, Joe Hines, said, "He looks like Spider-Man." Everybody heard that, and I've been "Spider" ever since. Even my family calls me Spider. It's pretty funny.

Affectionately known by his nickname "Spider," Brad Caldwell was the senior student manager for the 1986 national champions and stayed on as an assistant equipment manager, ascending to the top position in 2001. *Photo courtesy of Brad Caldwell.*

My senior year was 1986. I was graduating in December, and by then I was the head student manager. When we lost to Oklahoma in the Orange Bowl after the 1985 season, the next morning some of the guys that could have left early for the NFL, including Shane Conlan and D. J. Dozier, went to Joe's hotel room and knocked on the door. When Joe opened the door, they said, "Coach, we just want you to know, we're definitely coming back next year because we're not going to let this happen again."

From January 3 on, that team was on a mission. When we got back to the national championship game against Miami in the Fiesta Bowl, there was so much hoopla around it and every day at practice, you'd just bite your nails. Practice was so tight and tense because you just couldn't wait for the game.

I remember leaping up when Pete Giftopoulos made that final interception. My glasses went flying off, and I couldn't see a thing. I was trying to celebrate, and when my glasses are gone, I'm blind as a bat. I got a tap on my shoulder, and some guy gave me my glasses. I put them on, and here it was

David Hartman from *Good Morning America*. Just the feeling in that locker room after the game was something I'll never forget. I get goosebumps just talking about it.

Some of my memories are something that we actually call "bites," and they are getting bit by Joe. Joe is so intense in practices and in games, and he's always had that high-pitched scream, yelling for something. It was 1989 and we were playing Syracuse in the Carrier Dome. Right before halftime, we were winning and in field-goal range.

Joe wanted to get five yards closer, so he called this little five-yard hitch pass out to the sideline to get out of bounds and kick the field goal. Well, Tony Sacca, who was the quarterback at the time, threw a wobbly duck pass, and it was intercepted. Joe was just screaming going off the field. I was already in the locker room and had opened the door for the team to come in.

Well, Tony told Joe that the football was wet. In came Joe and he saw me in the back corner. He yelled, "Spider, why are the footballs wet? The footballs are wet! The footballs are wet! Who's running the footballs [to the referees]?"

I said, "Well, the Syracuse managers are running them."

He said, "What do you mean, the Syracuse managers are running them? You've got to get somebody on that!"

351

He was just going nuts and the whole team was now in the locker room, sitting down, watching me just get destroyed by Coach Paterno. He was so upset that he actually stormed out. There was total silence when Jerry Sandusky, the defensive coordinator, looked over to me and said, "The football's wet? How can a football be wet when we're playing inside the Carrier Dome?" The whole locker room just erupted in laughter, and I said, "Yeah, that's right." I didn't even think about it because I was just in shock.

At that point, we would only take six managers to away games. From that game on, we've taken eight managers to away games and two of them run balls. To this day, I still don't live down the wet ball in the Carrier Dome.

One of the most thrilling things that happened to me here is I had a chance to go to the White House with the team in February 1987 and meet President Reagan and Vice President Bush. They had taken 44 players and the White House had said 50 people could come. Myself and the other head manager got to go because we were in charge of the buses. Being a small-town guy, just to be able to meet the president of the United States in the White House was an absolute thrill for me.

I actually graduated with a degree in recreation and parks management, and I love the outdoors. I've always thought it would be neat to be a park ranger, and I think as a retirement sort of thing, I hope to do that for a few years just as something different. But I really think I was meant to do this.

My wife and I don't have any children. She's a teacher and has elementary kids, and I've seen so many guys go through here. I've watched them go from boys to men. The guys make you stay young, and I think that's why Joe's still hopping around.

Before the Ohio State game in 2005, my dad, who sits in the press box, said, "When you come out on the field, you never wave." So I walked out onto the field when the team was already out there. I was probably the only person on the field, and I thought, "I better wave to Dad up there." He got so choked up. My dad never gets choked up, but he said that meant the most to him.

Coming from a small town and having the birth defect that I had and to be given this opportunity by the university and Coach Paterno, it's really been a dream for me. I used to drive through this area when I was a kid. To drive by that stadium now and to think that I actually have the keys to it…to come in here and see the history and all of the legends that have come through here and to know that I'm a part of this, it's just an indescribable feeling.

A 1986 graduate of Penn State, Brad Caldwell will be in his 20th season as a full-time equipment manager with the team in 2006. He and his wife Karen live in Port Matilda. An English teacher, Karen Caldwell does all of the football team's sewing on the side. Her husband answers the phone at the Lasch Building as "Spider."

GENE WETTSTONE
NITTANY LION MASCOT
1939

I WAS THE THIRD NITTANY LION MASCOT, but I'm better known at Penn State as the men's gymnastics coach. I coached gymnastics from 1939 until my retirement in 1976, and during that time my teams won [a record] nine NCAA championships.

I came from the University of Iowa in 1938 to teach physical education and run a circus at Penn State for Dean [Carl] Schott, who was head of the Department of Physical Education. He asked me to run the circus to promote our physical education majors.

At that time, jobs were hard to get. He thought that if we had a big circus, a big physical education event in the spring, he could invite the superintendents of schools in Pennsylvania to see it, and after they watched what our physical education majors could do, they would hire more of them in their high schools. How I became the Nittany Lion mascot was really part of starting and running the circus.

We had a circus at Iowa, and I also had some experience with the Swiss Society in Union City, New Jersey, where we put on exhibitions all the time with all kinds of acrobatic stuff. So I had my phys ed majors all hepped up in the classes, and we started to figure out some of the things we should have for a circus and the acts we should put on.

I started to order stuff for things done at the circus, like a trapeze and a tight wire. I had a guy at the machine shop make these pieces of equipment

The Nittany Lion Mascot makes his debut on October 22, 1922, at New York's Polo Grounds before Penn State's first-ever game against Syracuse. The teams tied 0–0.

for me. I really was a gymnast, so I knew what would be good and what gymnasts could do that would be like circus acts, like hanging a bar trapeze and doing a muscle grind where a guy goes around and around a bar up high. We also had a rope climber and a guy on flying rings. So we designed some very interesting acts for the first show.

The first circus was in the spring [April] of 1939. We had an entrance fee of 25¢, as I remember, and maybe 10¢ for children, and it went over big. I

Gene Wettstone, above as the Nittany Lion Mascot in the only photograph that has been found of Wettstone's tenure as the third mascot in 1939, and, right, as the head gymnastics coach in Rec Hall in the 1970s.

had two bands. I had a string ensemble in one corner of Rec Hall and a platform in the far corner with another circus band that was made up of the guys from the Blue Band. Bill Jeffrey, our soccer coach, who was a character, was the ringmaster all dressed up in his red-and-white suit with a top hat.

We immediately started planning for the next circus the following spring. We had clowns in our first circus and we started thinking about adding animals. I thought a lion act would excite the crowd.

The school mascot was a Nittany Lion, but there wasn't any one [person] who was the mascot. I learned later that we had a mascot in 1922 and another a couple of years later, but everyone had forgotten about that in 1939. [The Nittany Lion was chosen by the student body in 1907 to be Penn State's official mascot after a campaign led by senior Joe Mason. On October 22, 1922, senior Dick Hoffman became the first mascot when he showed up impromptu in an African lion's costume at New York's Polo Grounds for Penn State's first game ever with Syracuse. In 1927 Leon Skinner pranced along the sidelines of Beaver Field in an African lion costume at a few games.]

In the meantime, I was full of school spirit and wondered what we could do for the football team that would bring more spirit to the team. At that time, they didn't have scholarships, either. There were football players in my class. I would even excuse them from Saturday morning class because they had a Saturday afternoon game. I knew I had to get the spirit for that team. I wondered, "Why don't they have a mascot?" I didn't know anything about the earlier mascots.

Schott liked the idea, so in early September he sent me to a costume house in New York City to get a suit made. I can't even tell you the name of the shop. My memory fails me, but I think I went by train. They measured me and fit me, and I went back to State College. It took about two or three weeks to make the suit. Then it came, but it looked more like an African lion. I asked the dean who should wear the suit for the football games, and he said something like, "If it fits, wear it." I was full of energy and thought I could do anything in those days, so I was very enthusiastic.

I wore it first at the Lewistown–State College [high school] game [on October 6, 1939] in Lewistown. Nothing happened. I just ran around and made some acts and so forth. I don't think too many people noticed me and it didn't make much difference.

I am having a hard time remembering when I wore it next. I'm told I wore it for a Penn State pep rally the night before the Lehigh game [at home] the next week because there was a *Daily Collegian* story about the mascot planning to show up. But I don't remember the pep rally or the game.

I vaguely remember there was some game where I wore it until I heard some whispers that the students were going to get me, strip me, and capture me. So I left the game. That may have been the Maryland game [November 4] before the team played at the University of Pennsylvania [November 11], because I did wear it when they played Penn.

I went down to Philadelphia. That's where the students stripped me. They got me and they took my suit off, and I had nothing on but underwear. I went back to the seat I was occupying before I went out onto the field, and there was a guy there from Penn State. He had a raincoat, and he gave it to me. We got the suit back, but that was the end of me wearing the [Nittany Lion] suit.

We got smarter the next year. By then we had a committee to choose the Lion. We wanted to see how he would run across the floor and watch his actions as a lion. We thought it was a big thing. We also chose him on the basis of an interview in which he would tell us what he would do if he were the Lion, what acts he'd put on, and so forth.

357

I was always the one to supervise him, to see what he's going to do, and to give him some real ideas. We screwed around doing all kinds of things, which we thought were funny. We pulled off some stuff in those days that you wouldn't believe.

I remember we built a chariot, and the Lion would ride around the outer perimeter of the football stadium, whipping the three or four cheerleaders pulling the chariot.

Once we had the Lion in some kind of balloon, and we filled the balloon with some kind of gas until the guy inside the suit got intoxicated, and we had to drag him out or he might have died.

The first few mascots who followed me were gymnasts. But after that, gymnasts were not really the funny ones. We picked them out of the fraternities or chose anybody who wanted to be the Lion. We changed every year. In time, they did some exploring and found out the real Nittany Lion was a mountain lion, not an African lion, and slowly we began to improve the appearance of the Lion.

Nowadays, the Nittany Lion mascot is known everywhere. I still go to some football and basketball games and gymnastics meets, and I still get a kick out of seeing the mascot parade around, doing his acts and his push-ups. Someone told me I'm a real Nittany Lion and will be a Nittany Lion forever. I guess that's true.

Gene Wettstone turned Penn State into a gymnastics powerhouse, coaching 35 individual NCAA champions and 14 Olympians. He was the head coach of the U.S. gymnastics teams in the 1948 and 1956 Olympics, an assistant coach in 1976, and a judge in 1968. Wettstone was inducted into the U.S. Gymnastics Hall of Fame in 1963. He turned 93 years old in 2006 and is still active in Penn State athletics affairs. He lives in State College.

WISNIEWSKI · ANDRE COLLINS · TERRY SMITH · O. J. MCDUFFI

M · JEFF HARTINGS · COURTNEY BROWN · LARRY JOHNSON · JI

· LENNY MOORE · DAN RADAKOVICH · MILT PLUM · RICHIE LUC

KWALICK · DENNIS ONKOTZ · CHARLIE PITTMAN · STEVE SMEAR

TI · MARK MARKOVICH · GREG MURPHY · CHRIS BAHR · GREG

K FUSINA · MATT MILLEN · MATT SUHEY · LEO WISNIEWSKI · SE

BLACKLEDGE · GREGG GARRITY · MARK ROBINSON · HARRY HA

SHAFFER · TREY BAUER · STEVE WISNIEWSKI · ANDRE COLLINS

R · KYLE BRADY · BOBBY ENGRAM · JEFF HARTINGS · COURTNEY

· MICHAEL ROBINSON · TAMBA HALI · PAUL POSLUSZNY · JIM O'H

Y MOORE · DAN RADAKOVICH · MILT PLUM · RICHIE LUCAS · BO

CK · DENNIS ONKOTZ · CHARLIE PITTMAN · STEVE SMEAR · NE

MARK MARKOVICH · GREG MURPHY · CHRIS BAHR · GREG BUTT

A · MATT MILLEN · MATT SUHEY · LEO WISNIEWSKI · SEAN FARREL

· GREGG GARRITY · MARK ROBINSON · HARRY HAMILTON · MI

REY BAUER · STEVE WISNIEWSKI · ANDRE COLLINS · TERRY SMIT

· BOBBY ENGRAM · JEFF HARTINGS · COURTNEY BROWN · LA

AEL ROBINSON · TAMBA HALI · PAUL POSLUSZNY · JIM O'HORA · S

E · DAN RADAKOVICH · MILT PLUM · RICHIE LUCAS · BOB MITIN